metro

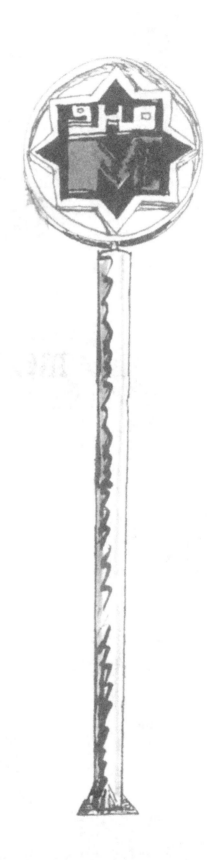

metro

A Story of Cairo

Magdy El Shafee

Translated by Chip Rossetti

Metropolitan Books

Henry Holt and Company

New York

Metropolitan Books
Henry Holt and Company, LLC
Publishers since 1866
175 Fifth Avenue
New York, New York 10010
www.henryholt.com

Metropolitan Books° and m° are registered trademarks of Henry Holt and Company, LLC.

Originally published in Egypt in 2008 by Malamih Publishing House, Cairo.

Library of Congress Cataloging-in-Publication data

Shafi'i, Majdi.
  [Mitru. English]
Metro : a story of Cairo / Magdy El Shafee ; translated by Chip Rossetti. — 1st U. S. ed.
    p. cm.
  ISBN 978-0-8050-9488-6
1. Egypt—Social conditions—21st century—Comic books, strips, etc. 2. Egypt—Politics and
government—21st century—Comic books, strips, etc. 3. Subways—Egypt—Cairo—Comic
books, strips, etc. 4. Graphic novels. I. Rossetti, Chip. II. Title.
  PN6790.E3S5313 2012
  741.5'962—dc23

                                                                    2012007732

Henry Holt books are available for special promotions and premiums.
For details contact: Director, Special Markets.

First U. S. Edition 2012
Designed by Meryl Sussman Levavi and Linda Kosarin
Hand-lettering by Rebecca Seltzer
Map of the Cairo metro by Jani Patokallio

To the memory of my father and mother,

and to Egypt's bloggers,

who give me hope that there is still light in the world

TRANSLATOR'S NOTE

Metro is sprinkled with current and cultural references, most of which would be instantly familiar to an Egyptian audience. The ring tones of the various cell phones in the book, for example, are often snippets of popular music. Thus on page 5, the young woman's cell phone in the third panel, second row, is playing a line from "Ahla Haga Feeki," or "The Best Thing About You," a 2007 hit by popular singer Mohammed Hamaki. The ring tone of the boy next to her is "Ooh, I love you, donkey," from "Bahebak Ya Himur"—literally, love song to a donkey, although, as in English, "donkey" could also refer to someone stupid. The singer is Sa'd El Soghayar, and the song appears in the 2006 comedy film *Aleya al-Tarab bil-Talaata*, loosely meaning "Musical Divorce." The ring tone in the final panel of that row is from "Enta Omri" ("You Are My Life"), a signature song of the great Umm Kulthoum, the Arab world's most renowned twentieth-century singer. On page 40, the radio is playing the opening line from "Lama el-Naseem"—"When the Wind"—by beloved contemporary Egyptian singer Mohammed Mounir.

There are several other references that warrant explanation: on page 19, Wannas takes offense when a boy hands him his "slipper." Wannas is a Sa'idi from Sa'id, or Upper Egypt, whose people are considered hicks and are often the target of Egyptian jokes. He wears a kind of rustic shoe known as a *shibshib*, and is inevitably insulted that the boy mistakes it for indoor footwear. On page 51 and elsewhere, mention is made of the Sayyida Zaynab metro station, district, and festival. This central

Cairo neighborhood is home to the Sayyida Zaynab Mosque, which is a shrine to Zaynab bint Ali, a descendant (or *sayyid*) of the prophet Muhammad. The district holds an annual festival in honor of Sayyida Zaynab's birthday.

Finally, the term "Hajj" (pronounced "hagg" in colloquial Egyptian) is formally bestowed on a Muslim who has made the hajj pilgrimage to Mecca. In informal usage, it signifies respect, but in the case of Ghareeb, the term is decidedly ironic.

metro

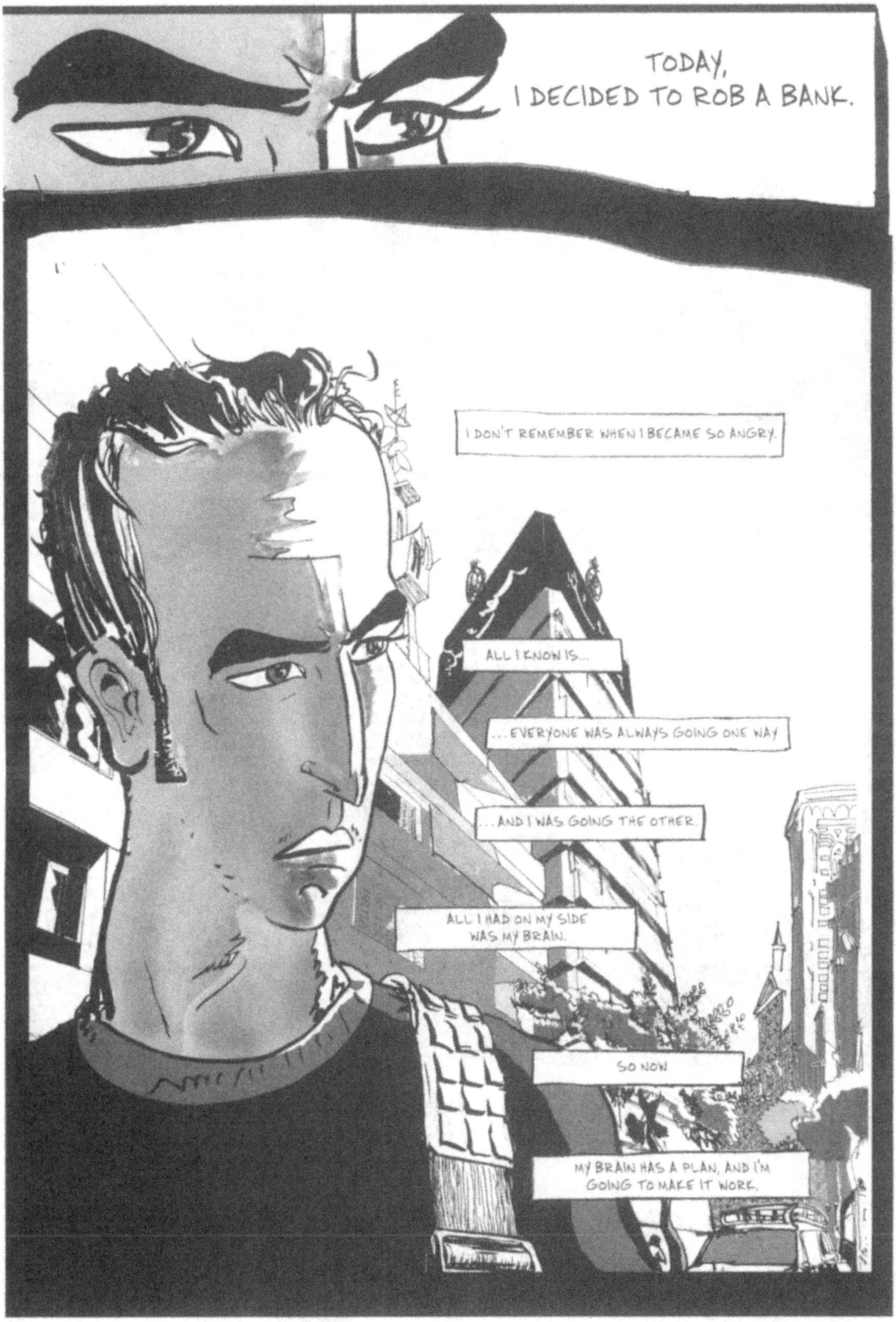
TODAY,
I DECIDED TO ROB A BANK.
I DON'T REMEMBER WHEN I BECAME SO ANGRY.
ALL I KNOW IS...
...EVERYONE WAS ALWAYS GOING ONE WAY
...AND I WAS GOING THE OTHER.
ALL I HAD ON MY SIDE
WAS MY BRAIN.
SO NOW
MY BRAIN HAS A PLAN, AND I'M
GOING TO MAKE IT WORK.

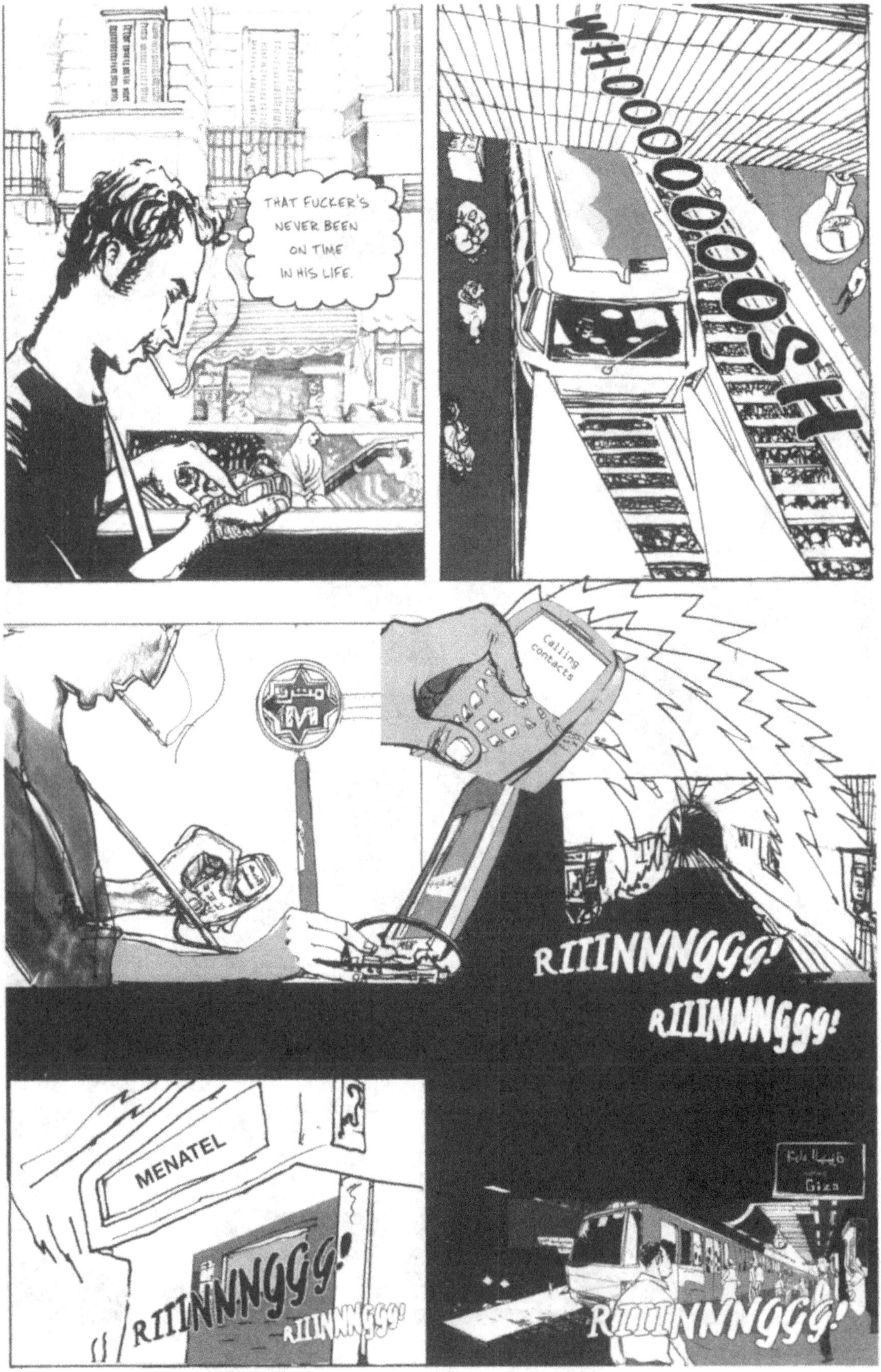
THAT FUCKER'S NEVER BEEN ON TIME IN HIS LIFE.
WHOOOOOOOOOSH
Calling contacts
RIIINNNGGG!
RIIINNNGGG!
MENATEL
RIIINNNGGG!
RIIINNNGGG!
Giza
RIIIINNNGGG!

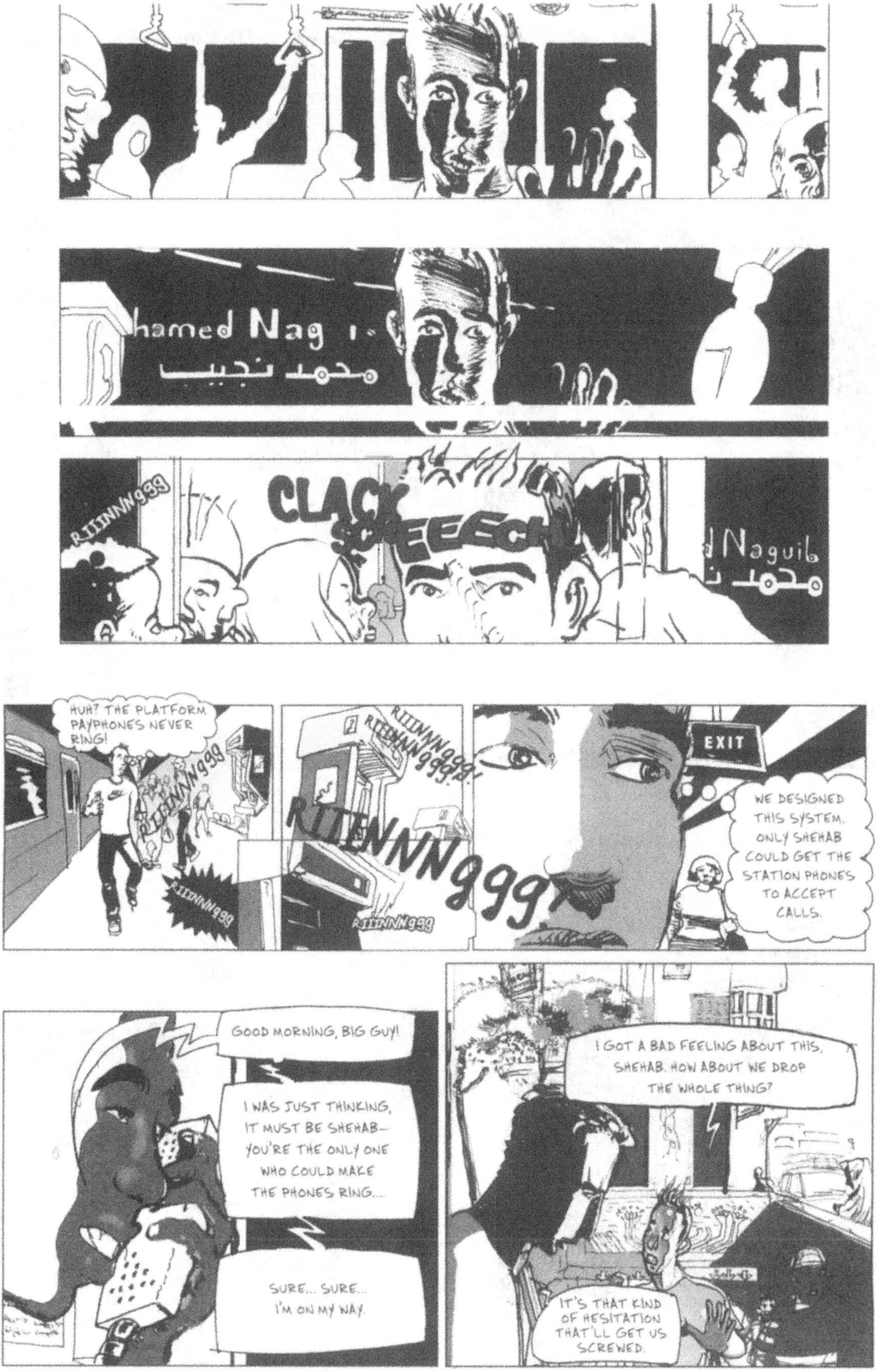
hamed Nag
محمد نجيب
RIIINNNggg
CLACK
SCREEECH
d Naguib
محمد ن
HUH? THE PLATFORM PAYPHONES NEVER RING!
RIIINNNggg
RIIINNNggg
RIIINNNggg
RIIINNNggg
RIIINNNggg
RIIENNNggg
EXIT
WE DESIGNED THIS SYSTEM. ONLY SHEHAB COULD GET THE STATION PHONES TO ACCEPT CALLS.
GOOD MORNING, BIG GUY!
I WAS JUST THINKING, IT MUST BE SHEHAB— YOU'RE THE ONLY ONE WHO COULD MAKE THE PHONES RING....
SURE... SURE... I'M ON MY WAY.
I GOT A BAD FEELING ABOUT THIS, SHEHAB. HOW ABOUT WE DROP THE WHOLE THING?
IT'S THAT KIND OF HESITATION THAT'LL GET US SCREWED.

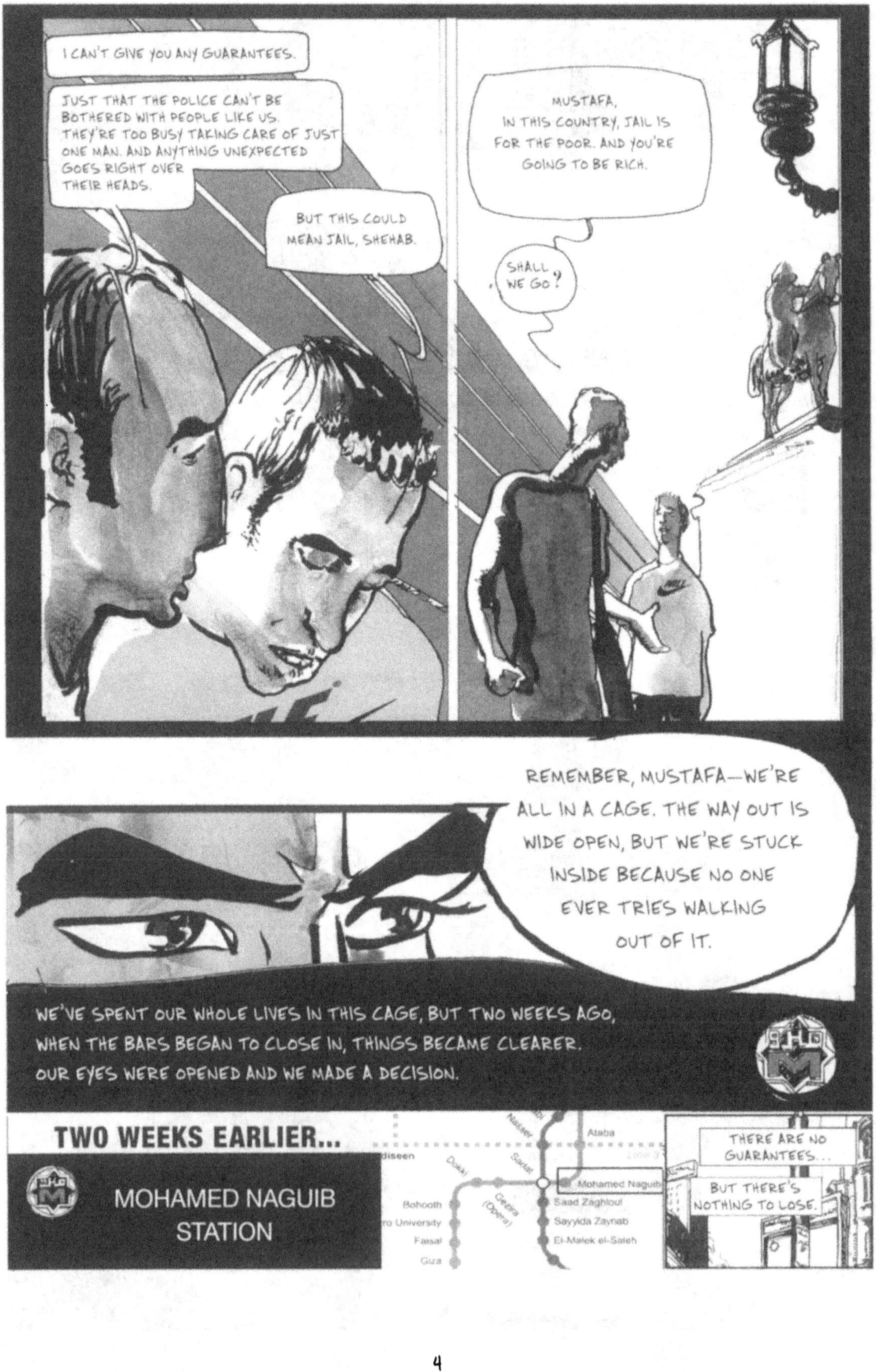

I CAN'T GIVE YOU ANY GUARANTEES.
JUST THAT THE POLICE CAN'T BE BOTHERED WITH PEOPLE LIKE US. THEY'RE TOO BUSY TAKING CARE OF JUST ONE MAN. AND ANYTHING UNEXPECTED GOES RIGHT OVER THEIR HEADS.
BUT THIS COULD MEAN JAIL, SHEHAB.
MUSTAFA, IN THIS COUNTRY, JAIL IS FOR THE POOR. AND YOU'RE GOING TO BE RICH.
SHALL WE GO?
REMEMBER, MUSTAFA—WE'RE ALL IN A CAGE. THE WAY OUT IS WIDE OPEN, BUT WE'RE STUCK INSIDE BECAUSE NO ONE EVER TRIES WALKING OUT OF IT.
WE'VE SPENT OUR WHOLE LIVES IN THIS CAGE, BUT TWO WEEKS AGO, WHEN THE BARS BEGAN TO CLOSE IN, THINGS BECAME CLEARER. OUR EYES WERE OPENED AND WE MADE A DECISION.
TWO WEEKS EARLIER...
MOHAMED NAGUIB STATION
Ataba
Mohamed Naguib
Saad Zaghloul
Sayyida Zaynab
El-Malek el-Saleh
Sadat
Dokki
Gezira (Opera)
Bohooth
Faisal
Giza
THERE ARE NO GUARANTEES...
BUT THERE'S NOTHING TO LOSE.

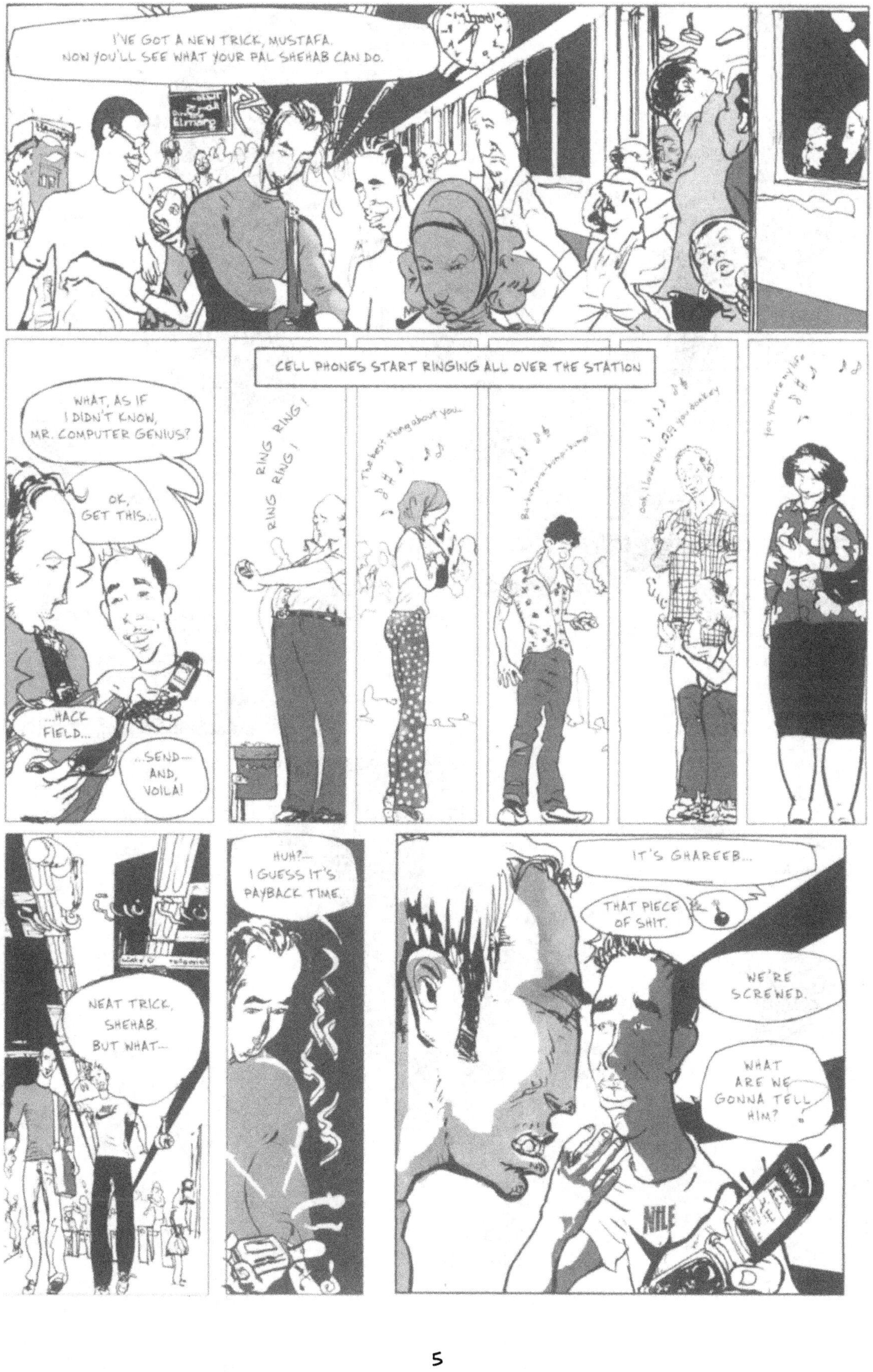
I'VE GOT A NEW TRICK, MUSTAFA. NOW YOU'LL SEE WHAT YOUR PAL SHEHAB CAN DO.
WHAT, AS IF I DIDN'T KNOW, MR. COMPUTER GENIUS?
OK, GET THIS...
...HACK FIELD...
...SEND— AND, VOILA!
CELL PHONES START RINGING ALL OVER THE STATION
RING RING! RING RING!
The best thing about you...
Bu-bump-a-bump-a-bump
you donkey
You you are my life
NEAT TRICK, SHEHAB. BUT WHAT...
HUH?... I GUESS IT'S PAYBACK TIME.
IT'S GHAREEB...
THAT PIECE OF SHIT.
WE'RE SCREWED.
WHAT ARE WE GONNA TELL HIM?
NILE

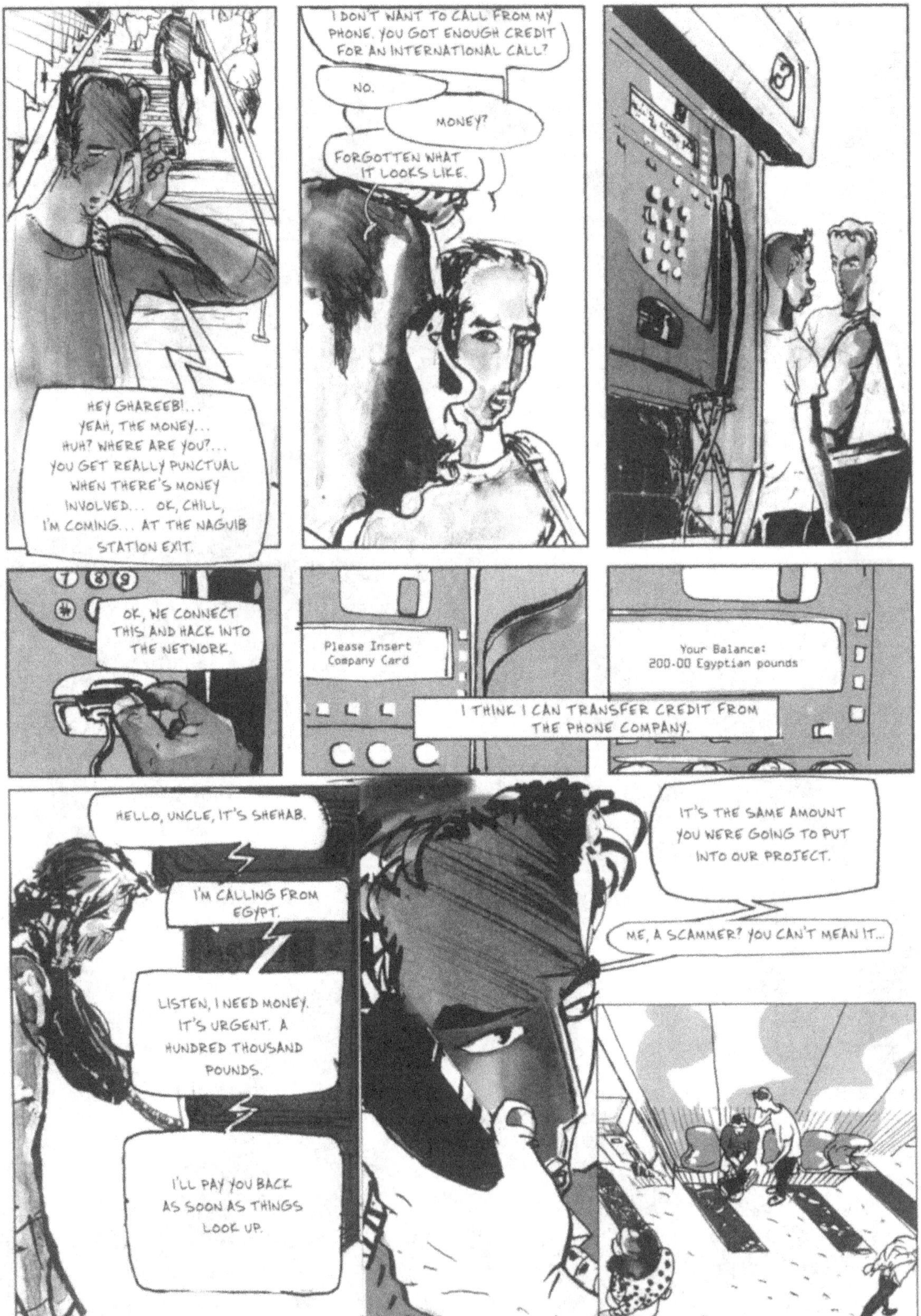
HEY GHAREEB!... YEAH, THE MONEY... HUH? WHERE ARE YOU?... YOU GET REALLY PUNCTUAL WHEN THERE'S MONEY INVOLVED... OK, CHILL, I'M COMING... AT THE NAGUIB STATION EXIT.
I DON'T WANT TO CALL FROM MY PHONE. YOU GOT ENOUGH CREDIT FOR AN INTERNATIONAL CALL?
NO.
MONEY?
FORGOTTEN WHAT IT LOOKS LIKE.
OK, WE CONNECT THIS AND HACK INTO THE NETWORK.
Please Insert Company Card
Your Balance: 200.00 Egyptian pounds
I THINK I CAN TRANSFER CREDIT FROM THE PHONE COMPANY.
HELLO, UNCLE, IT'S SHEHAB.
I'M CALLING FROM EGYPT.
LISTEN, I NEED MONEY. IT'S URGENT. A HUNDRED THOUSAND POUNDS.
I'LL PAY YOU BACK AS SOON AS THINGS LOOK UP.
IT'S THE SAME AMOUNT YOU WERE GOING TO PUT INTO OUR PROJECT.
ME, A SCAMMER? YOU CAN'T MEAN IT...

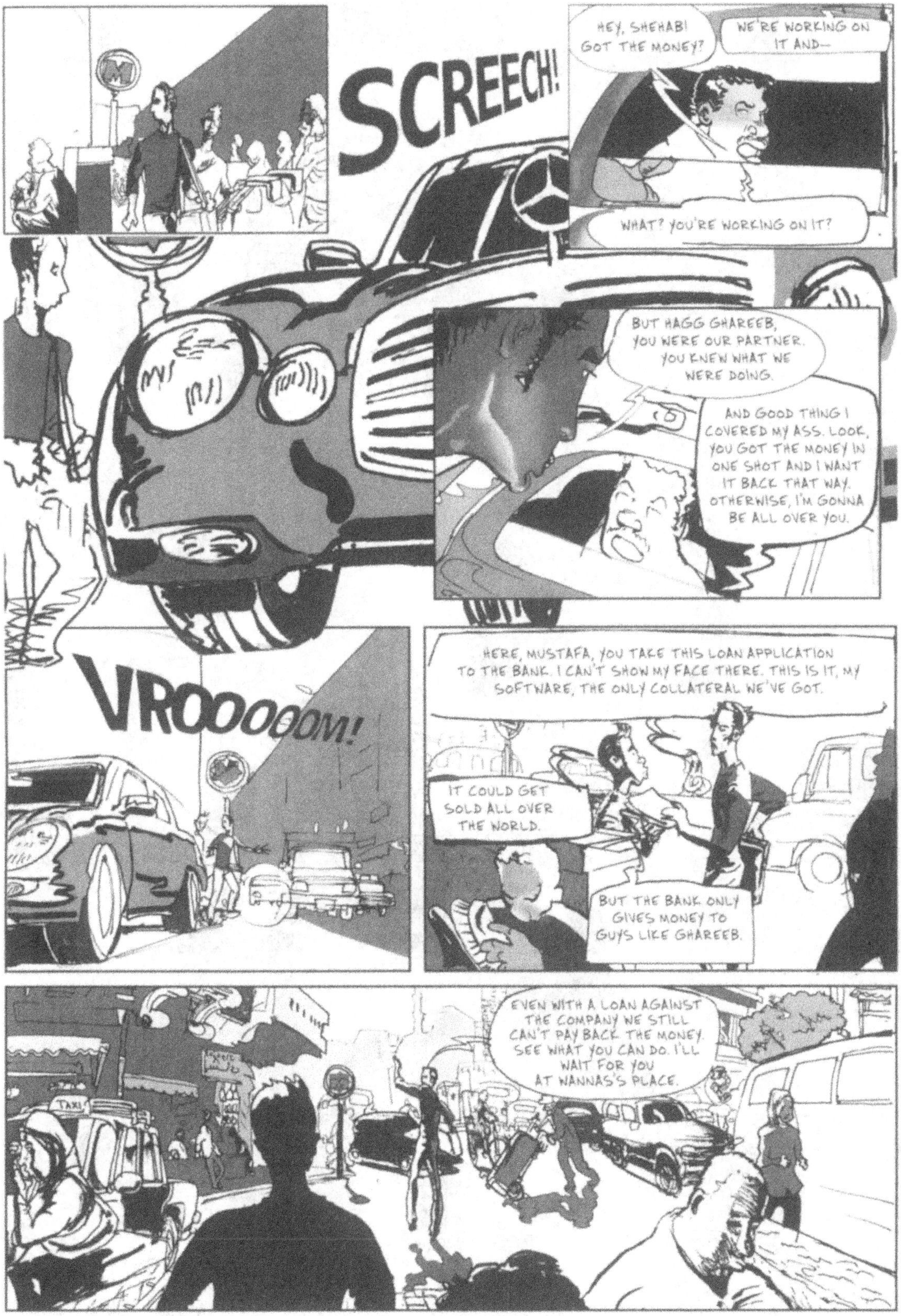
SCREECH!
HEY, SHEHAB! GOT THE MONEY?
WE'RE WORKING ON IT AND—
WHAT? YOU'RE WORKING ON IT?
BUT HAGG GHAREEB, YOU WERE OUR PARTNER. YOU KNEW WHAT WE WERE DOING.
AND GOOD THING I COVERED MY ASS. LOOK, YOU GOT THE MONEY IN ONE SHOT AND I WANT IT BACK THAT WAY. OTHERWISE, I'M GONNA BE ALL OVER YOU.
VROOOOOM!
HERE, MUSTAFA, YOU TAKE THIS LOAN APPLICATION TO THE BANK. I CAN'T SHOW MY FACE THERE. THIS IS IT, MY SOFTWARE, THE ONLY COLLATERAL WE'VE GOT.
IT COULD GET SOLD ALL OVER THE WORLD.
BUT THE BANK ONLY GIVES MONEY TO GUYS LIKE GHAREEB.
TAXI
EVEN WITH A LOAN AGAINST THE COMPANY WE STILL CAN'T PAY BACK THE MONEY. SEE WHAT YOU CAN DO. I'LL WAIT FOR YOU AT WANNAS'S PLACE.

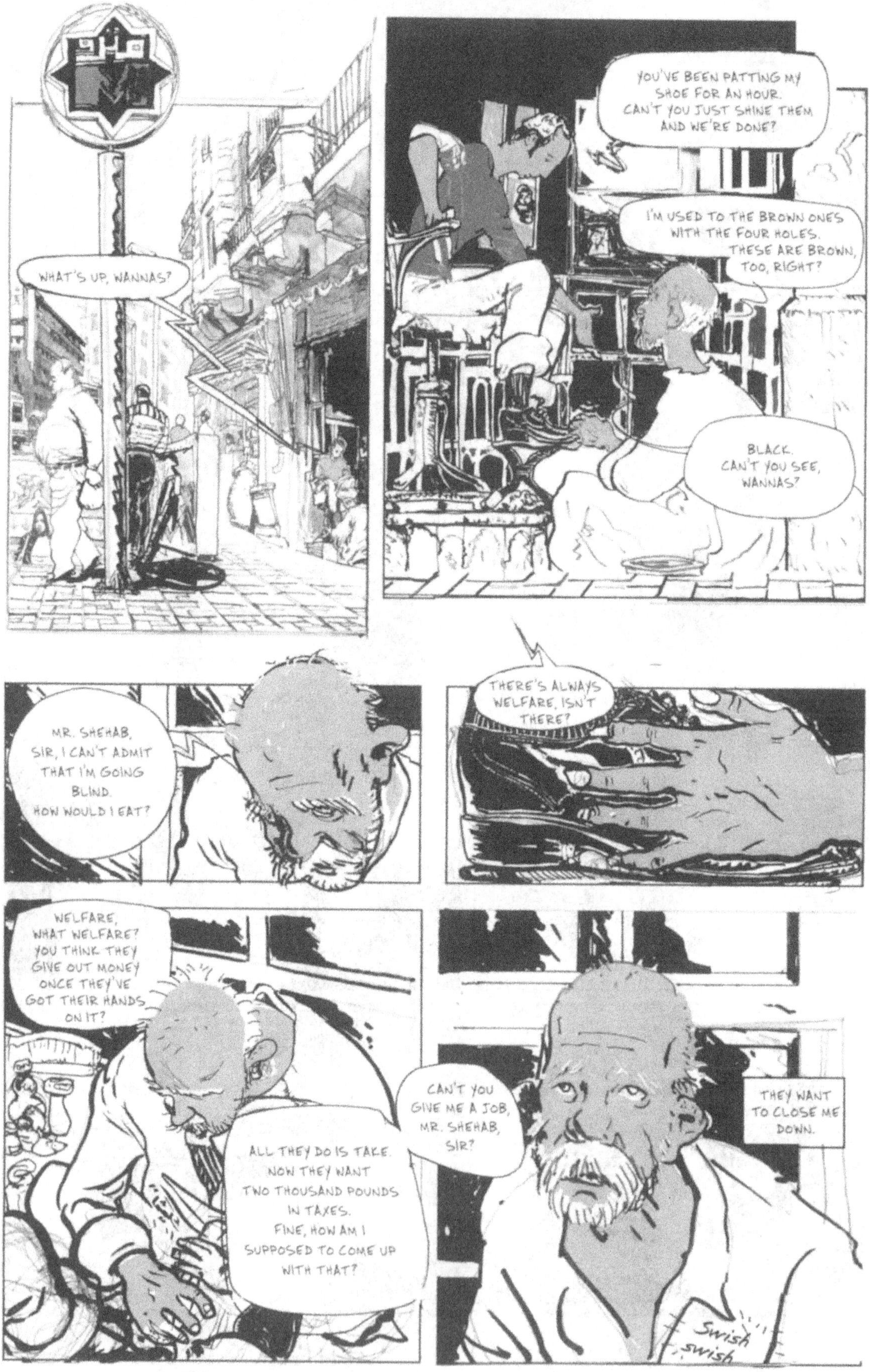
WHAT'S UP, WANNAS?
YOU'VE BEEN PATTING MY SHOE FOR AN HOUR. CAN'T YOU JUST SHINE THEM AND WE'RE DONE?
I'M USED TO THE BROWN ONES WITH THE FOUR HOLES. THESE ARE BROWN, TOO, RIGHT?
BLACK. CAN'T YOU SEE, WANNAS?
MR. SHEHAB, SIR, I CAN'T ADMIT THAT I'M GOING BLIND. HOW WOULD I EAT?
THERE'S ALWAYS WELFARE, ISN'T THERE?
WELFARE, WHAT WELFARE? YOU THINK THEY GIVE OUT MONEY ONCE THEY'VE GOT THEIR HANDS ON IT?
ALL THEY DO IS TAKE. NOW THEY WANT TWO THOUSAND POUNDS IN TAXES. FINE, HOW AM I SUPPOSED TO COME UP WITH THAT?
THEY WANT TO CLOSE ME DOWN.
CAN'T YOU GIVE ME A JOB, MR. SHEHAB, SIR?
Swish swish

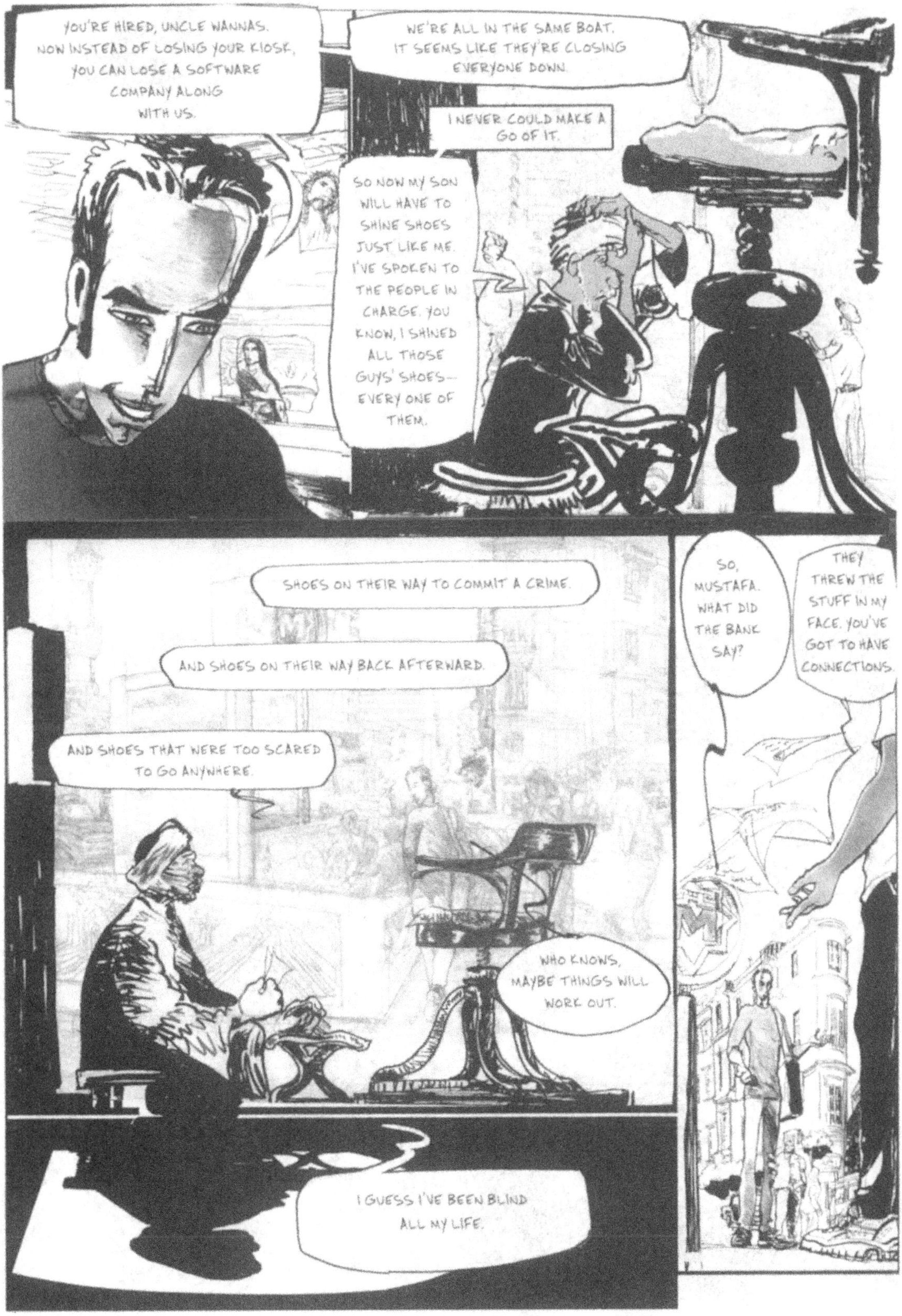
YOU'RE HIRED, UNCLE WANNAS. NOW INSTEAD OF LOSING YOUR KIOSK, YOU CAN LOSE A SOFTWARE COMPANY ALONG WITH US.
WE'RE ALL IN THE SAME BOAT. IT SEEMS LIKE THEY'RE CLOSING EVERYONE DOWN.
I NEVER COULD MAKE A GO OF IT.
SO NOW MY SON WILL HAVE TO SHINE SHOES JUST LIKE ME. I'VE SPOKEN TO THE PEOPLE IN CHARGE. YOU KNOW, I SHINED ALL THOSE GUYS' SHOES— EVERY ONE OF THEM.
SHOES ON THEIR WAY TO COMMIT A CRIME.
AND SHOES ON THEIR WAY BACK AFTERWARD.
AND SHOES THAT WERE TOO SCARED TO GO ANYWHERE.
WHO KNOWS, MAYBE THINGS WILL WORK OUT.
I GUESS I'VE BEEN BLIND ALL MY LIFE.
SO, MUSTAFA. WHAT DID THE BANK SAY?
THEY THREW THE STUFF IN MY FACE. YOU'VE GOT TO HAVE CONNECTIONS.

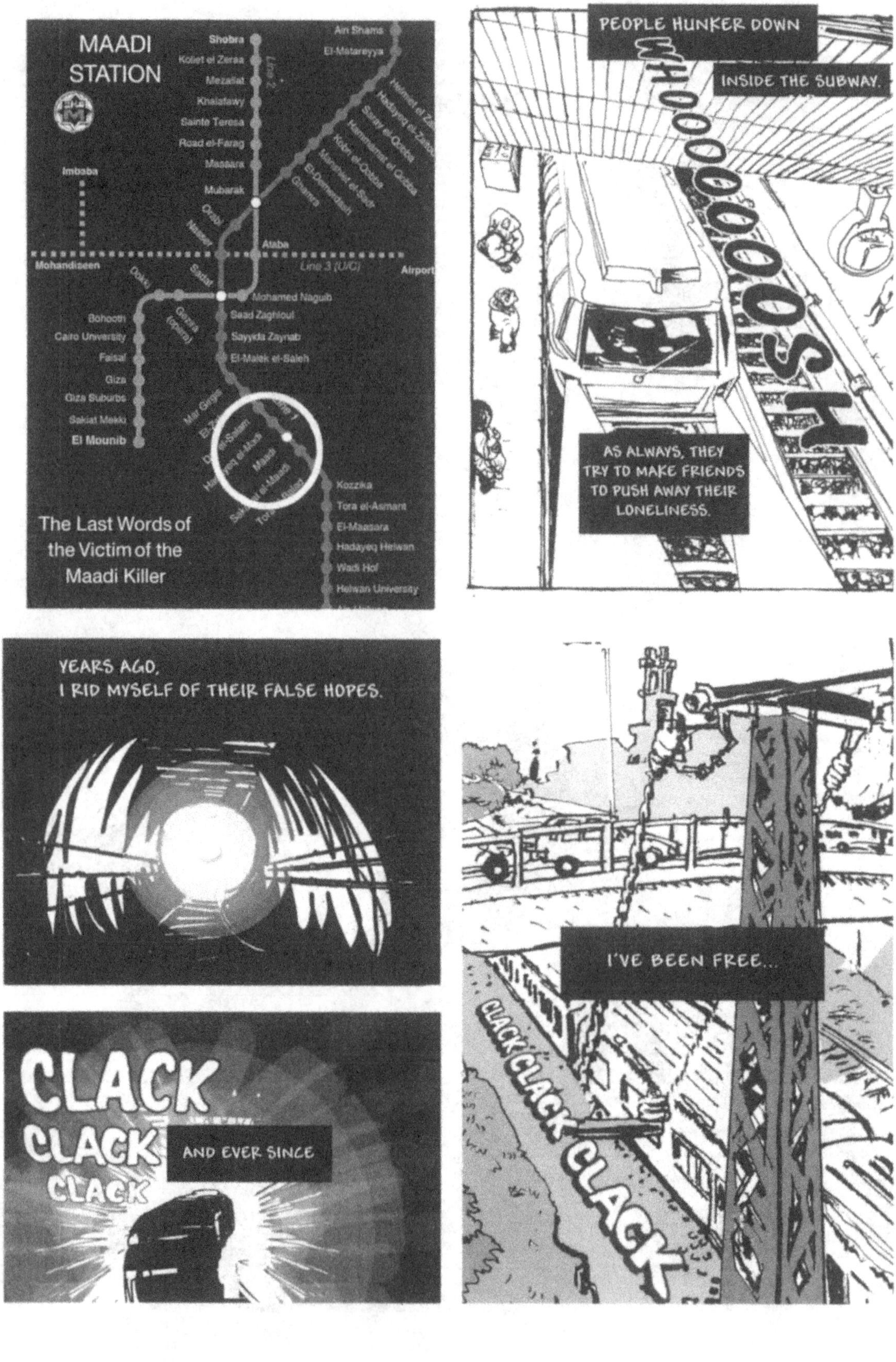
MAADI
STATION
Shobra
Koliet el Zeraa
Mezallat
Khalafawy
Sainte Teresa
Road el-Farag
Massara
Mubarak
Ataba
Imbaba
Mohandizeen
Line 3 (U/C)
Airport
Ain Shams
El-Matareyya
Line 2
Dokki
Sadat
Mohamed Naguib
Saad Zaghloul
Sayyida Zaynab
El-Malek el-Saleh
Bohooth
Cairo University
Faisal
Giza
Giza Suburbs
Sakiat Mekki
El Mounib
Gezira (Opera)
Mar Girgis
Kozzika
Tora el-Asmant
El-Maasara
Hadayeq Helwan
Wadi Hof
Helwan University
The Last Words of
the Victim of the
Maadi Killer
PEOPLE HUNKER DOWN
INSIDE THE SUBWAY.
WHOOOOOOOOOSH
AS ALWAYS, THEY TRY TO MAKE FRIENDS TO PUSH AWAY THEIR LONELINESS.
YEARS AGO, I RID MYSELF OF THEIR FALSE HOPES.
CLACK
CLACK
CLACK
AND EVER SINCE
I'VE BEEN FREE...
CLACK CLACK CLACK CLACK

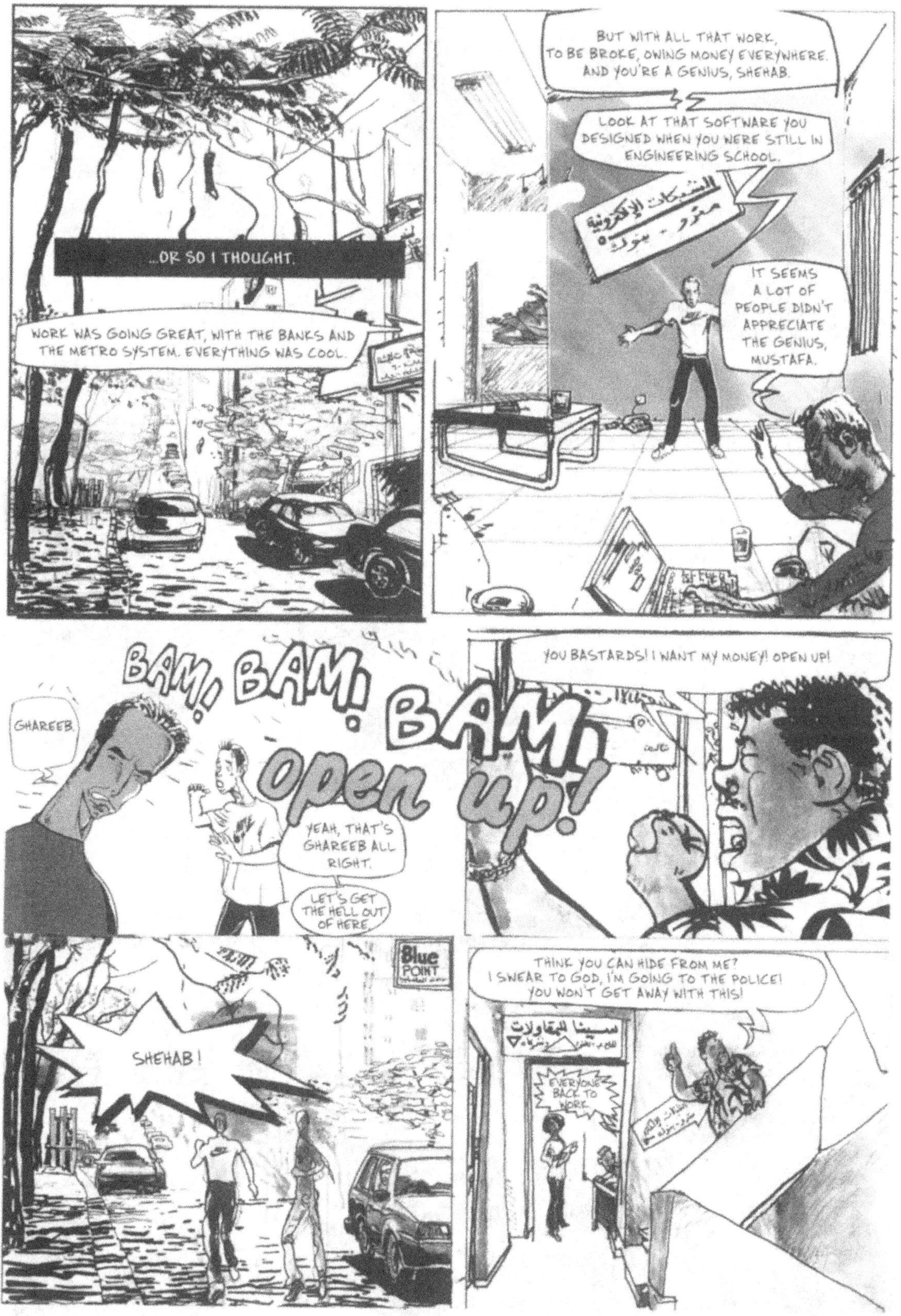
...OR SO I THOUGHT.
WORK WAS GOING GREAT, WITH THE BANKS AND THE METRO SYSTEM. EVERYTHING WAS COOL.
BUT WITH ALL THAT WORK, TO BE BROKE, OWING MONEY EVERYWHERE. AND YOU'RE A GENIUS, SHEHAB.
LOOK AT THAT SOFTWARE YOU DESIGNED WHEN YOU WERE STILL IN ENGINEERING SCHOOL.
IT SEEMS A LOT OF PEOPLE DIDN'T APPRECIATE THE GENIUS, MUSTAFA.
BAM! BAM! BAM!
open up!
YOU BASTARDS! I WANT MY MONEY! OPEN UP!
GHAREEB.
YEAH, THAT'S GHAREEB ALL RIGHT.
LET'S GET THE HELL OUT OF HERE.
Blue POINT
SHEHAB!
THINK YOU CAN HIDE FROM ME? I SWEAR TO GOD, I'M GOING TO THE POLICE! YOU WON'T GET AWAY WITH THIS!
سيناء للمقاولات
EVERYONE BACK TO WORK.

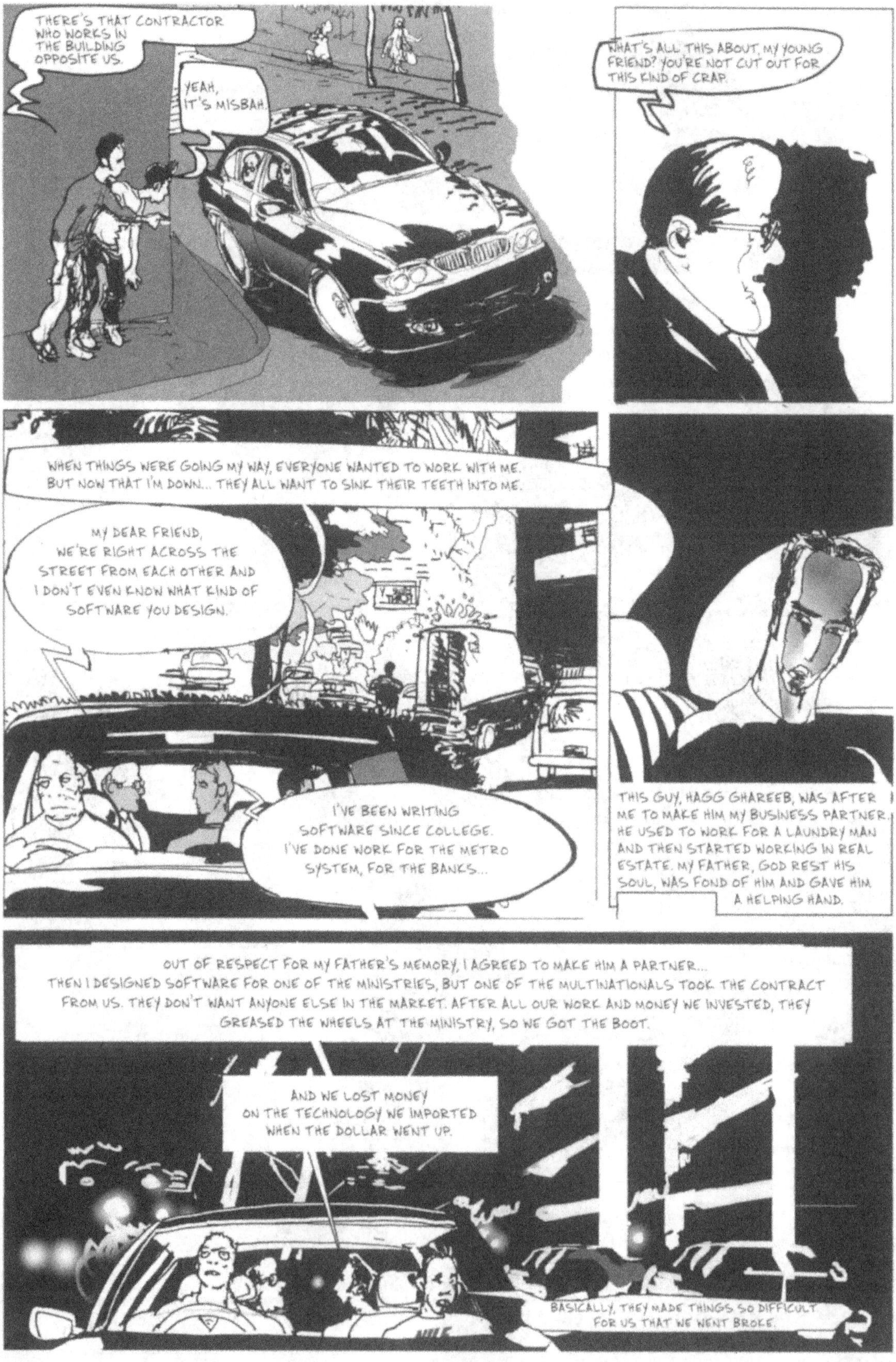
THERE'S THAT CONTRACTOR WHO WORKS IN THE BUILDING OPPOSITE US.
YEAH, IT'S MISBAH.
WHAT'S ALL THIS ABOUT, MY YOUNG FRIEND? YOU'RE NOT CUT OUT FOR THIS KIND OF CRAP.
WHEN THINGS WERE GOING MY WAY, EVERYONE WANTED TO WORK WITH ME. BUT NOW THAT I'M DOWN... THEY ALL WANT TO SINK THEIR TEETH INTO ME.
MY DEAR FRIEND, WE'RE RIGHT ACROSS THE STREET FROM EACH OTHER AND I DON'T EVEN KNOW WHAT KIND OF SOFTWARE YOU DESIGN.
I'VE BEEN WRITING SOFTWARE SINCE COLLEGE. I'VE DONE WORK FOR THE METRO SYSTEM, FOR THE BANKS...
THIS GUY, HAGG GHAREEB, WAS AFTER ME TO MAKE HIM MY BUSINESS PARTNER. HE USED TO WORK FOR A LAUNDRY MAN AND THEN STARTED WORKING IN REAL ESTATE. MY FATHER, GOD REST HIS SOUL, WAS FOND OF HIM AND GAVE HIM A HELPING HAND.
OUT OF RESPECT FOR MY FATHER'S MEMORY, I AGREED TO MAKE HIM A PARTNER... THEN I DESIGNED SOFTWARE FOR ONE OF THE MINISTRIES, BUT ONE OF THE MULTINATIONALS TOOK THE CONTRACT FROM US. THEY DON'T WANT ANYONE ELSE IN THE MARKET. AFTER ALL OUR WORK AND MONEY WE INVESTED, THEY GREASED THE WHEELS AT THE MINISTRY, SO WE GOT THE BOOT.
AND WE LOST MONEY ON THE TECHNOLOGY WE IMPORTED WHEN THE DOLLAR WENT UP.
BASICALLY, THEY MADE THINGS SO DIFFICULT FOR US THAT WE WENT BROKE.

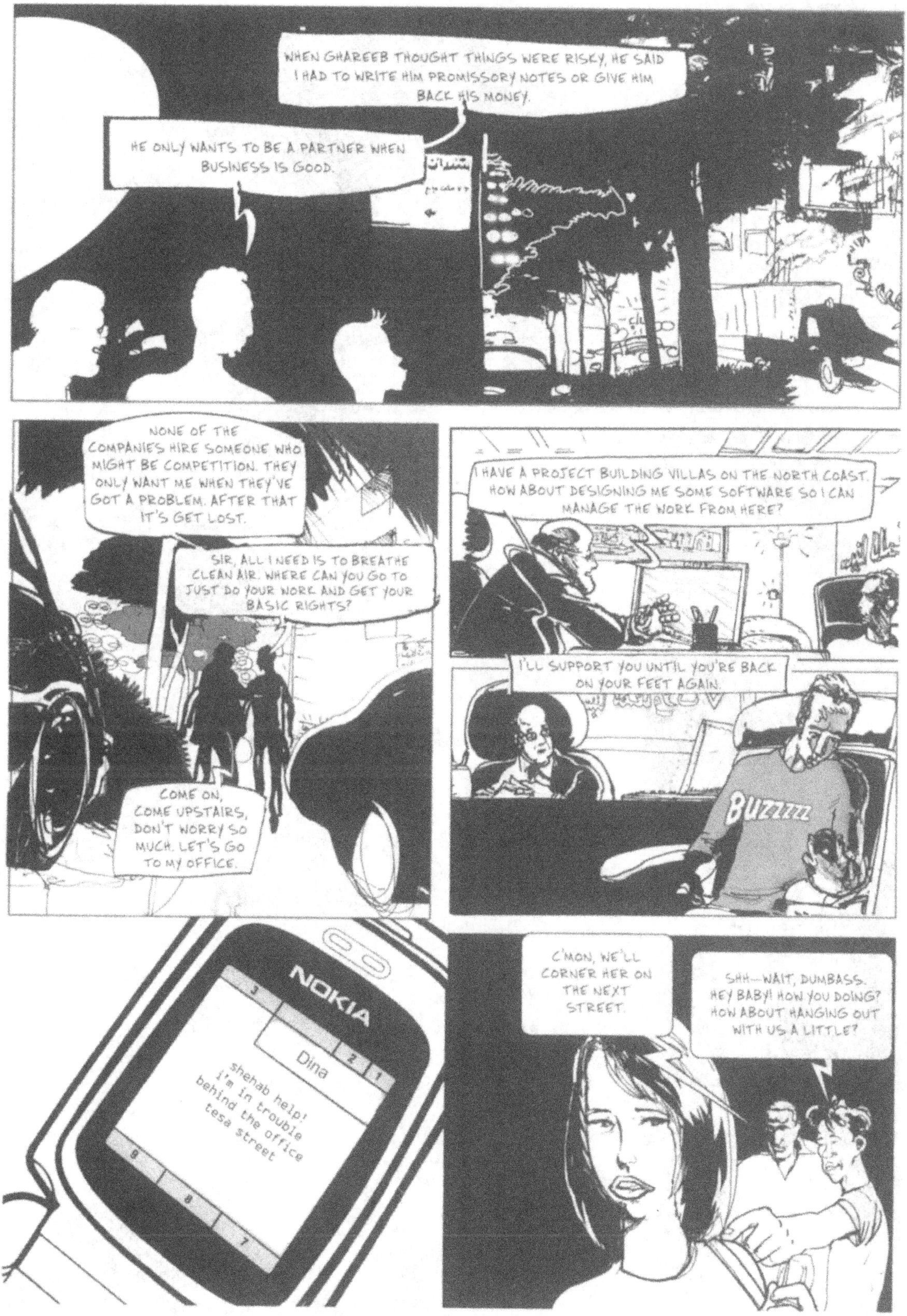
WHEN GHAREEB THOUGHT THINGS WERE RISKY, HE SAID I HAD TO WRITE HIM PROMISSORY NOTES OR GIVE HIM BACK HIS MONEY.
HE ONLY WANTS TO BE A PARTNER WHEN BUSINESS IS GOOD.
NONE OF THE COMPANIES HIRE SOMEONE WHO MIGHT BE COMPETITION. THEY ONLY WANT ME WHEN THEY'VE GOT A PROBLEM. AFTER THAT IT'S GET LOST.
SIR, ALL I NEED IS TO BREATHE CLEAN AIR. WHERE CAN YOU GO TO JUST DO YOUR WORK AND GET YOUR BASIC RIGHTS?
COME ON, COME UPSTAIRS, DON'T WORRY SO MUCH. LET'S GO TO MY OFFICE.
I HAVE A PROJECT BUILDING VILLAS ON THE NORTH COAST. HOW ABOUT DESIGNING ME SOME SOFTWARE SO I CAN MANAGE THE WORK FROM HERE?
I'LL SUPPORT YOU UNTIL YOU'RE BACK ON YOUR FEET AGAIN.
BUZZZZZ
NOKIA
Dina
shehab help! i'm in trouble behind the office tesa street
C'MON, WE'LL CORNER HER ON THE NEXT STREET.
SHH—WAIT, DUMBASS. HEY BABY! HOW YOU DOING? HOW ABOUT HANGING OUT WITH US A LITTLE?

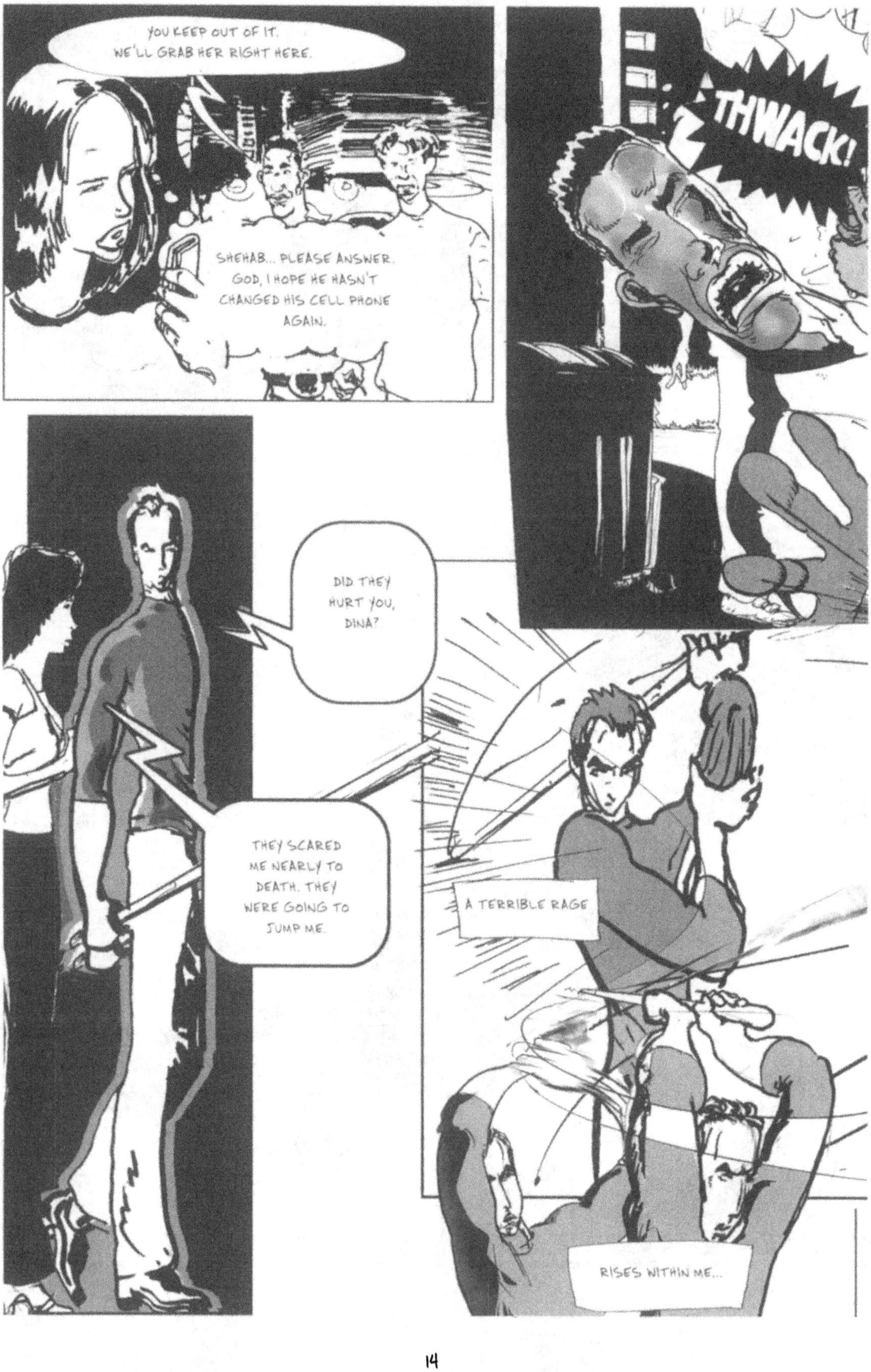
YOU KEEP OUT OF IT. WE'LL GRAB HER RIGHT HERE.
SHEHAB... PLEASE ANSWER. GOD, I HOPE HE HASN'T CHANGED HIS CELL PHONE AGAIN.
THWACK!
DID THEY HURT YOU, DINA?
THEY SCARED ME NEARLY TO DEATH. THEY WERE GOING TO JUMP ME.
A TERRIBLE RAGE
RISES WITHIN ME...

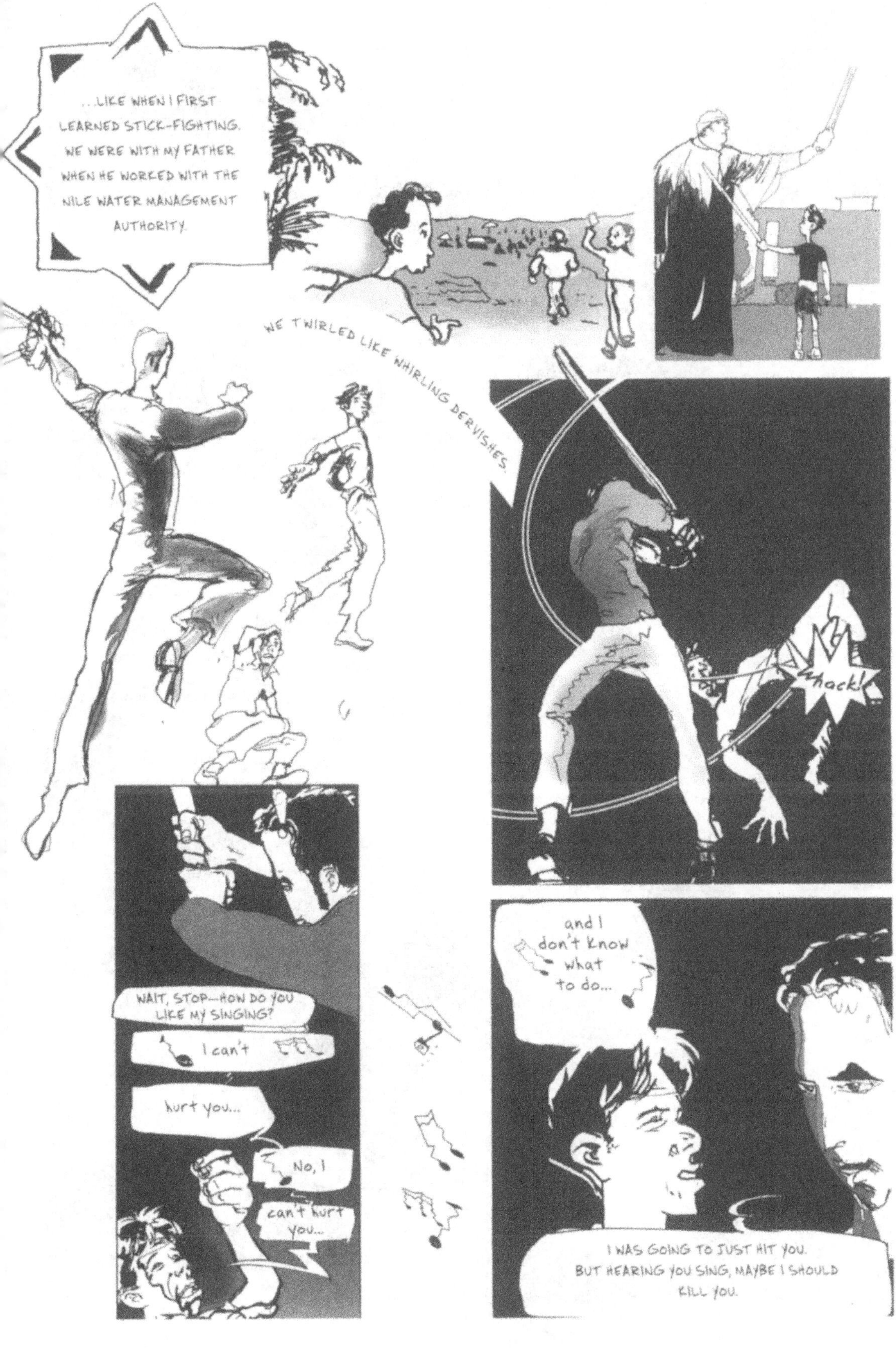

...LIKE WHEN I FIRST LEARNED STICK-FIGHTING. WE WERE WITH MY FATHER WHEN HE WORKED WITH THE NILE WATER MANAGEMENT AUTHORITY.
WE TWIRLED LIKE WHIRLING DERVISHES.
whack!
WAIT, STOP—HOW DO YOU LIKE MY SINGING?
I can't
hurt you...
No, I
can't hurt you...
and I don't know what to do...
I WAS GOING TO JUST HIT YOU. BUT HEARING YOU SING, MAYBE I SHOULD KILL YOU.

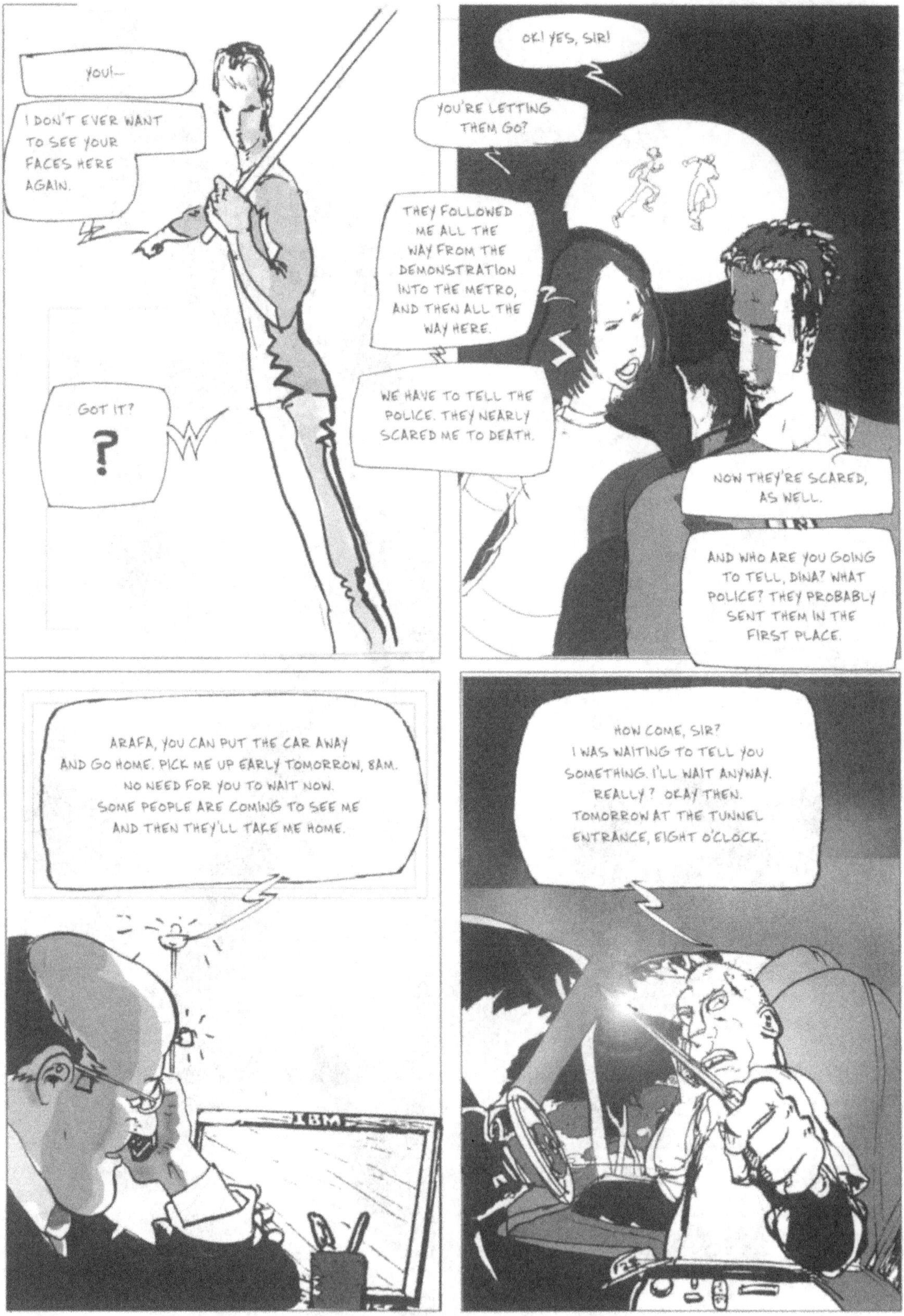
YOU!—
I DON'T EVER WANT TO SEE YOUR FACES HERE AGAIN.
GOT IT?
?
OK! YES, SIR!
YOU'RE LETTING THEM GO?
THEY FOLLOWED ME ALL THE WAY FROM THE DEMONSTRATION INTO THE METRO, AND THEN ALL THE WAY HERE.
WE HAVE TO TELL THE POLICE. THEY NEARLY SCARED ME TO DEATH.
NOW THEY'RE SCARED, AS WELL.
AND WHO ARE YOU GOING TO TELL, DINA? WHAT POLICE? THEY PROBABLY SENT THEM IN THE FIRST PLACE.
ARAFA, YOU CAN PUT THE CAR AWAY AND GO HOME. PICK ME UP EARLY TOMORROW, 8AM. NO NEED FOR YOU TO WAIT NOW. SOME PEOPLE ARE COMING TO SEE ME AND THEN THEY'LL TAKE ME HOME.
IBM
HOW COME, SIR? I WAS WAITING TO TELL YOU SOMETHING. I'LL WAIT ANYWAY. REALLY? OKAY THEN. TOMORROW AT THE TUNNEL ENTRANCE, EIGHT O'CLOCK.

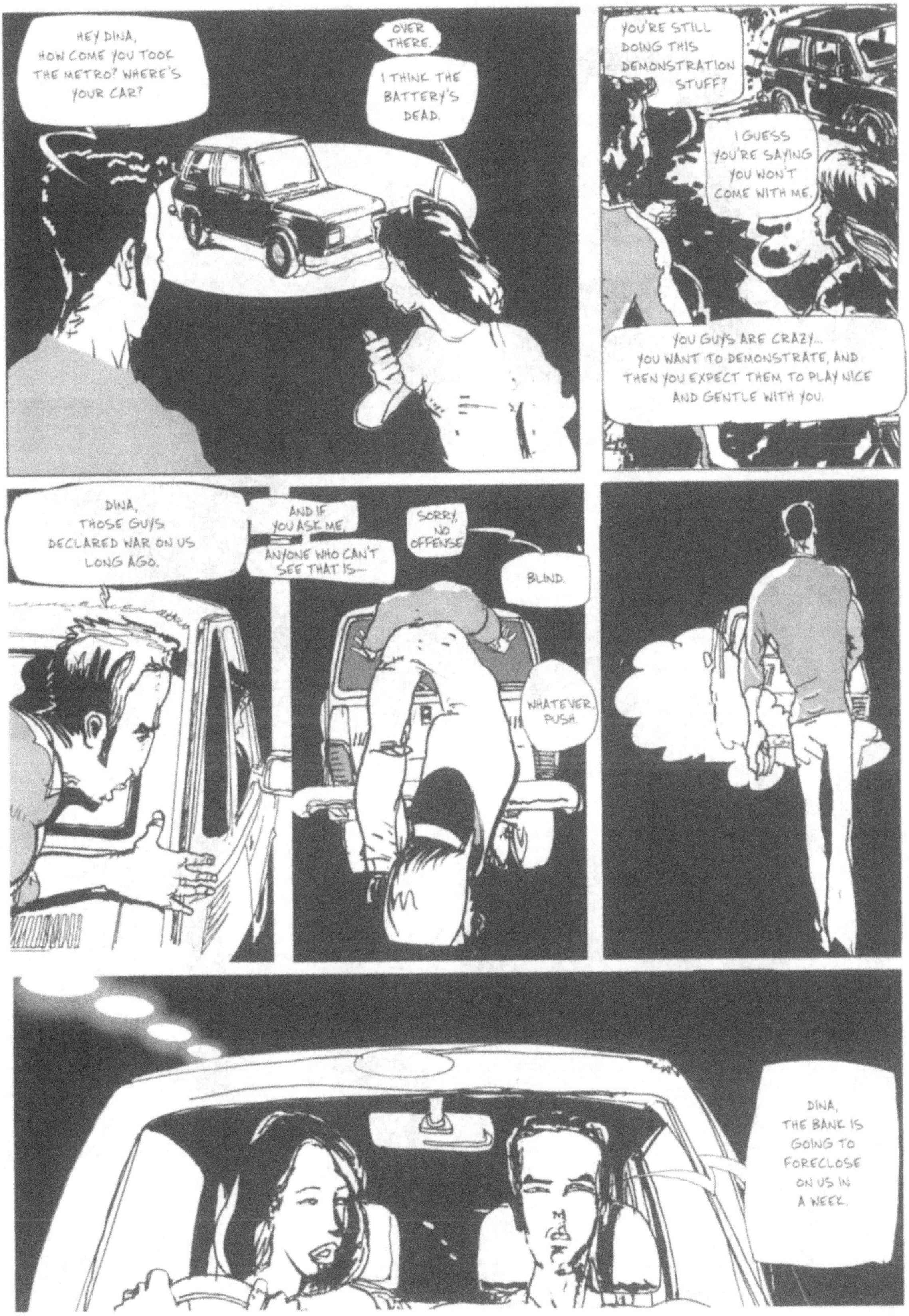
HEY DINA, HOW COME YOU TOOK THE METRO? WHERE'S YOUR CAR?
OVER THERE.
I THINK THE BATTERY'S DEAD.
YOU'RE STILL DOING THIS DEMONSTRATION STUFF?
I GUESS YOU'RE SAYING YOU WON'T COME WITH ME.
YOU GUYS ARE CRAZY... YOU WANT TO DEMONSTRATE, AND THEN YOU EXPECT THEM TO PLAY NICE AND GENTLE WITH YOU.
DINA, THOSE GUYS DECLARED WAR ON US LONG AGO.
AND IF YOU ASK ME,
ANYONE WHO CAN'T SEE THAT IS—
SORRY, NO OFFENSE
BLIND.
WHATEVER. PUSH.
DINA, THE BANK IS GOING TO FORECLOSE ON US IN A WEEK.

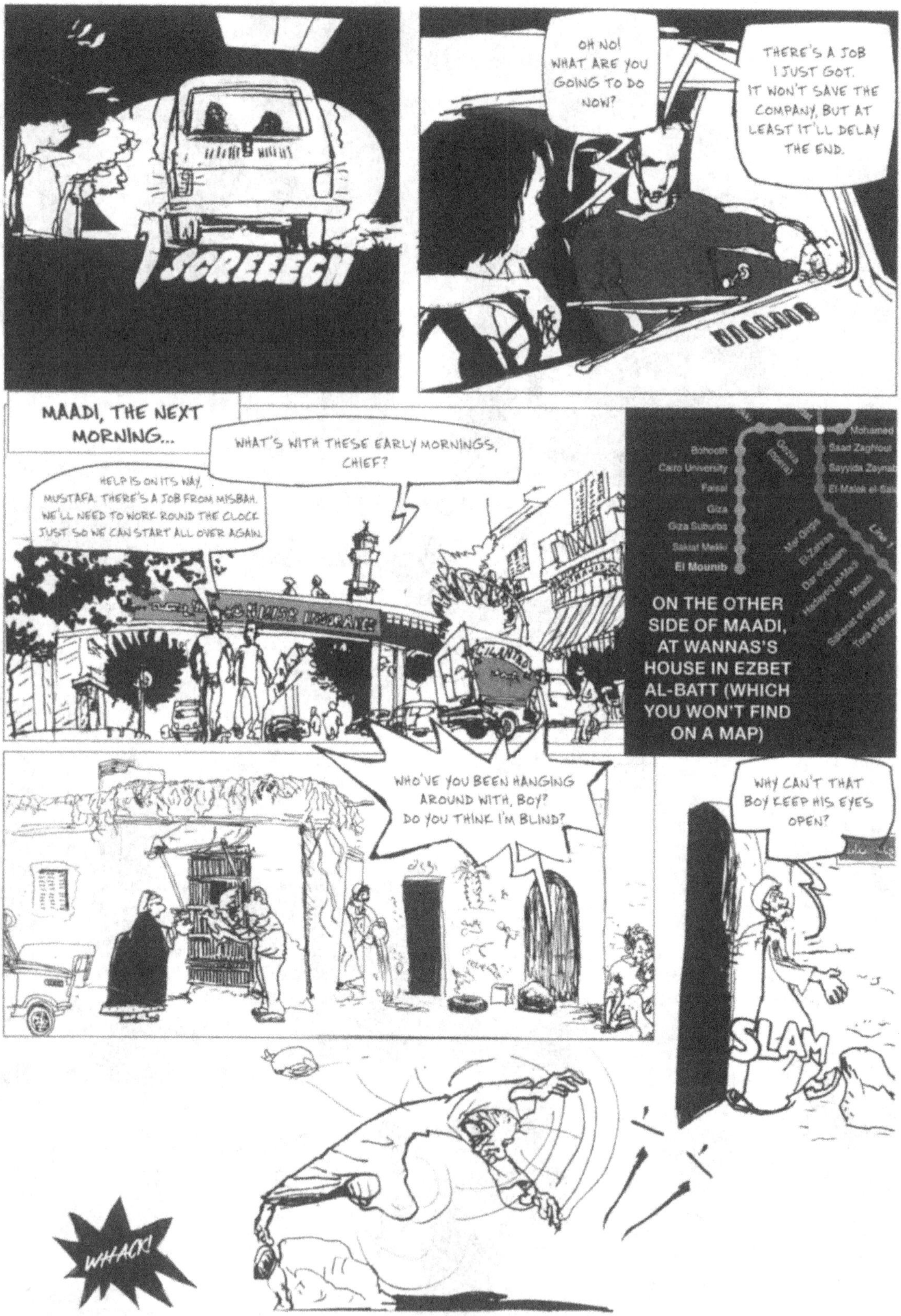
SCREEEECH
OH NO! WHAT ARE YOU GOING TO DO NOW?
THERE'S A JOB I JUST GOT. IT WON'T SAVE THE COMPANY, BUT AT LEAST IT'LL DELAY THE END.
MAADI, THE NEXT MORNING...
WHAT'S WITH THESE EARLY MORNINGS, CHIEF?
HELP IS ON ITS WAY, MUSTAFA. THERE'S A JOB FROM MISBAH. WE'LL NEED TO WORK ROUND THE CLOCK JUST SO WE CAN START ALL OVER AGAIN.
Bohooth
Cairo University
Faisal
Giza
Giza Suburbs
Sakiat Mekki
El Mounib
Saad Zaghloul
ON THE OTHER SIDE OF MAADI, AT WANNAS'S HOUSE IN EZBET AL-BATT (WHICH YOU WON'T FIND ON A MAP)
WHO'VE YOU BEEN HANGING AROUND WITH, BOY? DO YOU THINK I'M BLIND?
WHY CAN'T THAT BOY KEEP HIS EYES OPEN?
SLAM
WHACK!

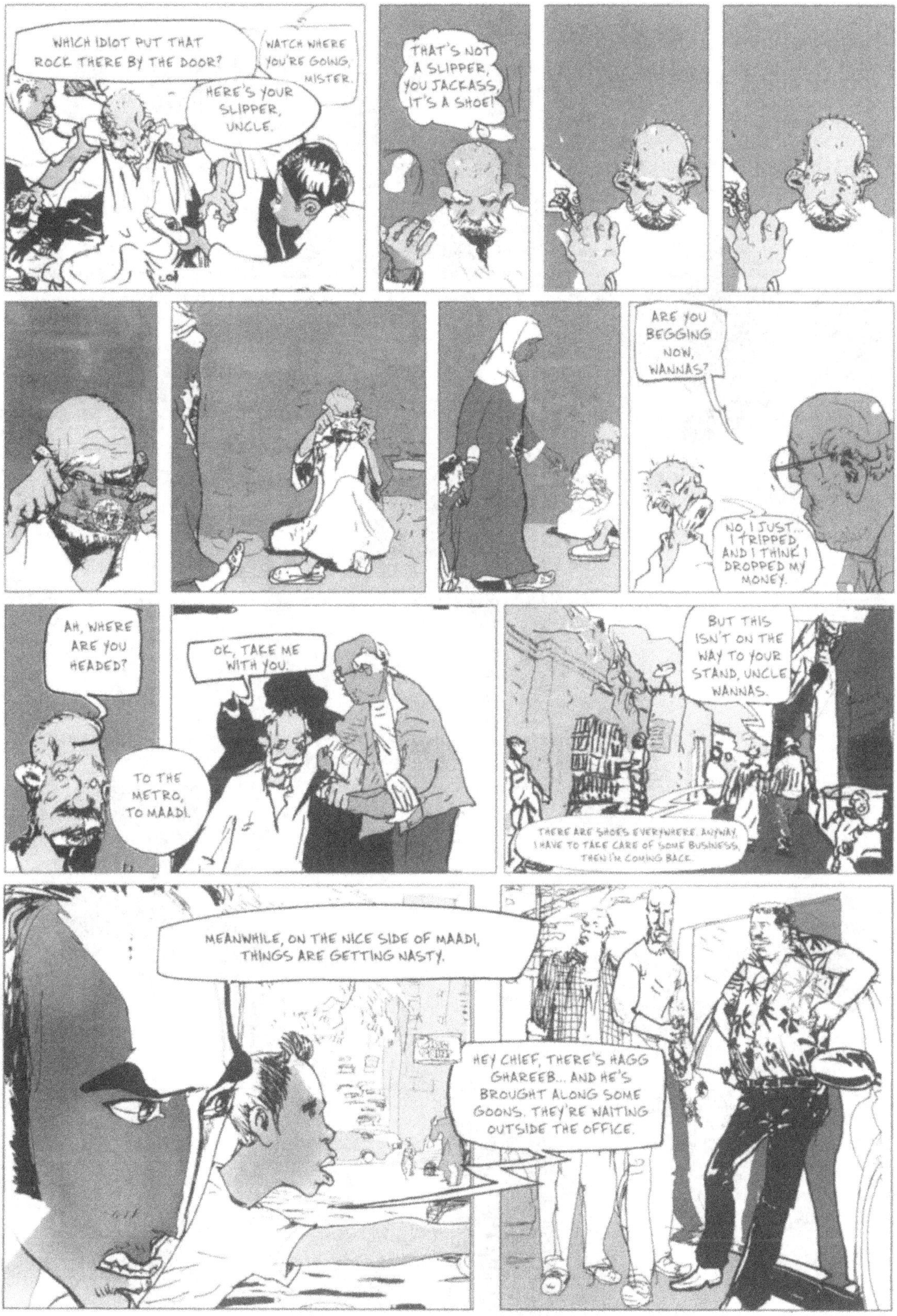
WHICH IDIOT PUT THAT ROCK THERE BY THE DOOR?
WATCH WHERE YOU'RE GOING, MISTER.
HERE'S YOUR SLIPPER, UNCLE.
THAT'S NOT A SLIPPER, YOU JACKASS, IT'S A SHOE!
ARE YOU BEGGING NOW, WANNAS?
NO, I JUST... I TRIPPED AND I THINK I DROPPED MY MONEY.
AH, WHERE ARE YOU HEADED?
TO THE METRO, TO MAADI.
OK, TAKE ME WITH YOU.
BUT THIS ISN'T ON THE WAY TO YOUR STAND, UNCLE WANNAS.
THERE ARE SHOES EVERYWHERE. ANYWAY, I HAVE TO TAKE CARE OF SOME BUSINESS, THEN I'M COMING BACK.
MEANWHILE, ON THE NICE SIDE OF MAADI, THINGS ARE GETTING NASTY.
HEY CHIEF, THERE'S HAGG GHAREEB... AND HE'S BROUGHT ALONG SOME GOONS. THEY'RE WAITING OUTSIDE THE OFFICE.

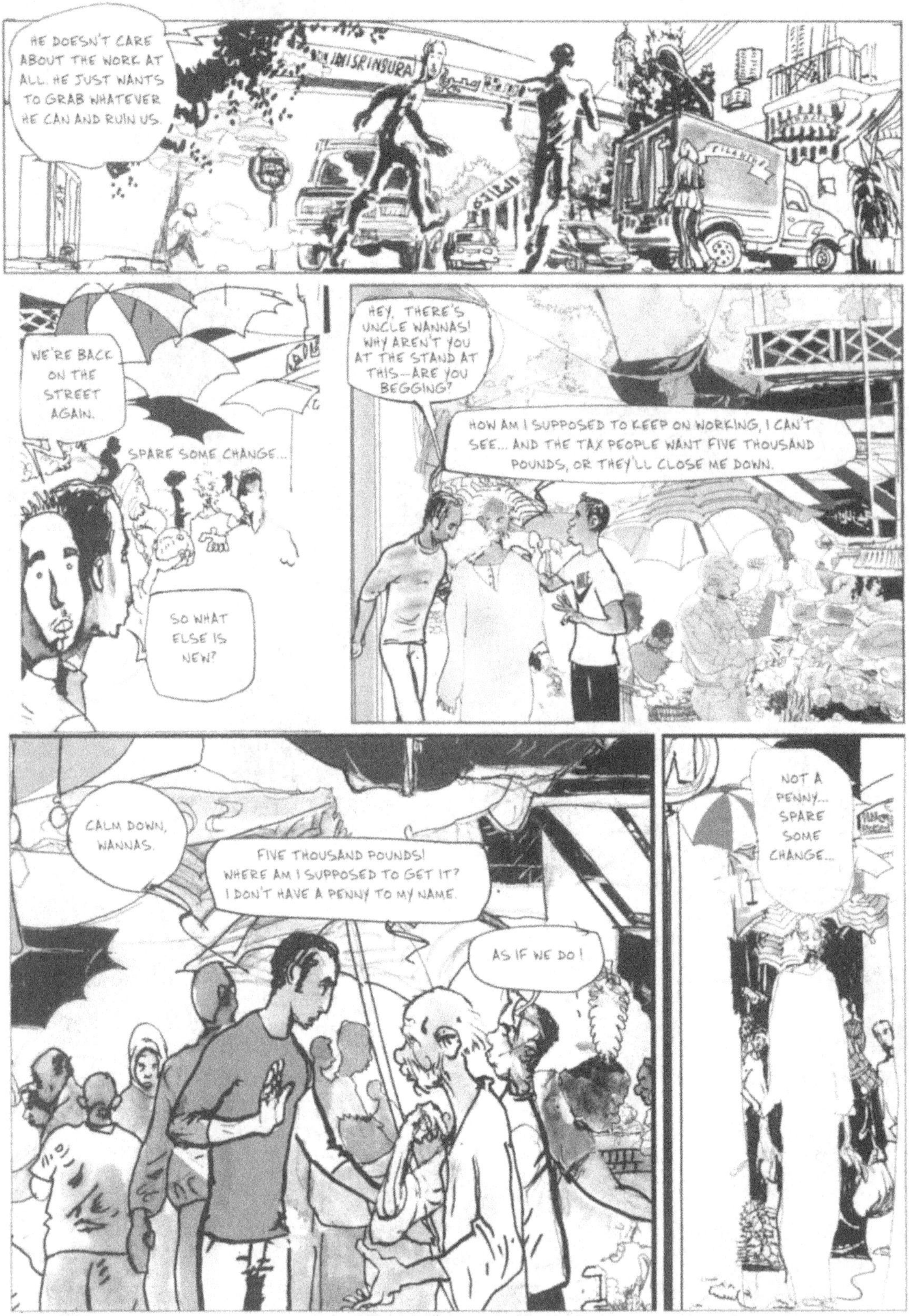
HE DOESN'T CARE ABOUT THE WORK AT ALL. HE JUST WANTS TO GRAB WHATEVER HE CAN AND RUIN US.
WE'RE BACK ON THE STREET AGAIN.
SPARE SOME CHANGE...
SO WHAT ELSE IS NEW?
HEY, THERE'S UNCLE WANNAS! WHY AREN'T YOU AT THE STAND AT THIS—ARE YOU BEGGING?
HOW AM I SUPPOSED TO KEEP ON WORKING, I CAN'T SEE... AND THE TAX PEOPLE WANT FIVE THOUSAND POUNDS, OR THEY'LL CLOSE ME DOWN.
CALM DOWN, WANNAS.
FIVE THOUSAND POUNDS! WHERE AM I SUPPOSED TO GET IT? I DON'T HAVE A PENNY TO MY NAME.
AS IF WE DO!
NOT A PENNY... SPARE SOME CHANGE...

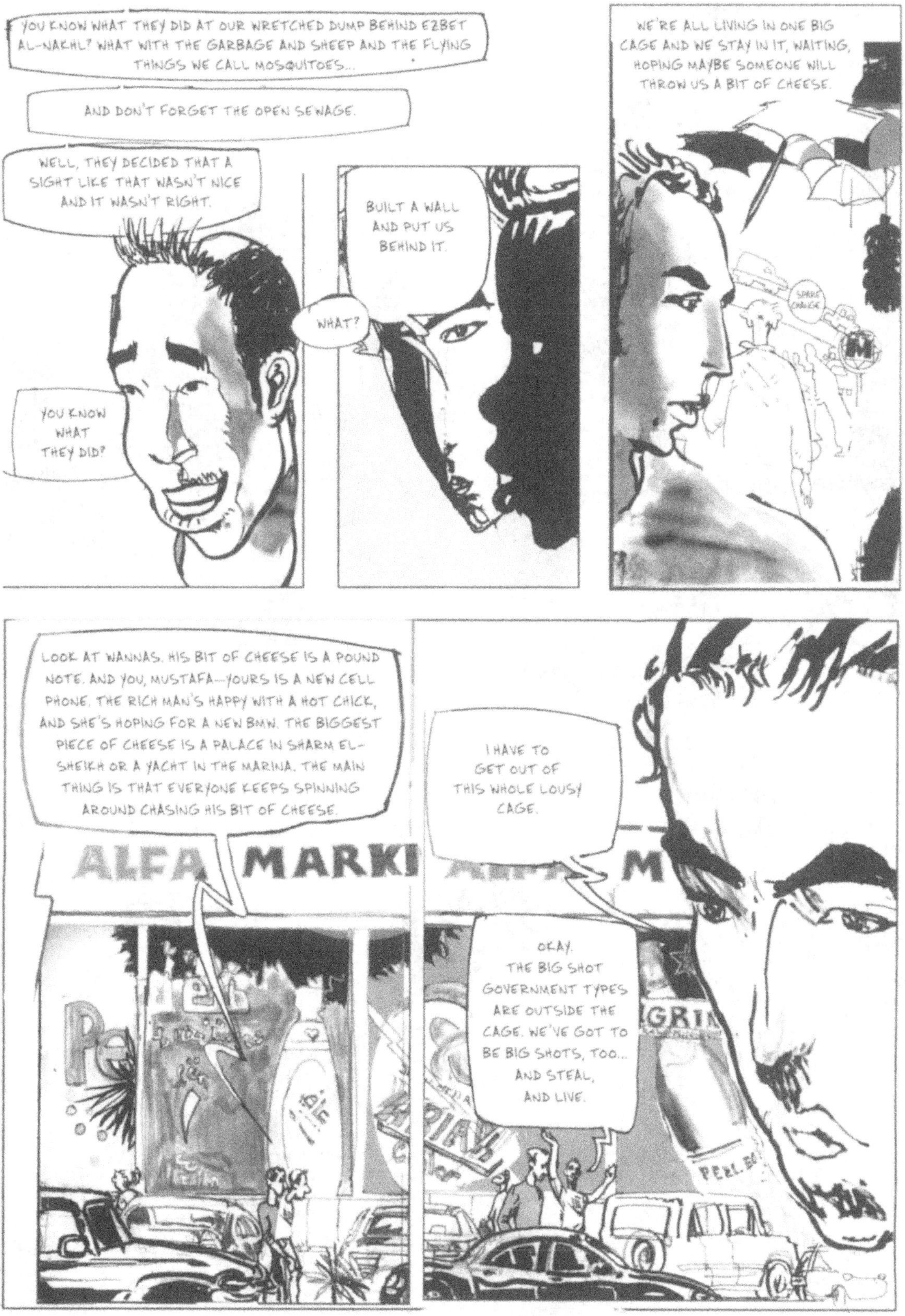
YOU KNOW WHAT THEY DID AT OUR WRETCHED DUMP BEHIND EZBET AL-NAKHL? WHAT WITH THE GARBAGE AND SHEEP AND THE FLYING THINGS WE CALL MOSQUITOES...
AND DON'T FORGET THE OPEN SEWAGE.
WELL, THEY DECIDED THAT A SIGHT LIKE THAT WASN'T NICE AND IT WASN'T RIGHT.
YOU KNOW WHAT THEY DID?
WHAT?
BUILT A WALL AND PUT US BEHIND IT.
WE'RE ALL LIVING IN ONE BIG CAGE AND WE STAY IN IT, WAITING, HOPING MAYBE SOMEONE WILL THROW US A BIT OF CHEESE.
LOOK AT WANNAS. HIS BIT OF CHEESE IS A POUND NOTE. AND YOU, MUSTAFA—YOURS IS A NEW CELL PHONE. THE RICH MAN'S HAPPY WITH A HOT CHICK, AND SHE'S HOPING FOR A NEW BMW. THE BIGGEST PIECE OF CHEESE IS A PALACE IN SHARM EL-SHEIKH OR A YACHT IN THE MARINA. THE MAIN THING IS THAT EVERYONE KEEPS SPINNING AROUND CHASING HIS BIT OF CHEESE.
I HAVE TO GET OUT OF THIS WHOLE LOUSY CAGE.
OKAY. THE BIG SHOT GOVERNMENT TYPES ARE OUTSIDE THE CAGE. WE'VE GOT TO BE BIG SHOTS, TOO... AND STEAL, AND LIVE.

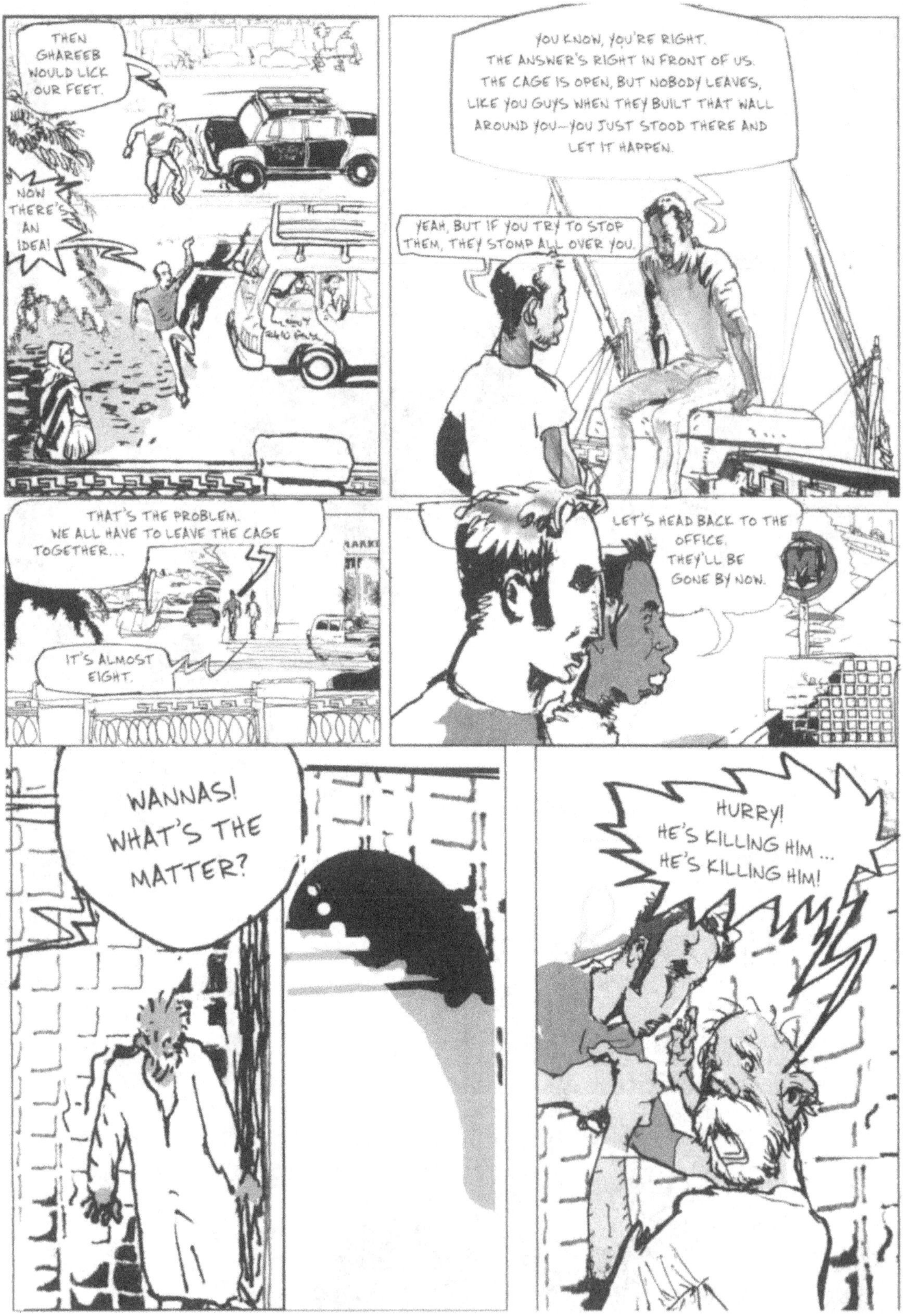
THEN GHAREEB WOULD LICK OUR FEET.
NOW THERE'S AN IDEA!
YOU KNOW, YOU'RE RIGHT. THE ANSWER'S RIGHT IN FRONT OF US. THE CAGE IS OPEN, BUT NOBODY LEAVES, LIKE YOU GUYS WHEN THEY BUILT THAT WALL AROUND YOU—YOU JUST STOOD THERE AND LET IT HAPPEN.
YEAH, BUT IF YOU TRY TO STOP THEM, THEY STOMP ALL OVER YOU.
THAT'S THE PROBLEM. WE ALL HAVE TO LEAVE THE CAGE TOGETHER...
IT'S ALMOST EIGHT.
LET'S HEAD BACK TO THE OFFICE. THEY'LL BE GONE BY NOW.
WANNAS! WHAT'S THE MATTER?
HURRY! HE'S KILLING HIM ... HE'S KILLING HIM!

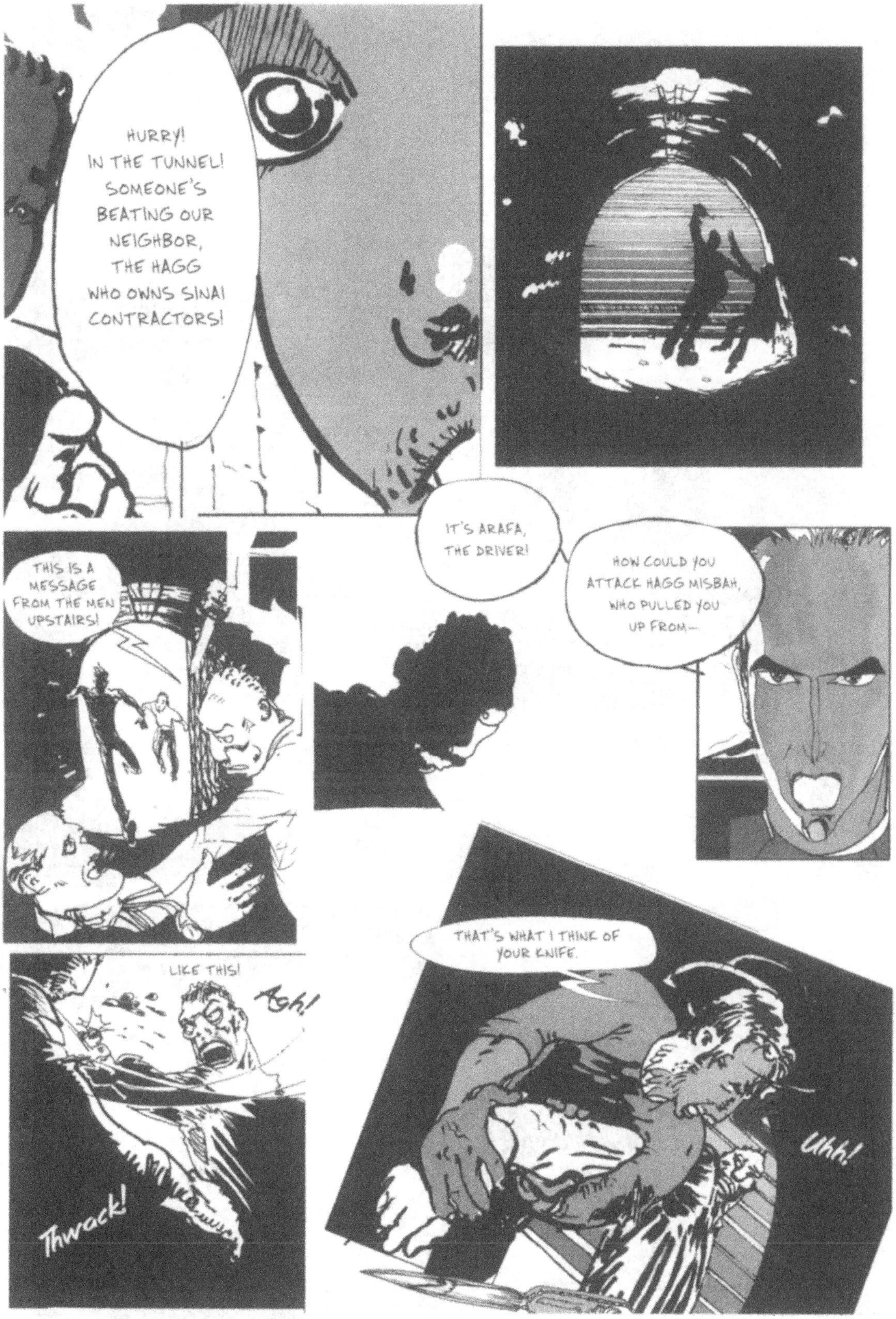
HURRY! IN THE TUNNEL! SOMEONE'S BEATING OUR NEIGHBOR, THE HAGG WHO OWNS SINAI CONTRACTORS!
THIS IS A MESSAGE FROM THE MEN UPSTAIRS!
IT'S ARAFA, THE DRIVER!
HOW COULD YOU ATTACK HAGG MISBAH, WHO PULLED YOU UP FROM—
LIKE THIS!
Agh!
Thwack!
THAT'S WHAT I THINK OF YOUR KNIFE.
Uhh!

WAIT...

I'M DYING...

DON'T WORRY— WE'RE GETTING AN AMBULANCE.

NO TIME... THE STABLE...

DON'T LOSE YOUR— THE WHAT? WHAT STABLE?

I GUESS THEY HAD TO...

...KILL ME...

....NOW UP TO YOU...

...AHHH...

...THE STABLE...

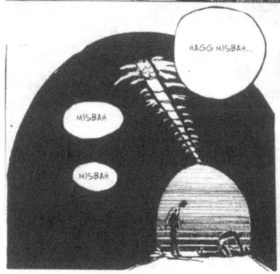

HAGG MISBAH...

MISBAH

MISBAH

SOMEONE'S COMING... WE GOTTA GET OUT OF HERE, SHEHAB, BEFORE THINGS GET ANY WORSE. WE'VE GOT ARAFA'S KNIFE... WE DON'T WANT MORE TROUBLE...

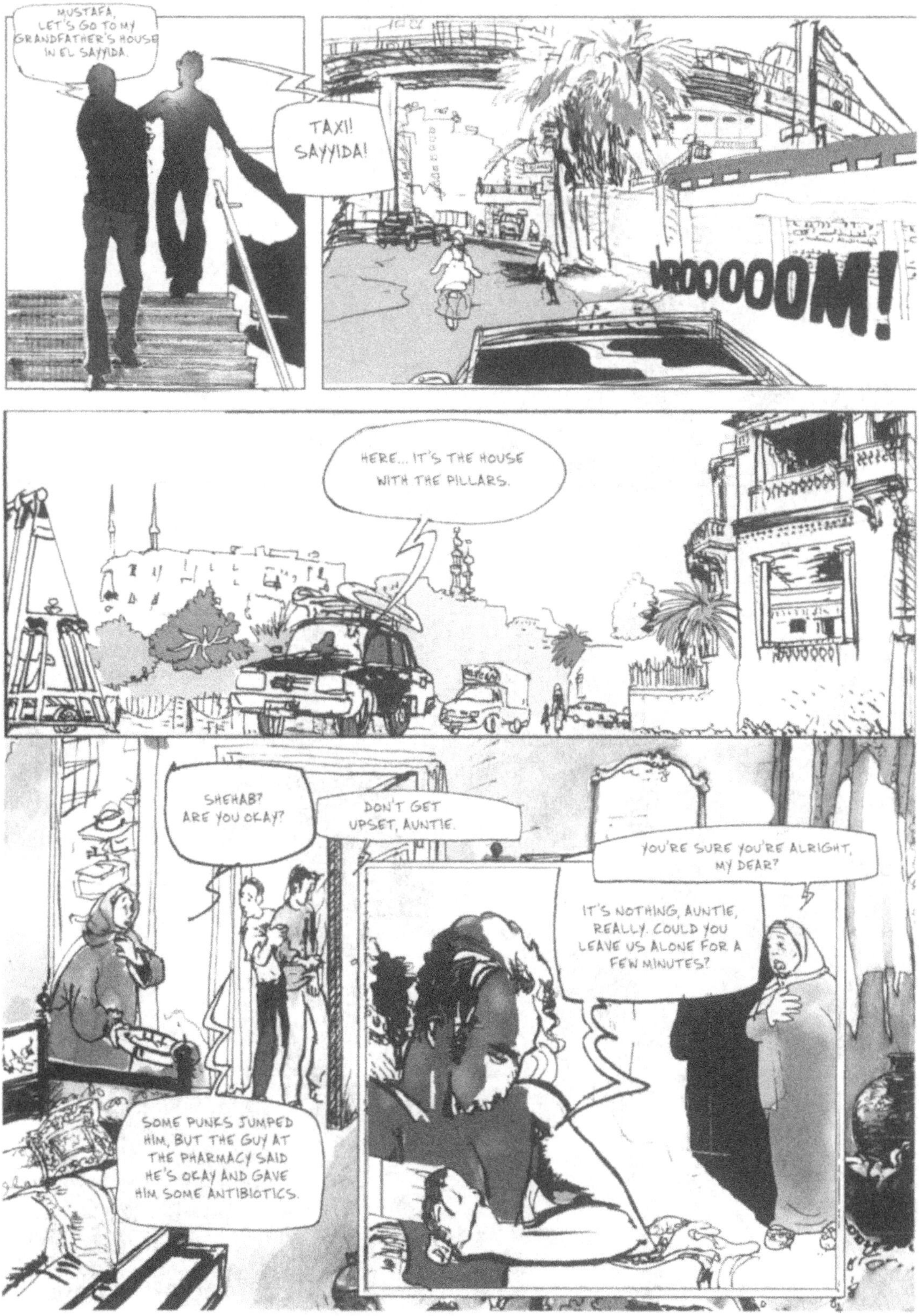

MUSTAFA, LET'S GO TO MY GRANDFATHER'S HOUSE IN EL SAYYIDA.
TAXI! SAYYIDA!
VROOOOOM!
HERE... IT'S THE HOUSE WITH THE PILLARS.
SHEHAB? ARE YOU OKAY?
DON'T GET UPSET, AUNTIE.
SOME PUNKS JUMPED HIM, BUT THE GUY AT THE PHARMACY SAID HE'S OKAY AND GAVE HIM SOME ANTIBIOTICS.
YOU'RE SURE YOU'RE ALRIGHT, MY DEAR?
IT'S NOTHING, AUNTIE, REALLY. COULD YOU LEAVE US ALONE FOR A FEW MINUTES?

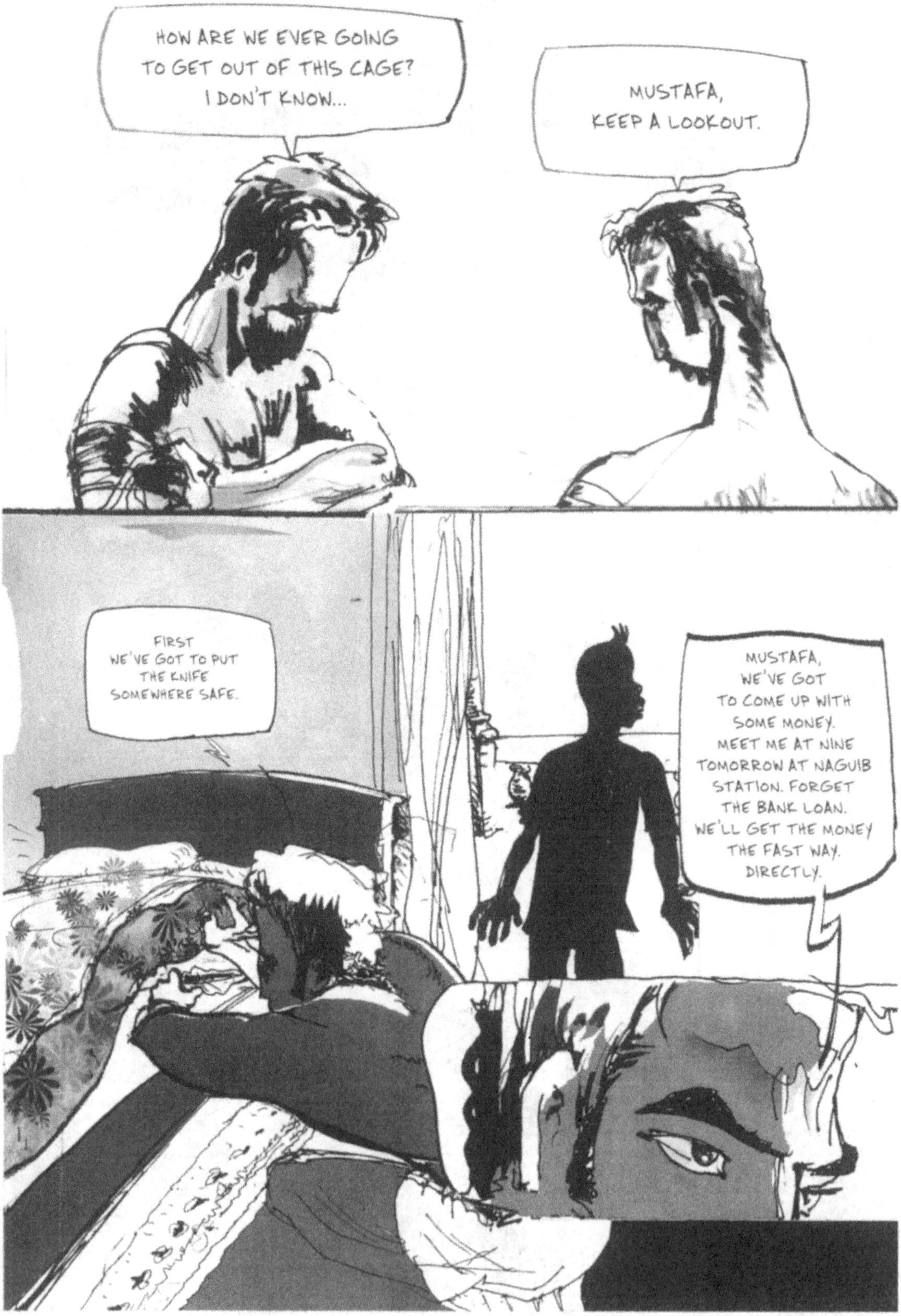
HOW ARE WE EVER GOING TO GET OUT OF THIS CAGE? I DON'T KNOW...
MUSTAFA, KEEP A LOOKOUT.
FIRST WE'VE GOT TO PUT THE KNIFE SOMEWHERE SAFE.
MUSTAFA, WE'VE GOT TO COME UP WITH SOME MONEY. MEET ME AT NINE TOMORROW AT NAGUIB STATION. FORGET THE BANK LOAN. WE'LL GET THE MONEY THE FAST WAY. DIRECTLY.

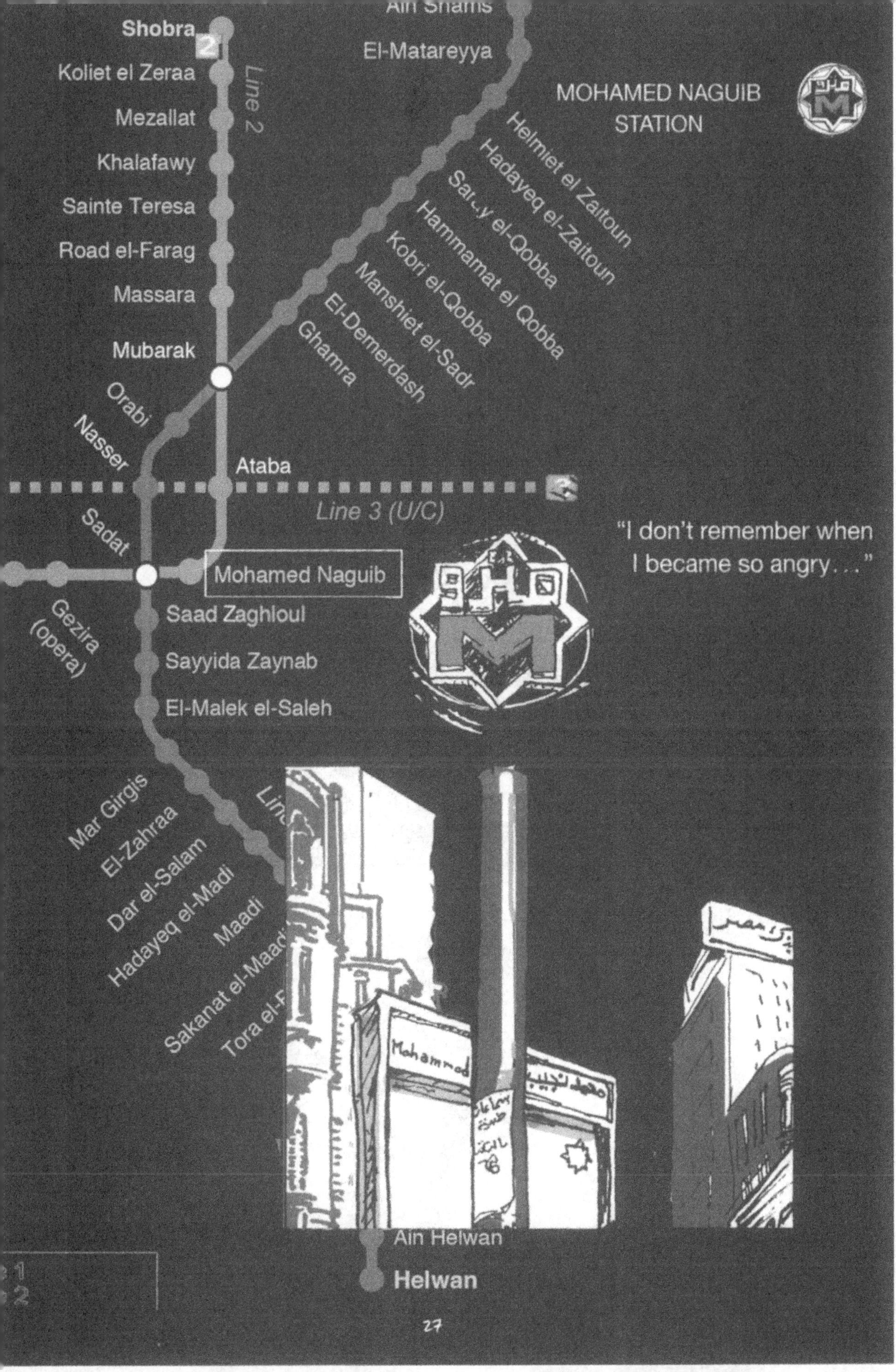
Ain Shams
El-Matareyya
MOHAMED NAGUIB
STATION
Shobra
2
Koliet el Zeraa
Mezallat
Khalafawy
Sainte Teresa
Road el-Farag
Massara
Mubarak
Line 2
Helmiet el Zaitoun
Hadayeq el-Zaitoun
Hammamat el Qobba
Kobri el-Qobba
Manshiet el-Sadr
El-Demerdash
Ghamra
Orabi
Nasser
Ataba
Line 3 (U/C)
Sadat
Mohamed Naguib
Saad Zaghloul
Sayyida Zaynab
El-Malek el-Saleh
Gezira
(opera)
"I don't remember when
I became so angry. . ."
Mar Girgis
El-Zahraa
Dar el-Salam
Hadayeq el-Madi
Maadi
Mohammed
Ain Helwan
Helwan

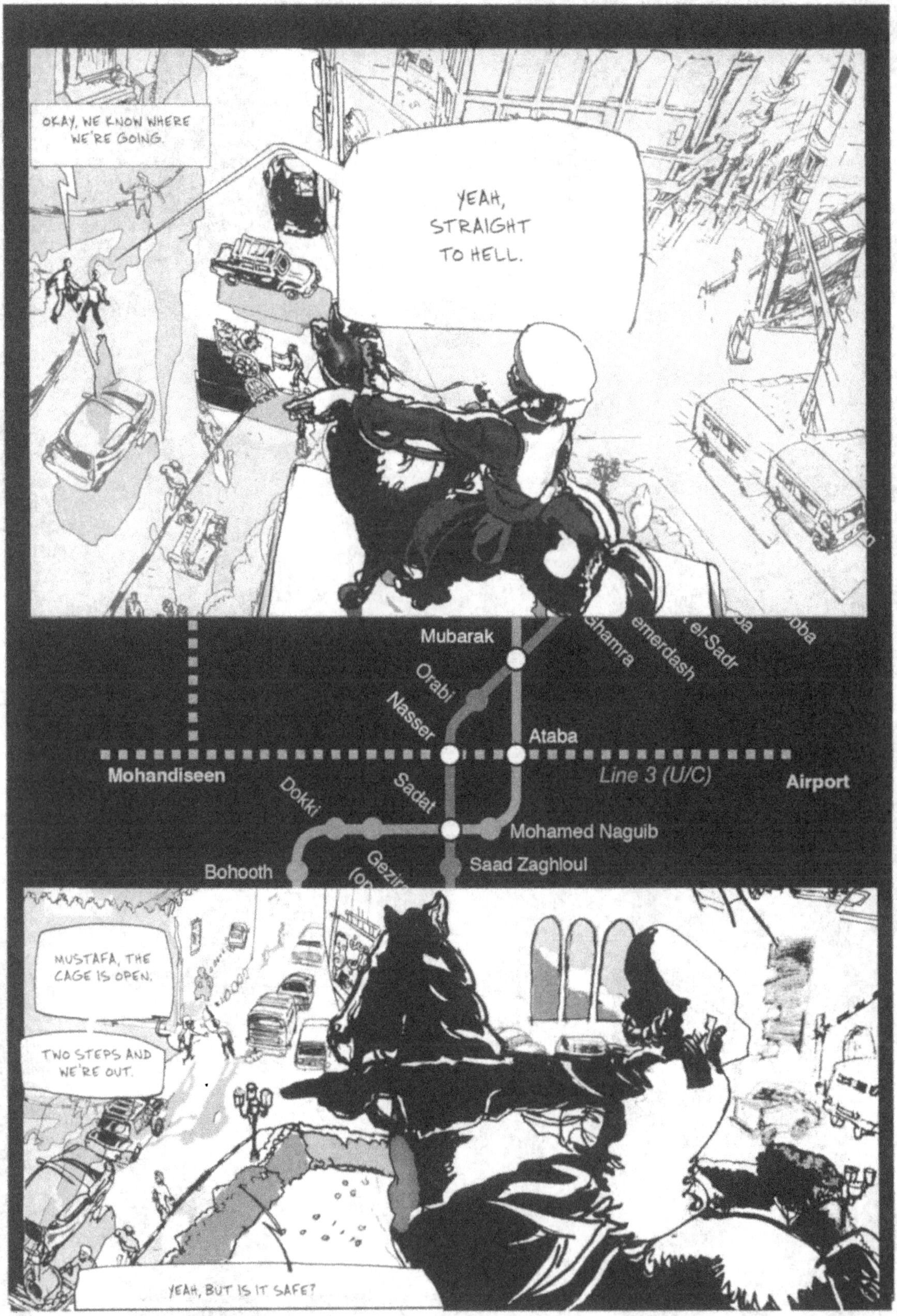
OKAY, WE KNOW WHERE WE'RE GOING.
YEAH, STRAIGHT TO HELL.
Mubarak
Orabi
Nasser
Ataba
Mohandiseen
Line 3 (U/C)
Airport
Dokki
Sadat
Mohamed Naguib
Bohooth
Saad Zaghloul
MUSTAFA, THE CAGE IS OPEN.
TWO STEPS AND WE'RE OUT.
YEAH, BUT IS IT SAFE?

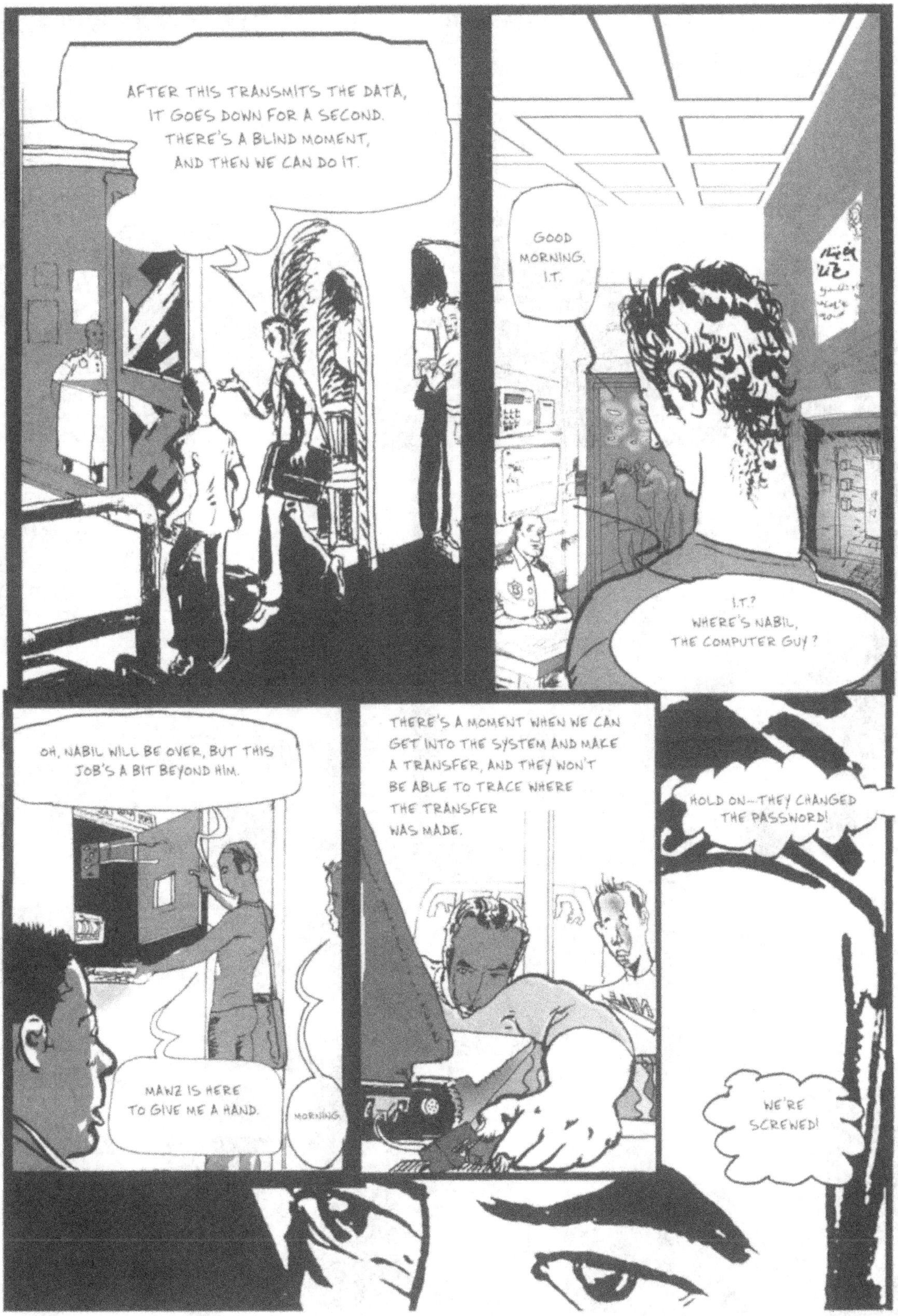

AFTER THIS TRANSMITS THE DATA, IT GOES DOWN FOR A SECOND. THERE'S A BLIND MOMENT, AND THEN WE CAN DO IT.
GOOD MORNING. I.T.
I.T.? WHERE'S NABIL, THE COMPUTER GUY?
OH, NABIL WILL BE OVER, BUT THIS JOB'S A BIT BEYOND HIM.
MAWZ IS HERE TO GIVE ME A HAND.
MORNING.
THERE'S A MOMENT WHEN WE CAN GET INTO THE SYSTEM AND MAKE A TRANSFER, AND THEY WON'T BE ABLE TO TRACE WHERE THE TRANSFER WAS MADE.
HOLD ON—THEY CHANGED THE PASSWORD!
WE'RE SCREWED!

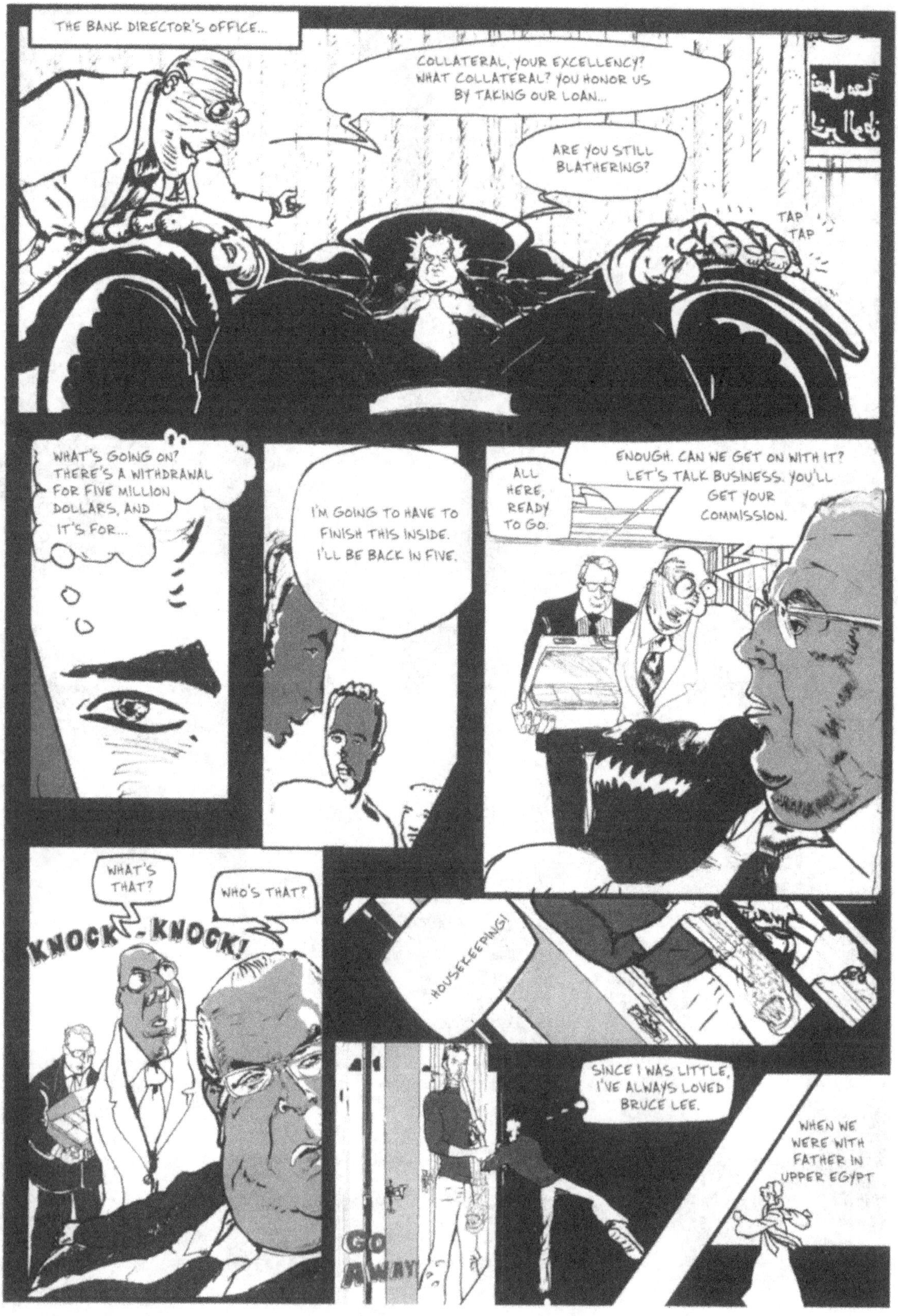

THE BANK DIRECTOR'S OFFICE...
COLLATERAL, YOUR EXCELLENCY? WHAT COLLATERAL? YOU HONOR US BY TAKING OUR LOAN...
ARE YOU STILL BLATHERING?
TAP TAP
WHAT'S GOING ON? THERE'S A WITHDRAWAL FOR FIVE MILLION DOLLARS, AND IT'S FOR...
I'M GOING TO HAVE TO FINISH THIS INSIDE. I'LL BE BACK IN FIVE.
ALL HERE, READY TO GO.
ENOUGH. CAN WE GET ON WITH IT? LET'S TALK BUSINESS. YOU'LL GET YOUR COMMISSION.
WHAT'S THAT?
WHO'S THAT?
KNOCK-KNOCK!
HOUSEKEEPING!
GO AWAY!
SINCE I WAS LITTLE, I'VE ALWAYS LOVED BRUCE LEE.
WHEN WE WERE WITH FATHER IN UPPER EGYPT

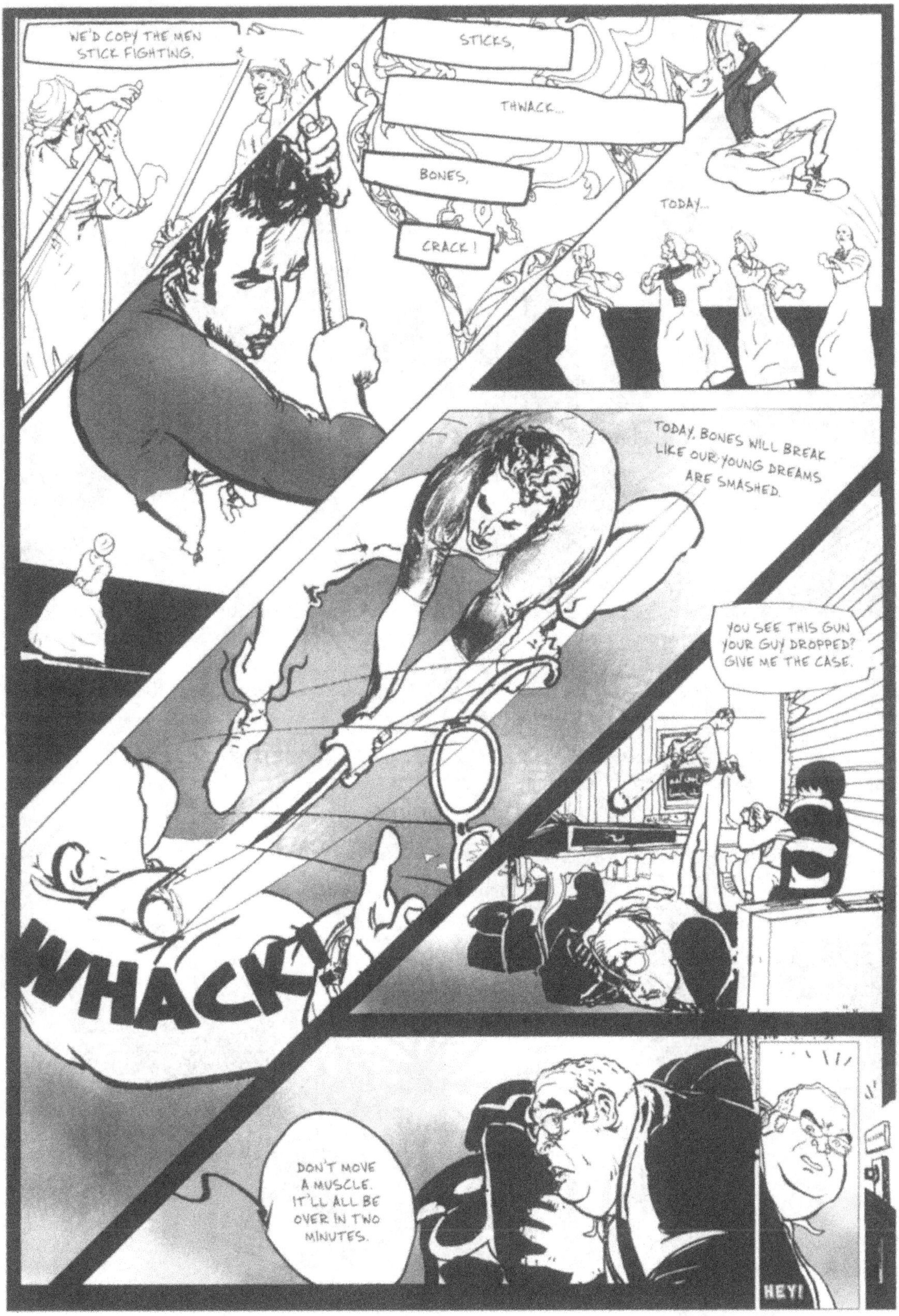
WE'D COPY THE MEN STICK FIGHTING.
STICKS,
THWACK...
BONES,
CRACK!
TODAY...
TODAY, BONES WILL BREAK LIKE OUR YOUNG DREAMS ARE SMASHED.
YOU SEE THIS GUN YOUR GUY DROPPED? GIVE ME THE CASE.
WHACK!
DON'T MOVE A MUSCLE. IT'LL ALL BE OVER IN TWO MINUTES.
HEY!

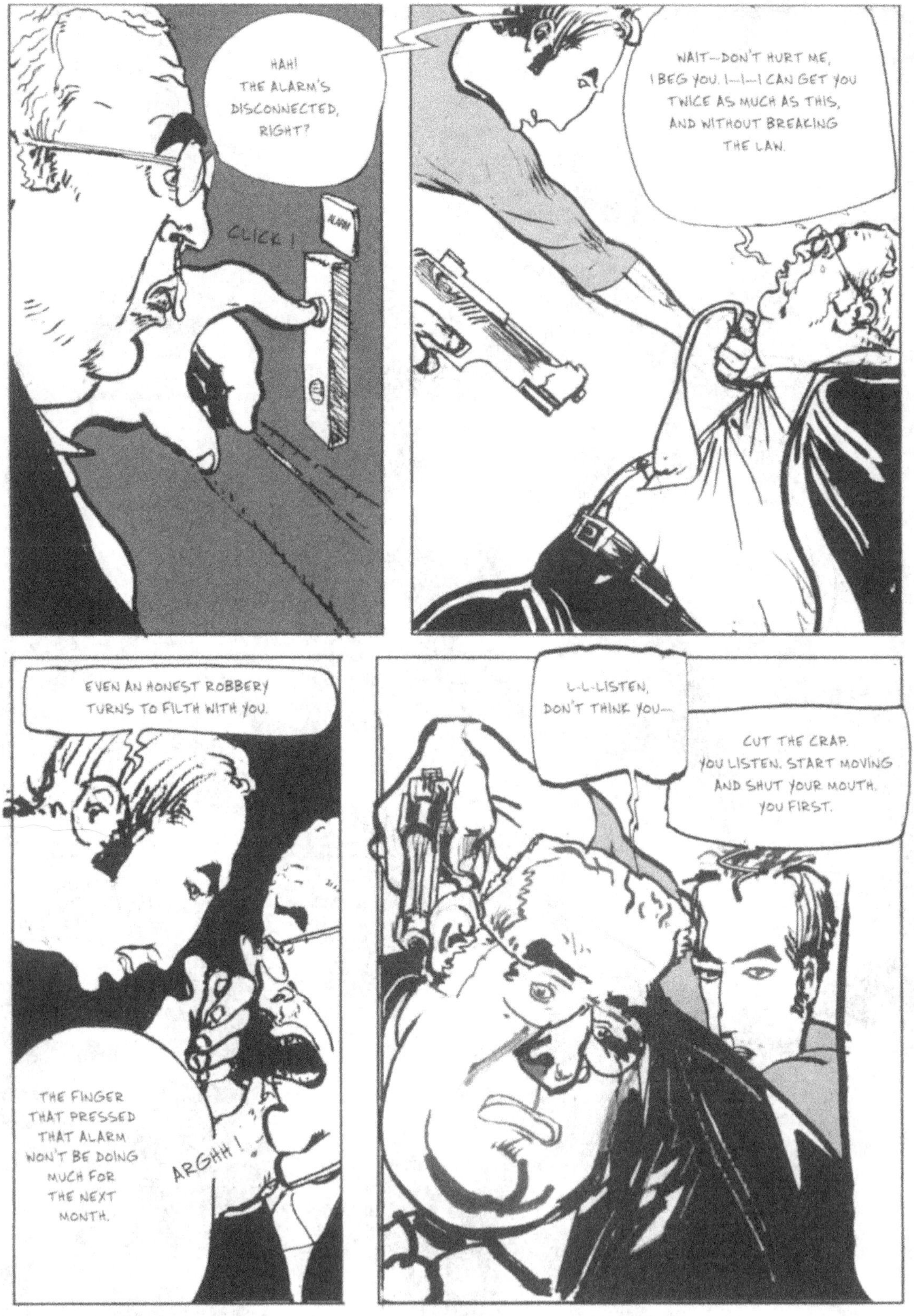
HAH!
THE ALARM'S
DISCONNECTED,
RIGHT?
ALARM
CLICK!
WAIT—DON'T HURT ME, I BEG YOU. I—I—I CAN GET YOU TWICE AS MUCH AS THIS, AND WITHOUT BREAKING THE LAW.
EVEN AN HONEST ROBBERY TURNS TO FILTH WITH YOU.
THE FINGER THAT PRESSED THAT ALARM WON'T BE DOING MUCH FOR THE NEXT MONTH.
ARGHH!
L-L-LISTEN, DON'T THINK YOU—
CUT THE CRAP. YOU LISTEN. START MOVING AND SHUT YOUR MOUTH. YOU FIRST.

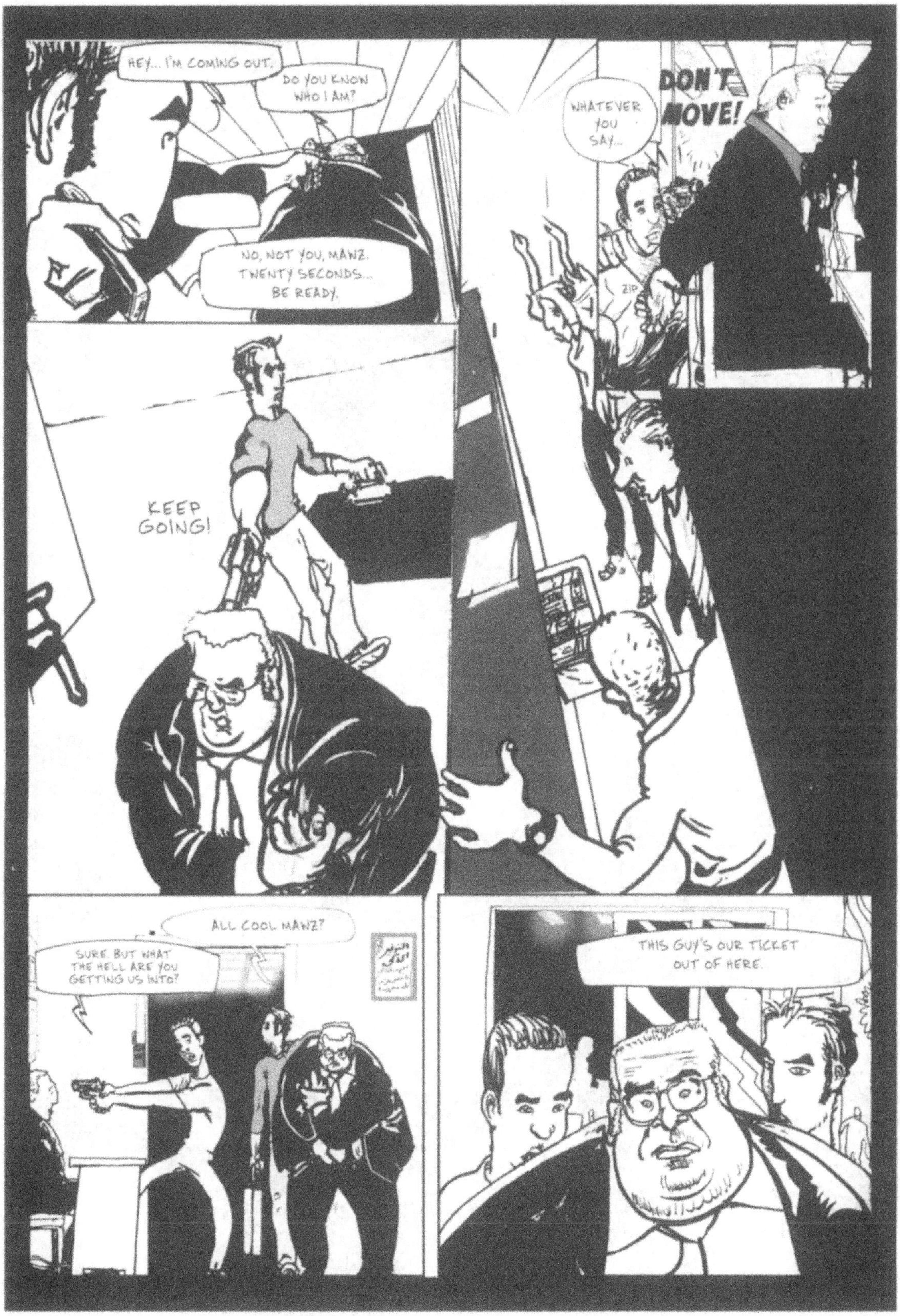
HEY... I'M COMING OUT.
DO YOU KNOW WHO I AM?
NO, NOT YOU, MAWZ. TWENTY SECONDS... BE READY.
WHATEVER YOU SAY...
DON'T MOVE!
ZIP
KEEP GOING!
ALL COOL MAWZ?
SURE. BUT WHAT THE HELL ARE YOU GETTING US INTO?
THIS GUY'S OUR TICKET OUT OF HERE.

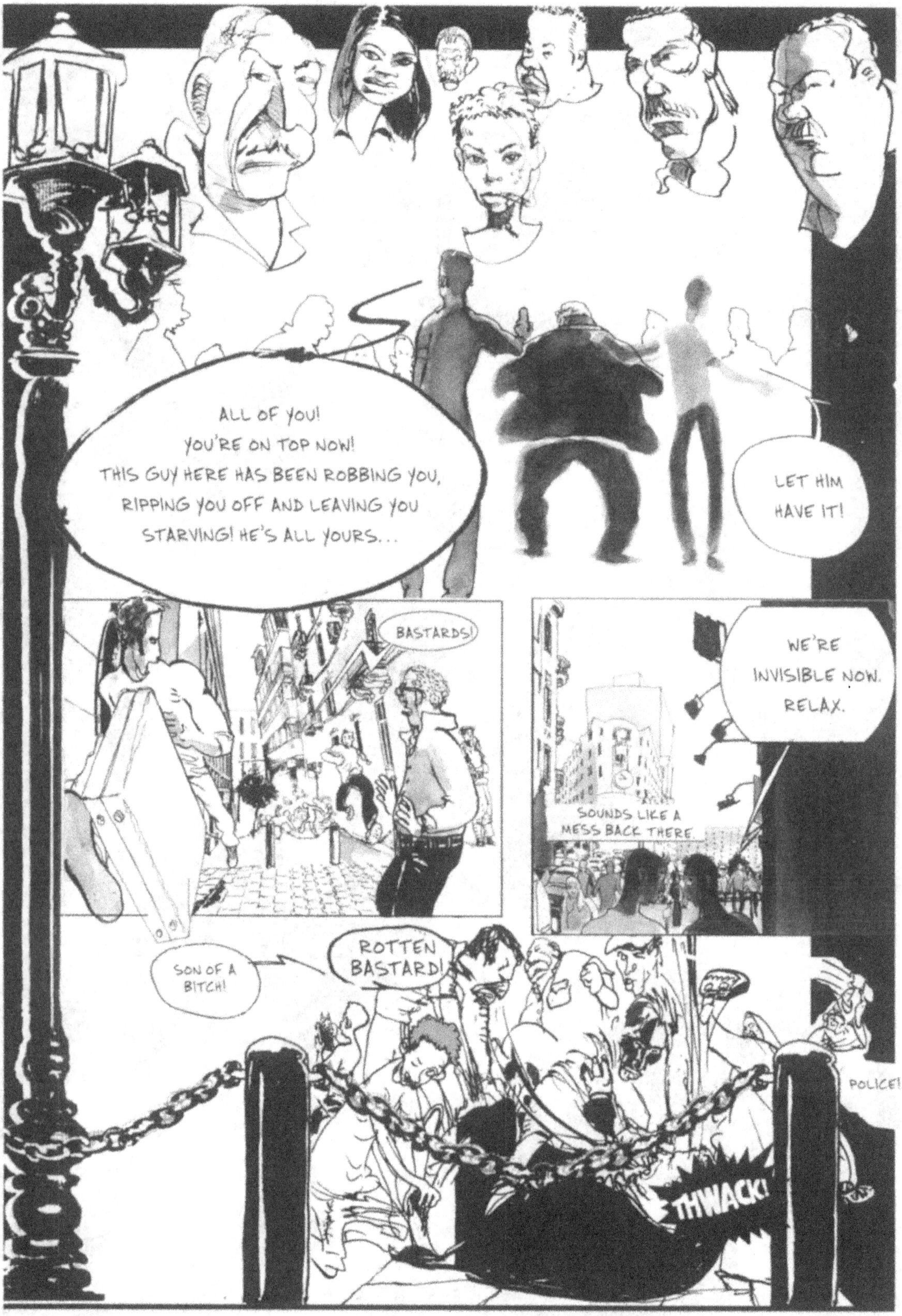
ALL OF YOU! YOU'RE ON TOP NOW! THIS GUY HERE HAS BEEN ROBBING YOU, RIPPING YOU OFF AND LEAVING YOU STARVING! HE'S ALL YOURS...
LET HIM HAVE IT!
BASTARDS!
WE'RE INVISIBLE NOW. RELAX.
SOUNDS LIKE A MESS BACK THERE.
SON OF A BITCH!
ROTTEN BASTARD!
POLICE!
THWACK!

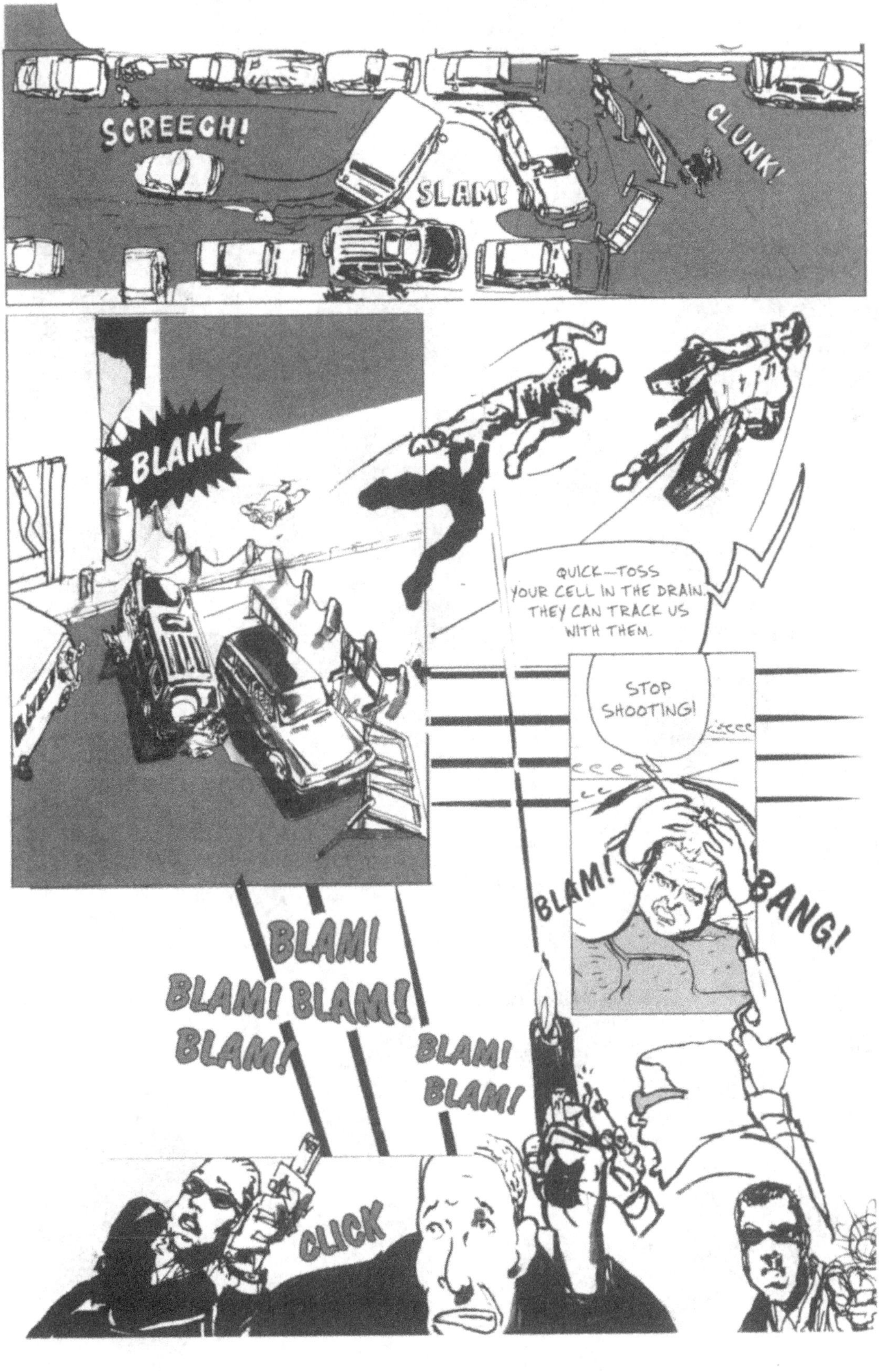
SCREECH!
SLAM!
CLUNK!
BLAM!
QUICK—TOSS YOUR CELL IN THE DRAIN. THEY CAN TRACK US WITH THEM.
STOP SHOOTING!
BLAM!
BANG!
BLAM!
BLAM! BLAM!
BLAM!
BLAM!
BLAM!
CLICK

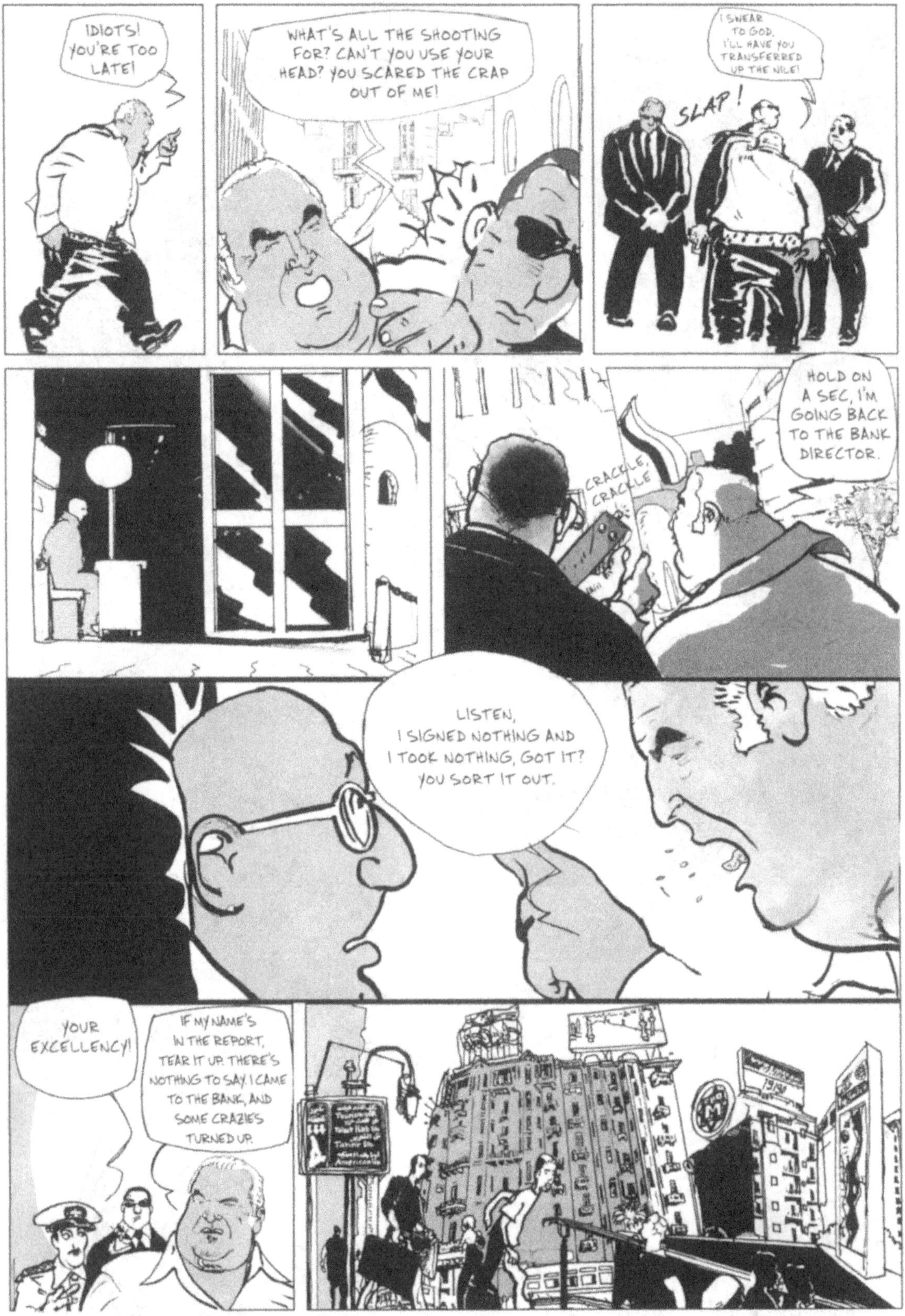
IDIOTS! YOU'RE TOO LATE!
WHAT'S ALL THE SHOOTING FOR? CAN'T YOU USE YOUR HEAD? YOU SCARED THE CRAP OUT OF ME!
I SWEAR TO GOD, I'LL HAVE YOU TRANSFERRED UP THE NILE!
SLAP!
CRACKLE, CRACKLE
HOLD ON A SEC, I'M GOING BACK TO THE BANK DIRECTOR.
LISTEN, I SIGNED NOTHING AND I TOOK NOTHING, GOT IT? YOU SORT IT OUT.
YOUR EXCELLENCY!
IF MY NAME'S IN THE REPORT, TEAR IT UP. THERE'S NOTHING TO SAY. I CAME TO THE BANK, AND SOME CRAZIES TURNED UP.

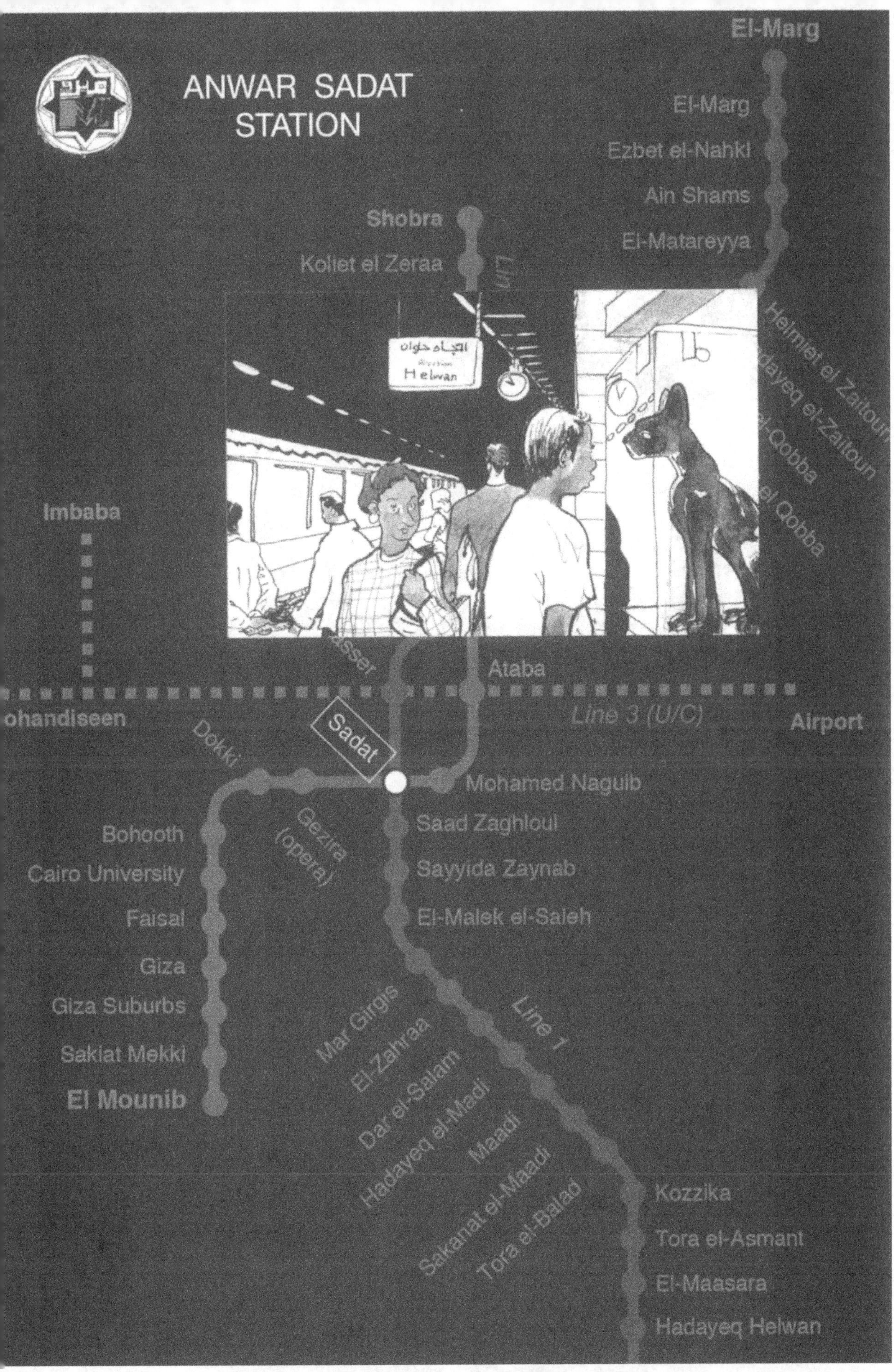

ANWAR SADAT
STATION

El-Marg

El-Marg

Ezbet el-Nahkl

Ain Shams

El-Matareyya

Shobra

Koliet el Zeraa

Helmiet el Zaitoun

Hadayeq el-Zaitoun

el-Qobba

el Qobba

Imbaba

Ataba

ohandiseen

Line 3 (U/C)

Airport

Dokki

Sadat

Mohamed Naguib

Bohooth

Gezira
(opera)

Saad Zaghloul

Cairo University

Sayyida Zaynab

Faisal

El-Malek el-Saleh

Giza

Giza Suburbs

Sakiat Mekki

El Mounib

Mar Girgis

El-Zahraa

Dar el-Salam

Hadayed el-Madi

Maadi

Line 1

Sakanat el-Maadi

Tora el-Balad

Kozzika

Tora el-Asmant

El-Maasara

Hadayeq Helwan

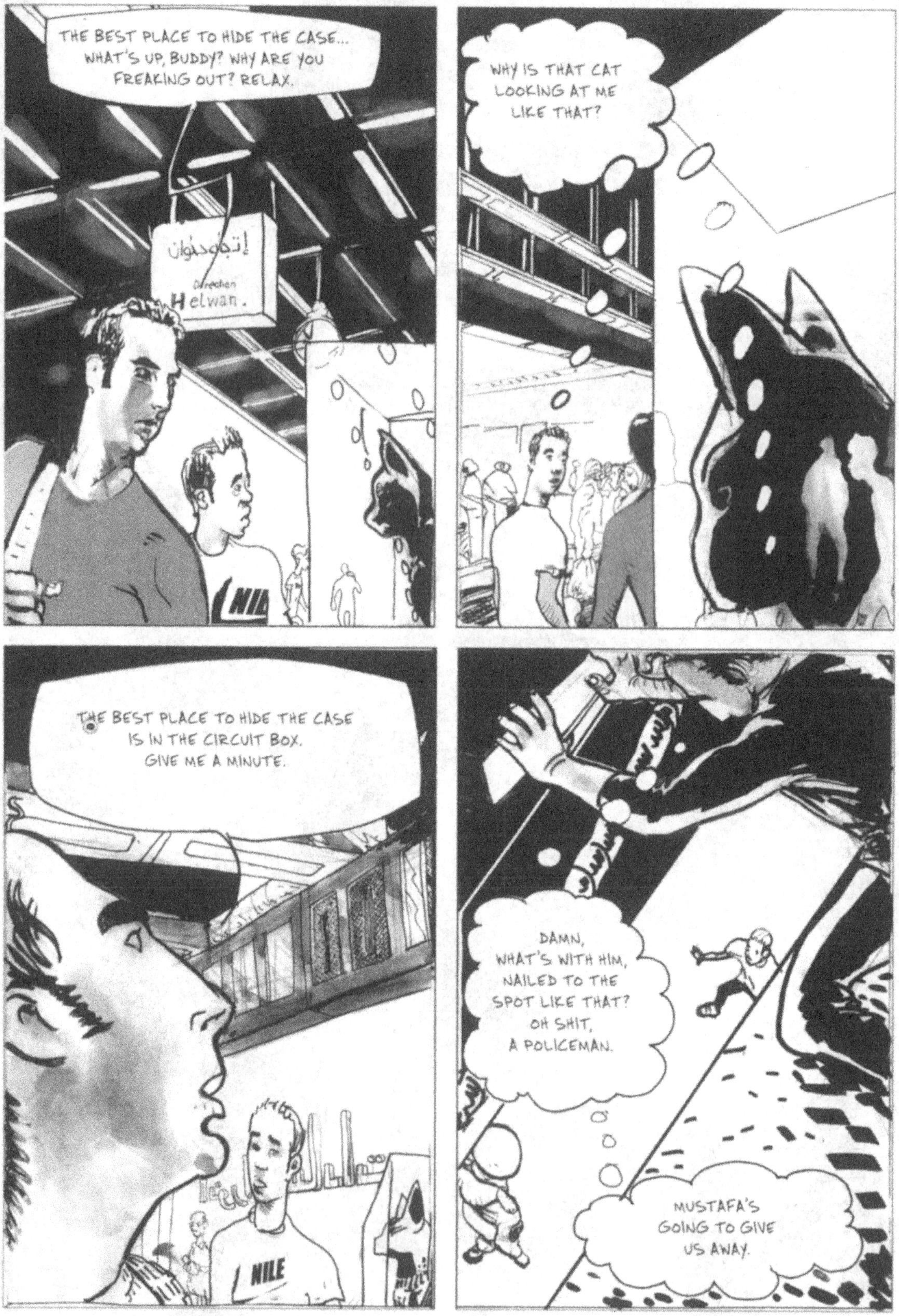
THE BEST PLACE TO HIDE THE CASE... WHAT'S UP, BUDDY? WHY ARE YOU FREAKING OUT? RELAX.
Direction
Helwan.
WHY IS THAT CAT LOOKING AT ME LIKE THAT?
THE BEST PLACE TO HIDE THE CASE IS IN THE CIRCUIT BOX. GIVE ME A MINUTE.
NILE
DAMN, WHAT'S WITH HIM, NAILED TO THE SPOT LIKE THAT? OH SHIT, A POLICEMAN.
MUSTAFA'S GOING TO GIVE US AWAY.

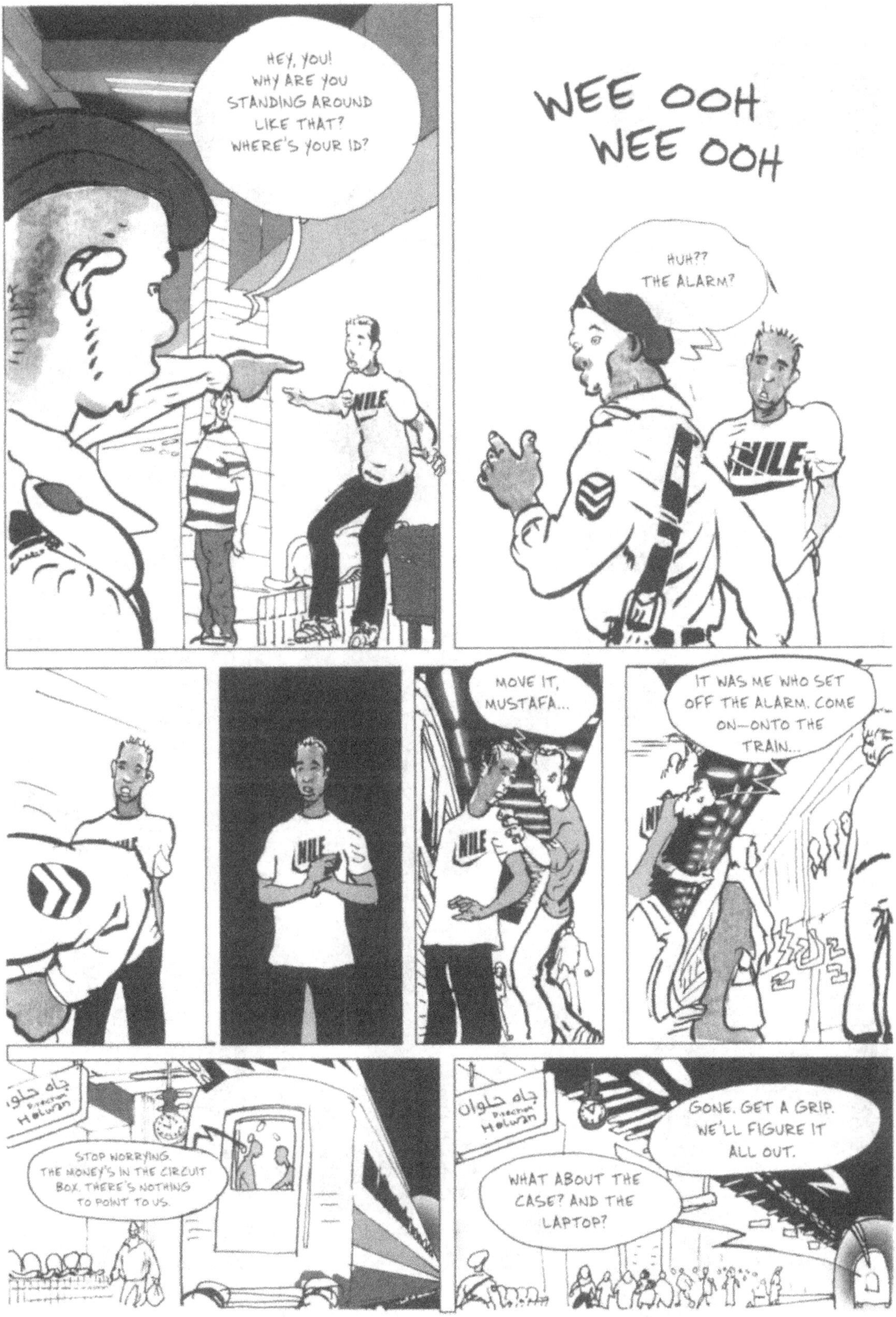
HEY, YOU! WHY ARE YOU STANDING AROUND LIKE THAT? WHERE'S YOUR ID?
WEE OOH WEE OOH
HUH?? THE ALARM?
NILE
MOVE IT, MUSTAFA...
IT WAS ME WHO SET OFF THE ALARM. COME ON—ONTO THE TRAIN...
جاه حلوان
Direction Helwan
STOP WORRYING. THE MONEY'S IN THE CIRCUIT BOX. THERE'S NOTHING TO POINT TO US.
WHAT ABOUT THE CASE? AND THE LAPTOP?
GONE. GET A GRIP. WE'LL FIGURE IT ALL OUT.

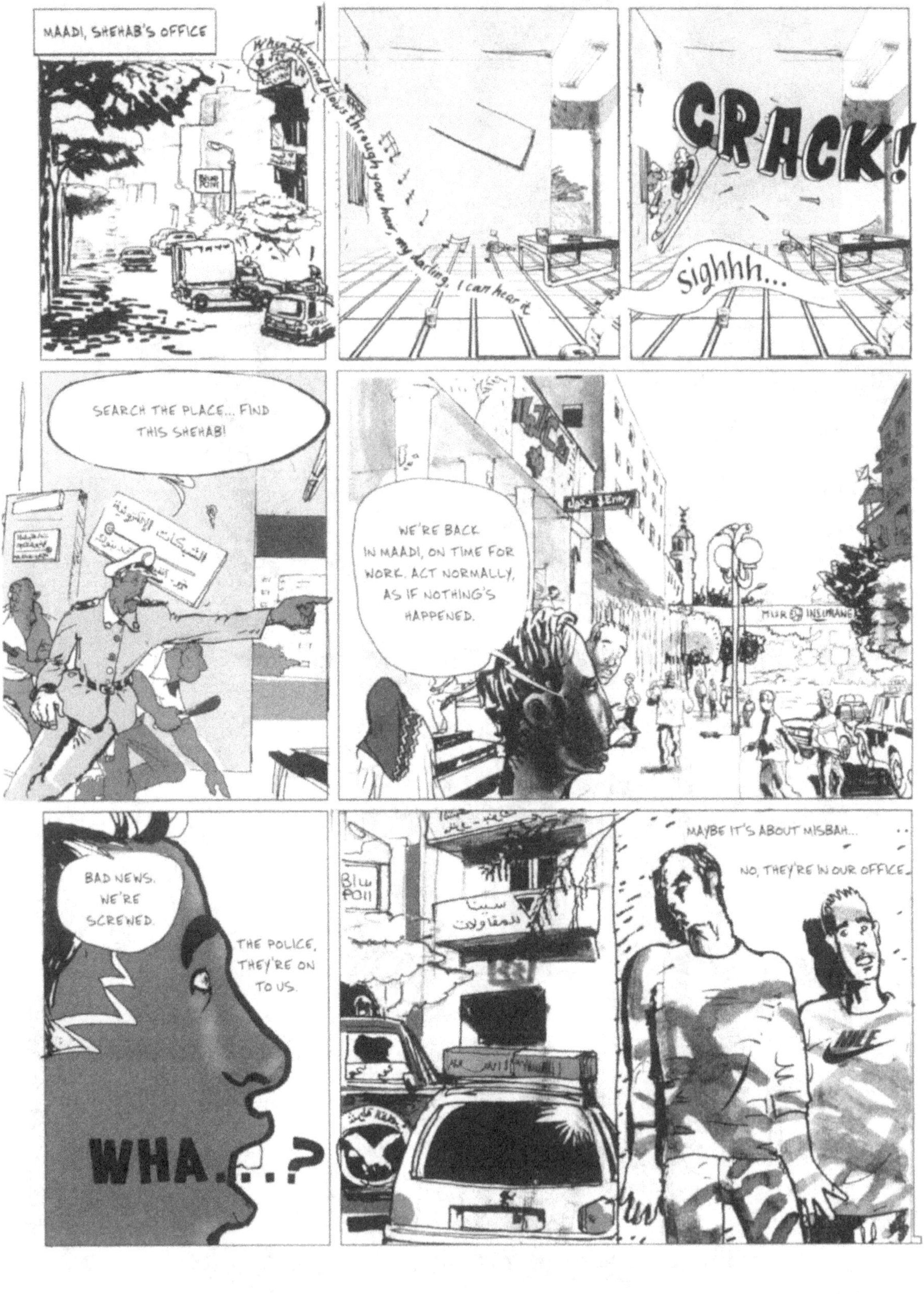
MAADI, SHEHAB'S OFFICE
When the wind blows through your hair, my darling, I can hear it
CRACK!
sighhh...
SEARCH THE PLACE... FIND THIS SHEHAB!
WE'RE BACK IN MAADI, ON TIME FOR WORK. ACT NORMALLY, AS IF NOTHING'S HAPPENED.
BAD NEWS. WE'RE SCREWED.
THE POLICE, THEY'RE ON TO US.
WHA...?
MAYBE IT'S ABOUT MISBAH...
NO, THEY'RE IN OUR OFFICE.

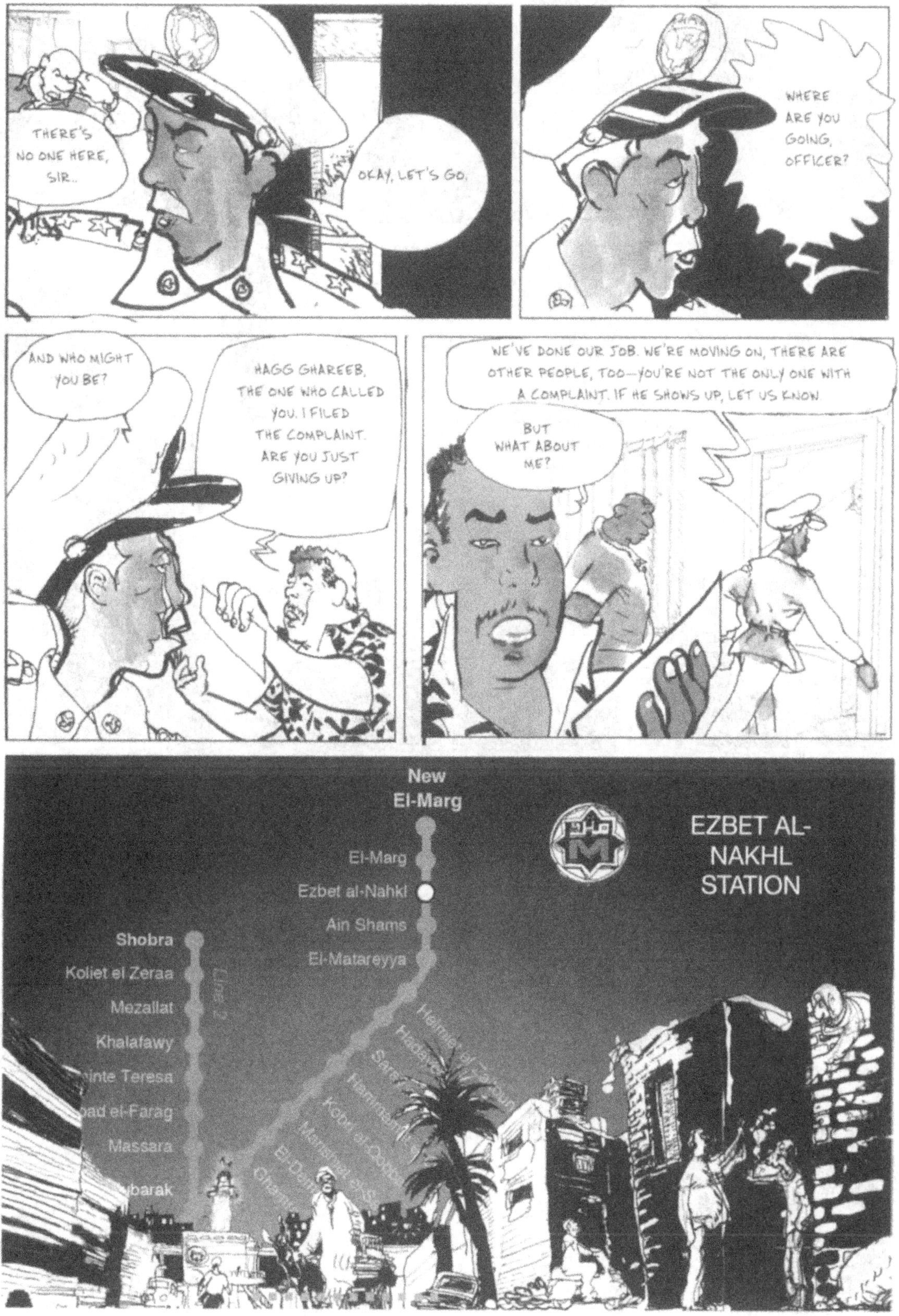
THERE'S NO ONE HERE, SIR..
OKAY, LET'S GO.
WHERE ARE YOU GOING, OFFICER?
AND WHO MIGHT YOU BE?
HAGG GHAREEB, THE ONE WHO CALLED YOU. I FILED THE COMPLAINT. ARE YOU JUST GIVING UP?
WE'VE DONE OUR JOB. WE'RE MOVING ON, THERE ARE OTHER PEOPLE, TOO—YOU'RE NOT THE ONLY ONE WITH A COMPLAINT. IF HE SHOWS UP, LET US KNOW.
BUT WHAT ABOUT ME?
New El-Marg
El-Marg
Ezbet al-Nakhl
Ain Shams
El-Matareyya
EZBET AL-NAKHL STATION
Shobra
Koliet el Zeraa
Mezallat
Khalafawy
Massara
Line 2

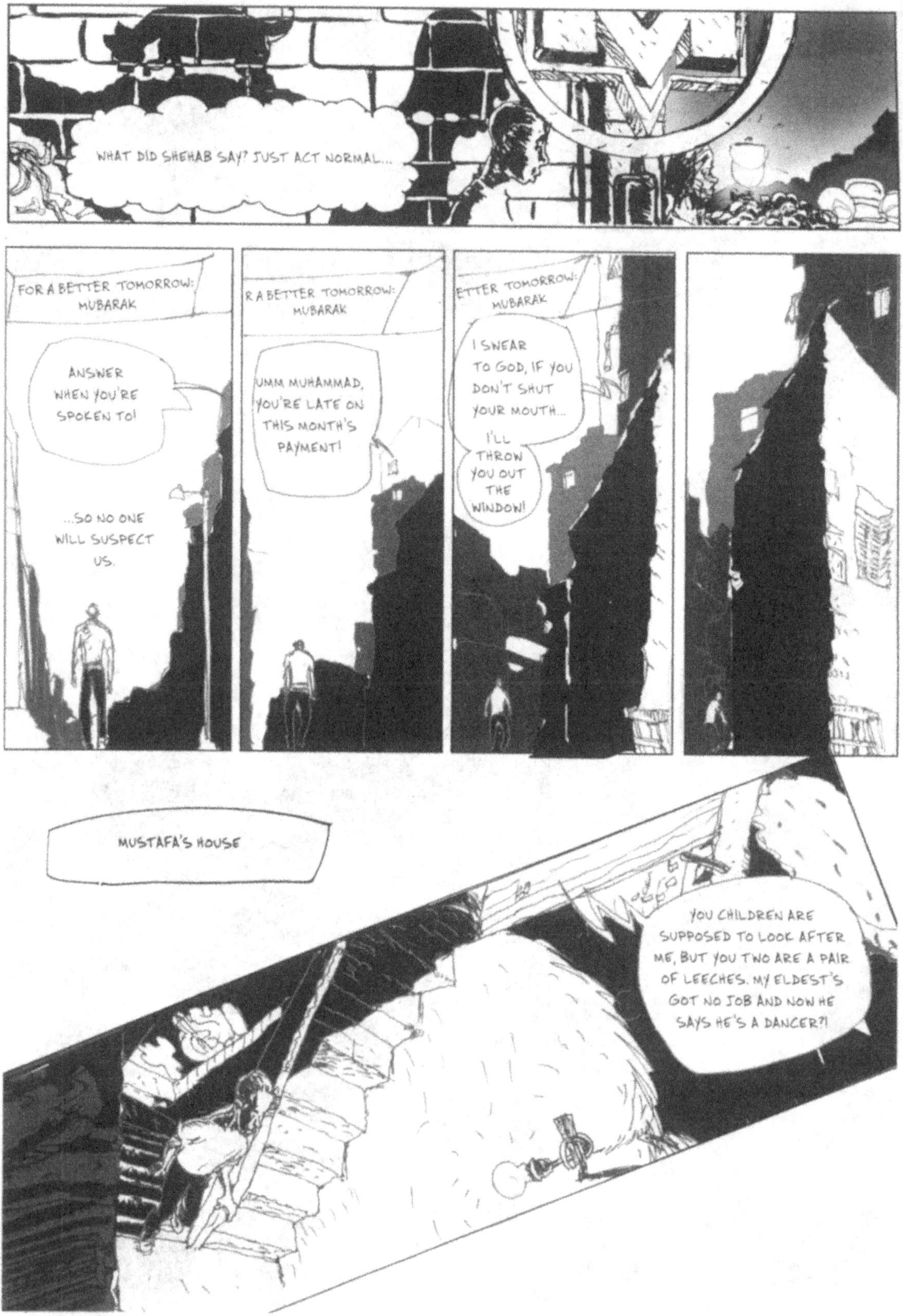
WHAT DID SHEHAB SAY? JUST ACT NORMAL...
FOR A BETTER TOMORROW: MUBARAK
ANSWER WHEN YOU'RE SPOKEN TO!
...SO NO ONE WILL SUSPECT US.
R A BETTER TOMORROW: MUBARAK
UMM MUHAMMAD, YOU'RE LATE ON THIS MONTH'S PAYMENT!
ETTER TOMORROW: MUBARAK
I SWEAR TO GOD, IF YOU DON'T SHUT YOUR MOUTH...
I'LL THROW YOU OUT THE WINDOW!
MUSTAFA'S HOUSE
YOU CHILDREN ARE SUPPOSED TO LOOK AFTER ME, BUT YOU TWO ARE A PAIR OF LEECHES. MY ELDEST'S GOT NO JOB AND NOW HE SAYS HE'S A DANCER?!

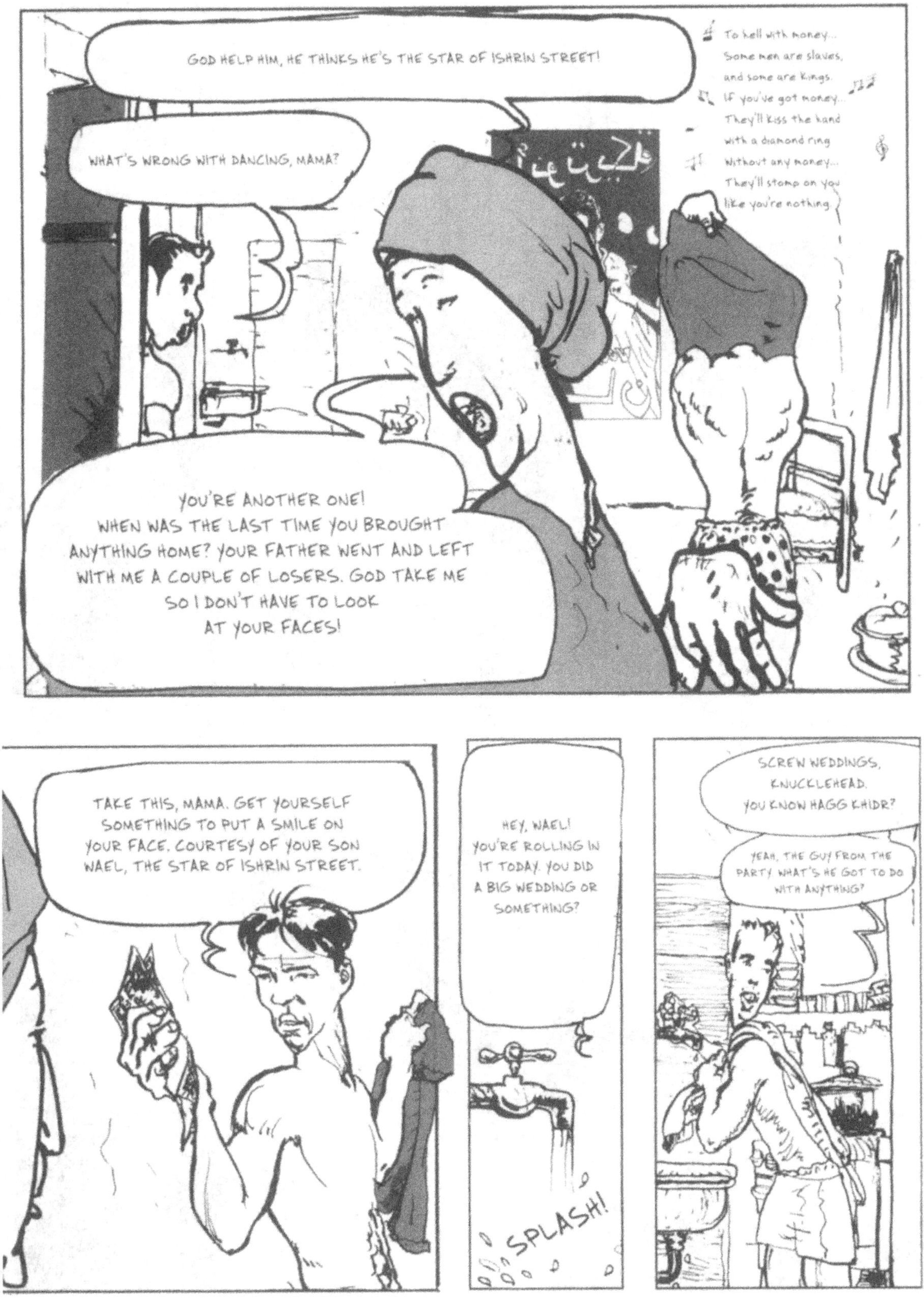
GOD HELP HIM, HE THINKS HE'S THE STAR OF ISHRIN STREET!
WHAT'S WRONG WITH DANCING, MAMA?
To hell with money... Some men are slaves, and some are kings. If you've got money... They'll kiss the hand with a diamond ring Without any money... They'll stomp on you like you're nothing.
YOU'RE ANOTHER ONE! WHEN WAS THE LAST TIME YOU BROUGHT ANYTHING HOME? YOUR FATHER WENT AND LEFT WITH ME A COUPLE OF LOSERS. GOD TAKE ME SO I DON'T HAVE TO LOOK AT YOUR FACES!
TAKE THIS, MAMA. GET YOURSELF SOMETHING TO PUT A SMILE ON YOUR FACE. COURTESY OF YOUR SON WAEL, THE STAR OF ISHRIN STREET.
HEY, WAEL! YOU'RE ROLLING IN IT TODAY. YOU DID A BIG WEDDING OR SOMETHING?
SPLASH!
SCREW WEDDINGS, KNUCKLEHEAD. YOU KNOW HAGG KHIDR?
YEAH, THE GUY FROM THE PARTY. WHAT'S HE GOT TO DO WITH ANYTHING?

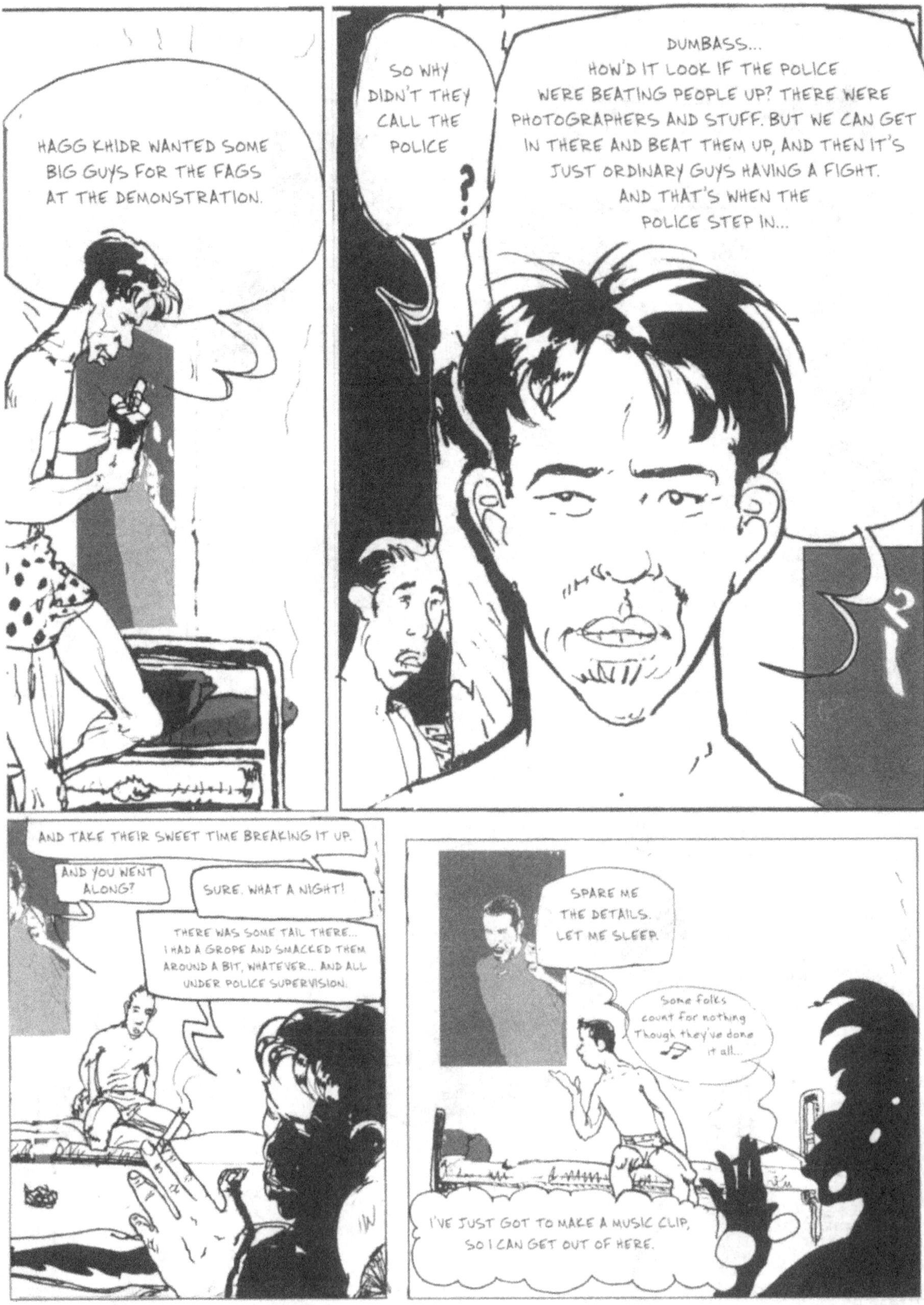
HAGG KHIDR WANTED SOME BIG GUYS FOR THE FAGS AT THE DEMONSTRATION.
SO WHY DIDN'T THEY CALL THE POLICE
?
DUMBASS... HOW'D IT LOOK IF THE POLICE WERE BEATING PEOPLE UP? THERE WERE PHOTOGRAPHERS AND STUFF. BUT WE CAN GET IN THERE AND BEAT THEM UP, AND THEN IT'S JUST ORDINARY GUYS HAVING A FIGHT. AND THAT'S WHEN THE POLICE STEP IN...
AND TAKE THEIR SWEET TIME BREAKING IT UP.
AND YOU WENT ALONG?
SURE. WHAT A NIGHT!
THERE WAS SOME TAIL THERE... I HAD A GROPE AND SMACKED THEM AROUND A BIT, WHATEVER... AND ALL UNDER POLICE SUPERVISION.
SPARE ME THE DETAILS. LET ME SLEEP.
Some folks count for nothing Though they've done it all...
I'VE JUST GOT TO MAKE A MUSIC CLIP, SO I CAN GET OUT OF HERE.

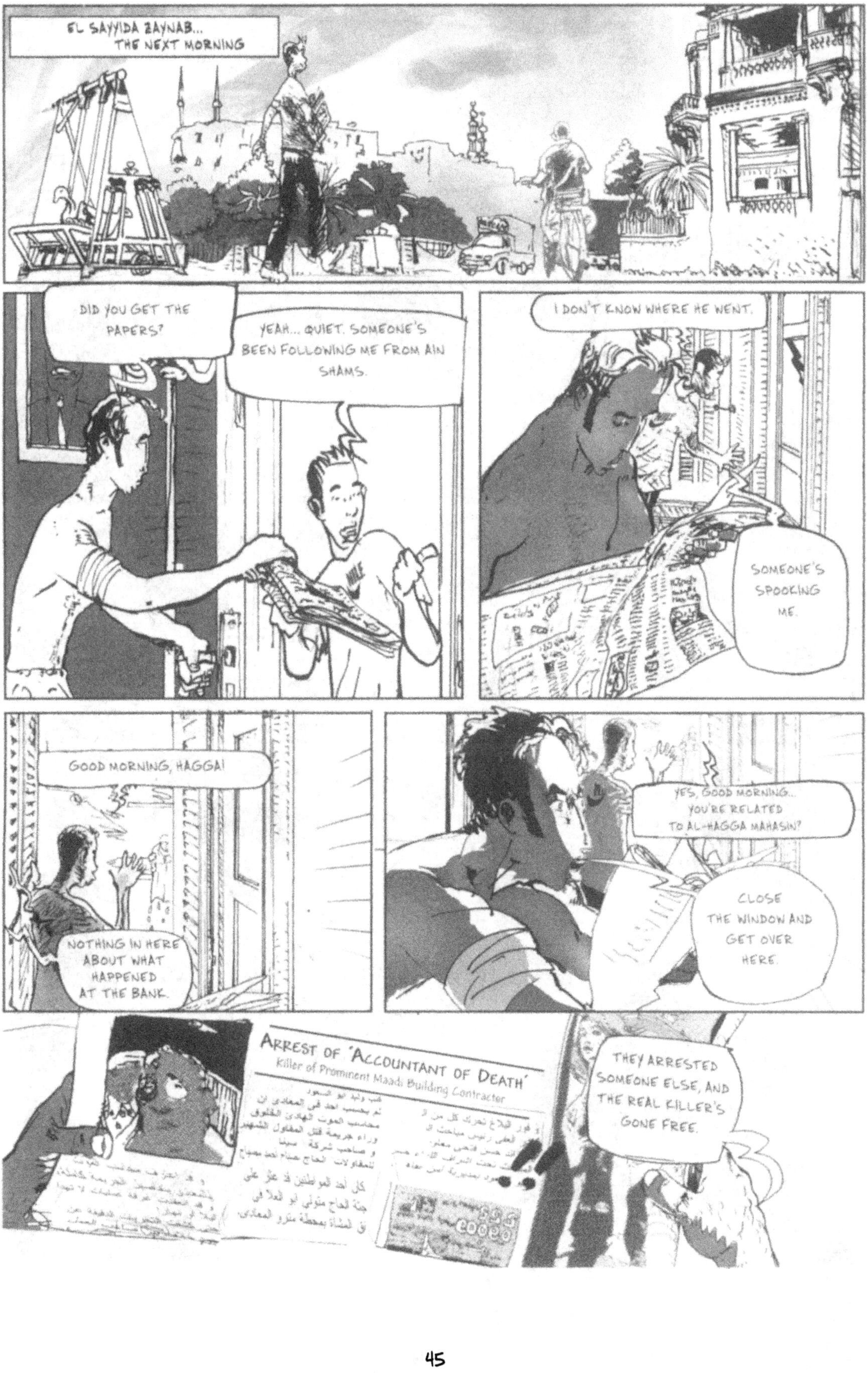
EL SAYYIDA ZAYNAB... THE NEXT MORNING
DID YOU GET THE PAPERS?
YEAH... QUIET. SOMEONE'S BEEN FOLLOWING ME FROM AIN SHAMS.
I DON'T KNOW WHERE HE WENT.
SOMEONE'S SPOOKING ME.
GOOD MORNING, HAGGA!
NOTHING IN HERE ABOUT WHAT HAPPENED AT THE BANK.
YES, GOOD MORNING... YOU'RE RELATED TO AL-HAGGA MAHASIN?
CLOSE THE WINDOW AND GET OVER HERE.
ARREST OF 'ACCOUNTANT OF DEATH'
Killer of Prominent Maadi Building Contractor
THEY ARRESTED SOMEONE ELSE, AND THE REAL KILLER'S GONE FREE.

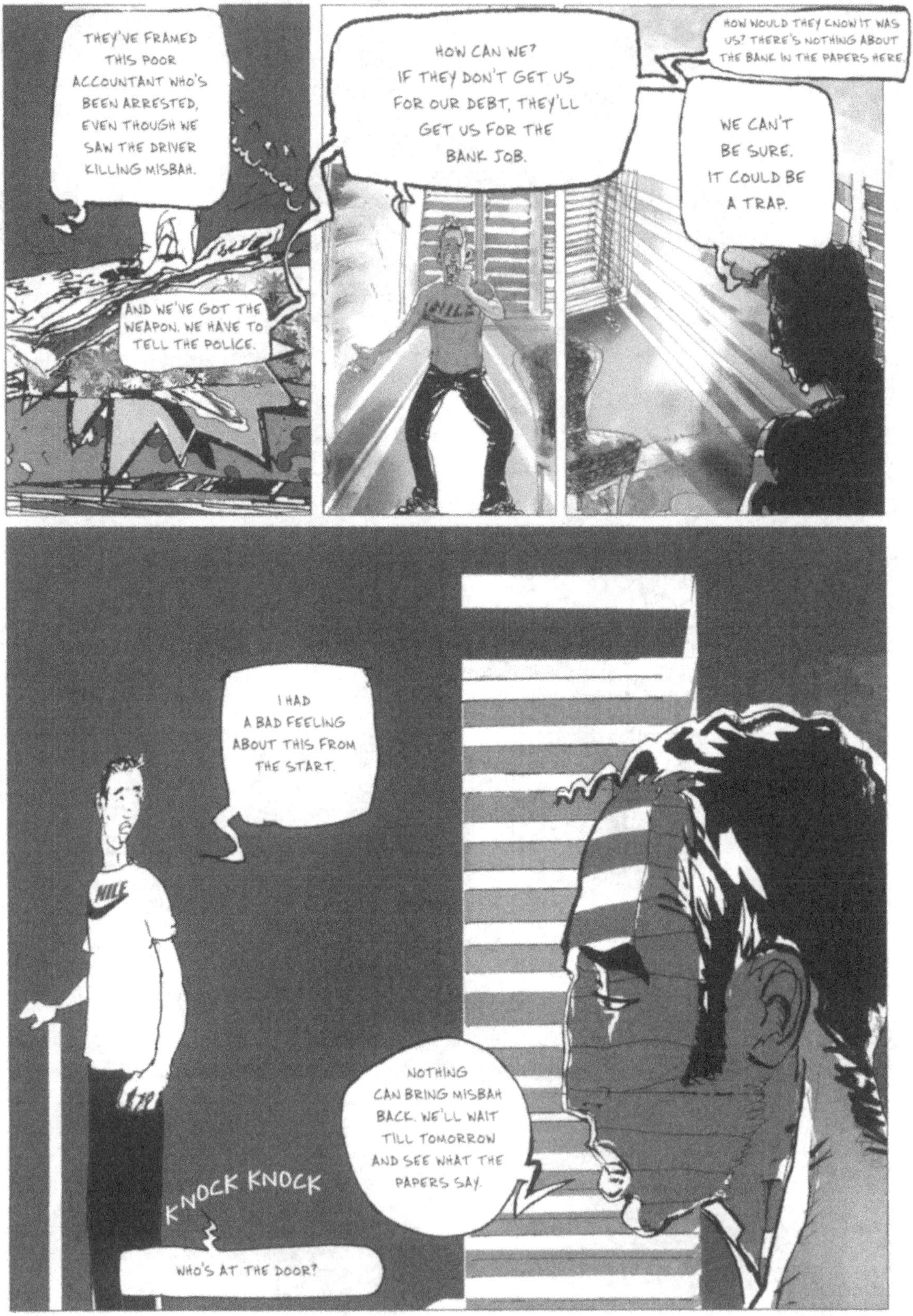
THEY'VE FRAMED THIS POOR ACCOUNTANT WHO'S BEEN ARRESTED, EVEN THOUGH WE SAW THE DRIVER KILLING MISBAH.
AND WE'VE GOT THE WEAPON. WE HAVE TO TELL THE POLICE.
HOW CAN WE? IF THEY DON'T GET US FOR OUR DEBT, THEY'LL GET US FOR THE BANK JOB.
HOW WOULD THEY KNOW IT WAS US? THERE'S NOTHING ABOUT THE BANK IN THE PAPERS HERE.
WE CAN'T BE SURE. IT COULD BE A TRAP.
I HAD A BAD FEELING ABOUT THIS FROM THE START.
NOTHING CAN BRING MISBAH BACK. WE'LL WAIT TILL TOMORROW AND SEE WHAT THE PAPERS SAY.
KNOCK KNOCK
WHO'S AT THE DOOR?

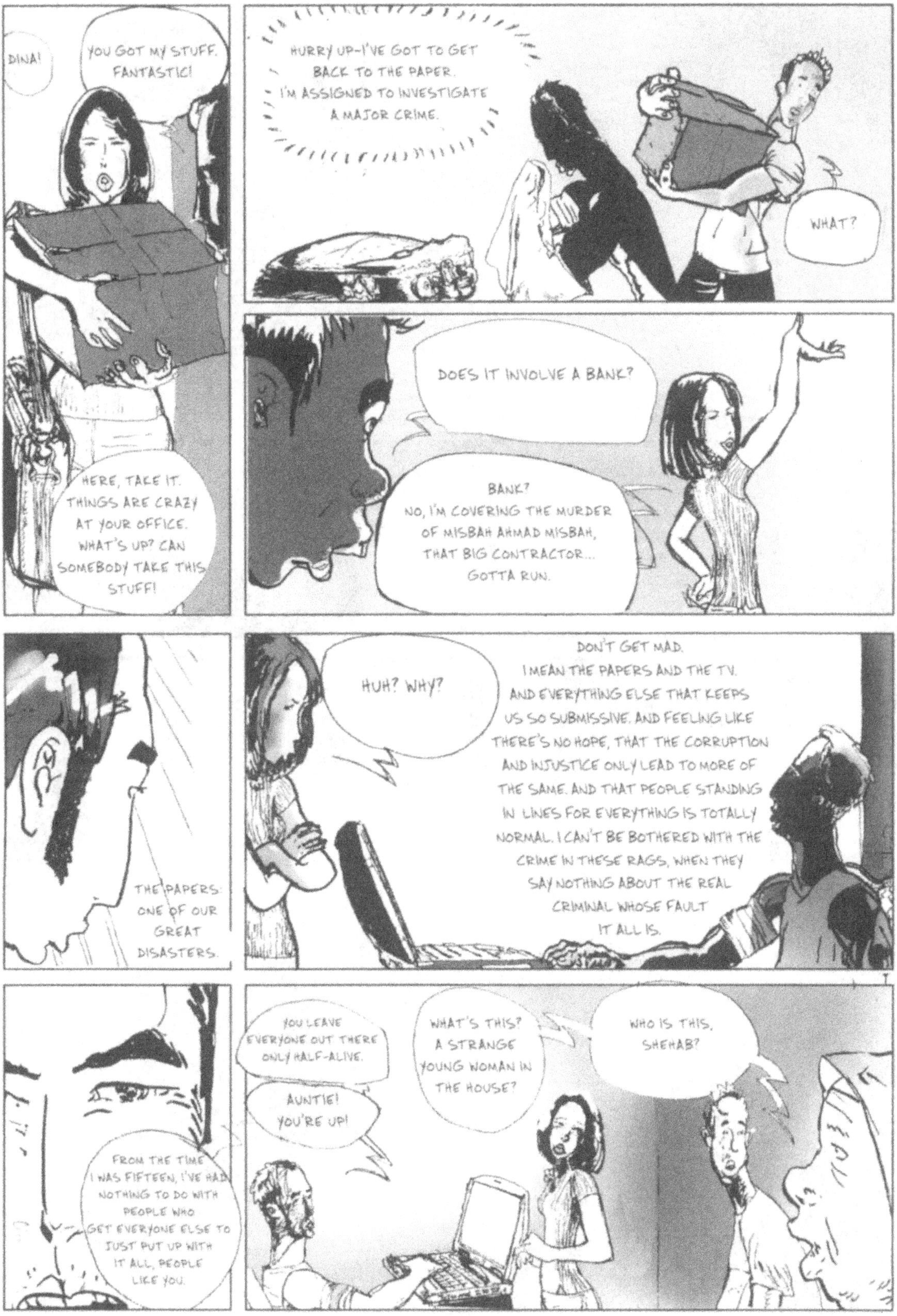

DINA!
YOU GOT MY STUFF. FANTASTIC!
HERE, TAKE IT. THINGS ARE CRAZY AT YOUR OFFICE. WHAT'S UP? CAN SOMEBODY TAKE THIS STUFF!
HURRY UP—I'VE GOT TO GET BACK TO THE PAPER. I'M ASSIGNED TO INVESTIGATE A MAJOR CRIME.
WHAT?
DOES IT INVOLVE A BANK?
BANK? NO, I'M COVERING THE MURDER OF MISBAH AHMAD MISBAH, THAT BIG CONTRACTOR... GOTTA RUN.
THE PAPERS: ONE OF OUR GREAT DISASTERS.
HUH? WHY?
DON'T GET MAD. I MEAN THE PAPERS AND THE TV. AND EVERYTHING ELSE THAT KEEPS US SO SUBMISSIVE. AND FEELING LIKE THERE'S NO HOPE, THAT THE CORRUPTION AND INJUSTICE ONLY LEAD TO MORE OF THE SAME. AND THAT PEOPLE STANDING IN LINES FOR EVERYTHING IS TOTALLY NORMAL. I CAN'T BE BOTHERED WITH THE CRIME IN THESE RAGS, WHEN THEY SAY NOTHING ABOUT THE REAL CRIMINAL WHOSE FAULT IT ALL IS.
FROM THE TIME I WAS FIFTEEN, I'VE HAD NOTHING TO DO WITH PEOPLE WHO GET EVERYONE ELSE TO JUST PUT UP WITH IT ALL, PEOPLE LIKE YOU.
YOU LEAVE EVERYONE OUT THERE ONLY HALF-ALIVE.
AUNTIE! YOU'RE UP!
WHAT'S THIS? A STRANGE YOUNG WOMAN IN THE HOUSE?
WHO IS THIS, SHEHAB?

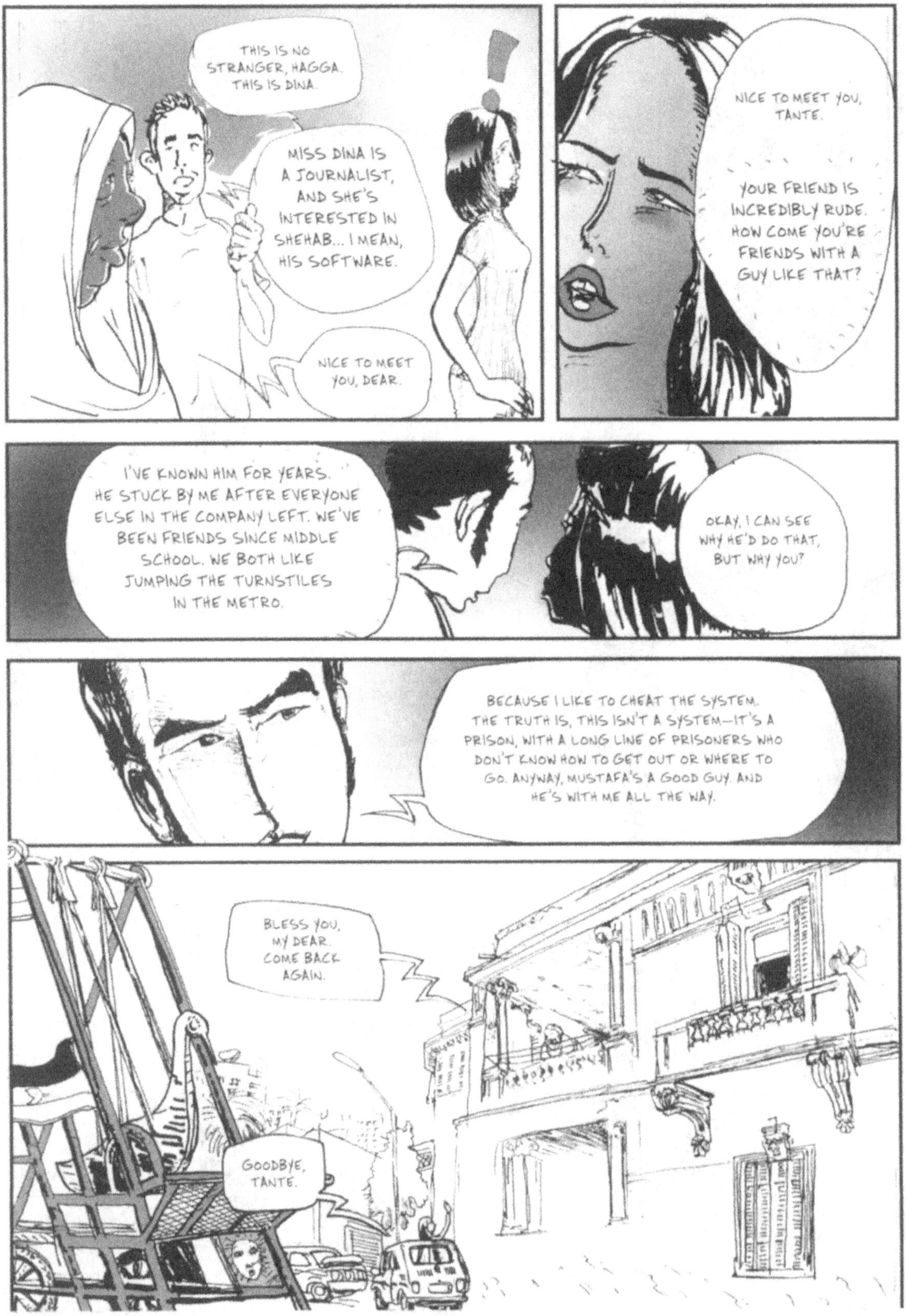
THIS IS NO STRANGER, HAGGA. THIS IS DINA.
MISS DINA IS A JOURNALIST, AND SHE'S INTERESTED IN SHEHAB... I MEAN, HIS SOFTWARE.
!
NICE TO MEET YOU, DEAR.
NICE TO MEET YOU, TANTE.
YOUR FRIEND IS INCREDIBLY RUDE. HOW COME YOU'RE FRIENDS WITH A GUY LIKE THAT?
I'VE KNOWN HIM FOR YEARS. HE STUCK BY ME AFTER EVERYONE ELSE IN THE COMPANY LEFT. WE'VE BEEN FRIENDS SINCE MIDDLE SCHOOL. WE BOTH LIKE JUMPING THE TURNSTILES IN THE METRO.
OKAY, I CAN SEE WHY HE'D DO THAT, BUT WHY YOU?
BECAUSE I LIKE TO CHEAT THE SYSTEM. THE TRUTH IS, THIS ISN'T A SYSTEM—IT'S A PRISON, WITH A LONG LINE OF PRISONERS WHO DON'T KNOW HOW TO GET OUT OR WHERE TO GO. ANYWAY, MUSTAFA'S A GOOD GUY. AND HE'S WITH ME ALL THE WAY.
BLESS YOU, MY DEAR. COME BACK AGAIN.
GOODBYE, TANTE.

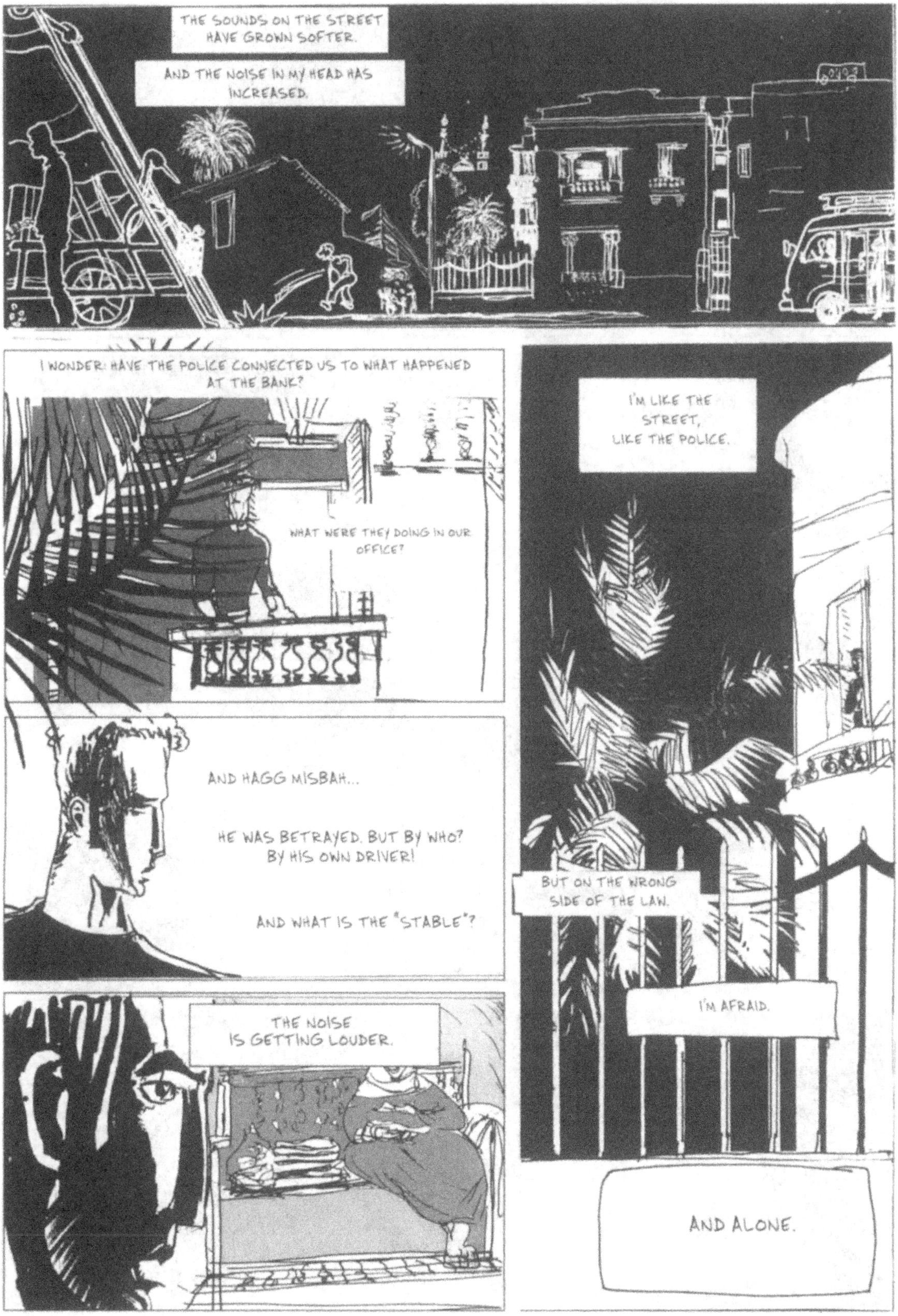
THE SOUNDS ON THE STREET HAVE GROWN SOFTER.
AND THE NOISE IN MY HEAD HAS INCREASED.
I WONDER: HAVE THE POLICE CONNECTED US TO WHAT HAPPENED AT THE BANK?
WHAT WERE THEY DOING IN OUR OFFICE?
AND HAGG MISBAH...
HE WAS BETRAYED. BUT BY WHO? BY HIS OWN DRIVER!
AND WHAT IS THE "STABLE"?
THE NOISE IS GETTING LOUDER.
I'M LIKE THE STREET, LIKE THE POLICE.
BUT ON THE WRONG SIDE OF THE LAW.
I'M AFRAID.
AND ALONE.

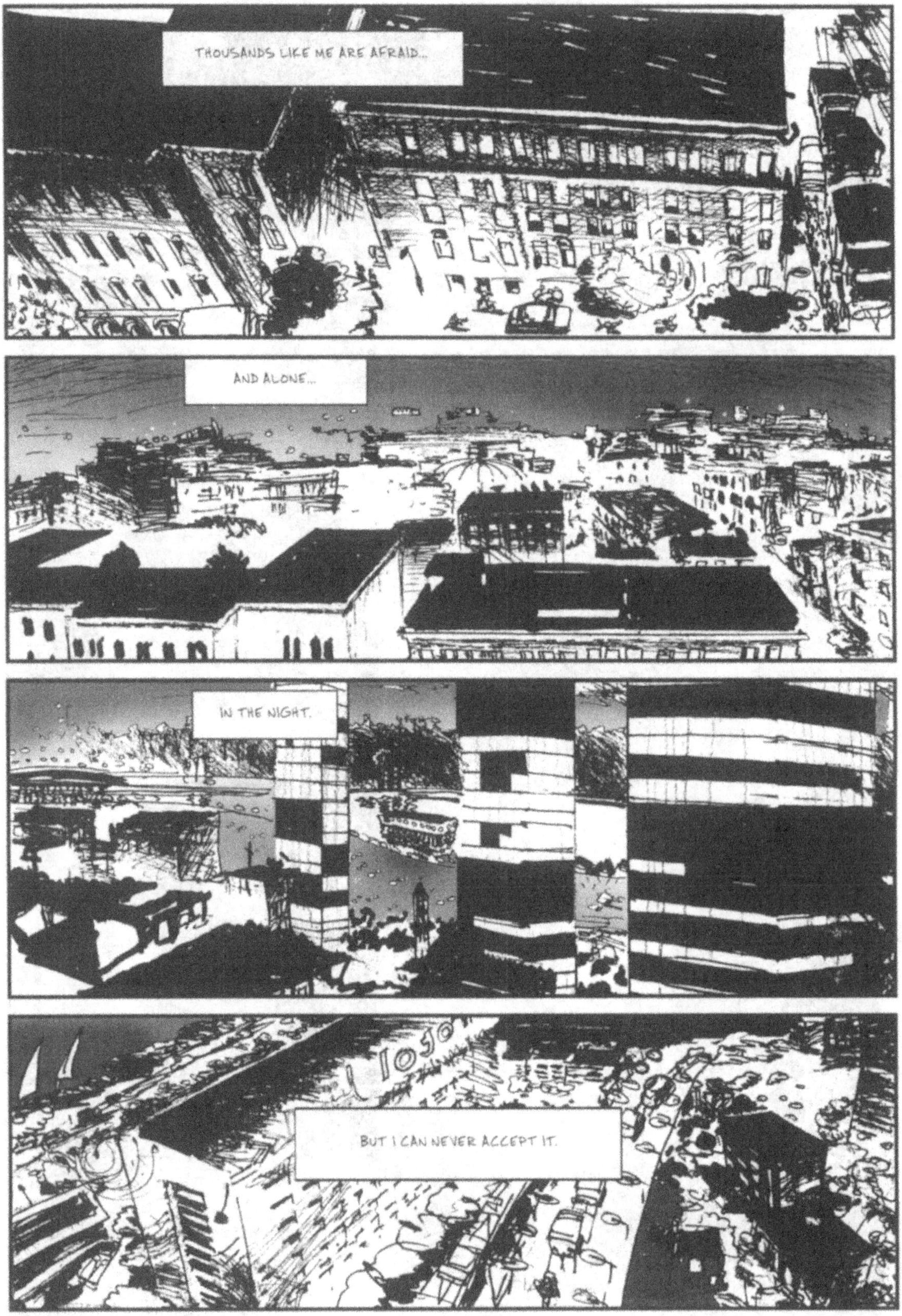
THOUSANDS LIKE ME ARE AFRAID...
AND ALONE...
IN THE NIGHT.
BUT I CAN NEVER ACCEPT IT.

SAYYIDA ZAYNAB STATION

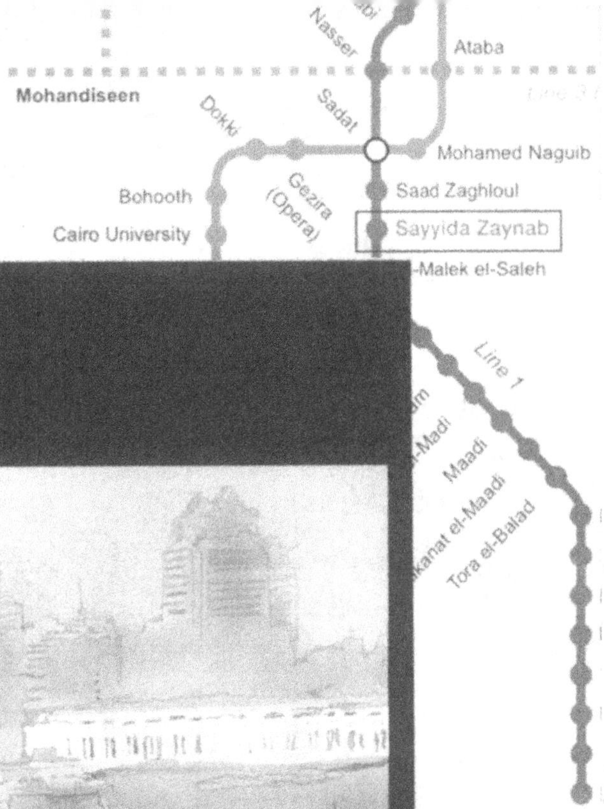

Nasser
Ataba
Mohandiseen
Line 3
Dokki
Sadat
Mohamed Naguib
Bohooth
Gezira (Opera)
Saad Zaghloul
Cairo University
Sayyida Zaynab
Malek el-Saleh
Line 1
Maadi
Tora el-Balad

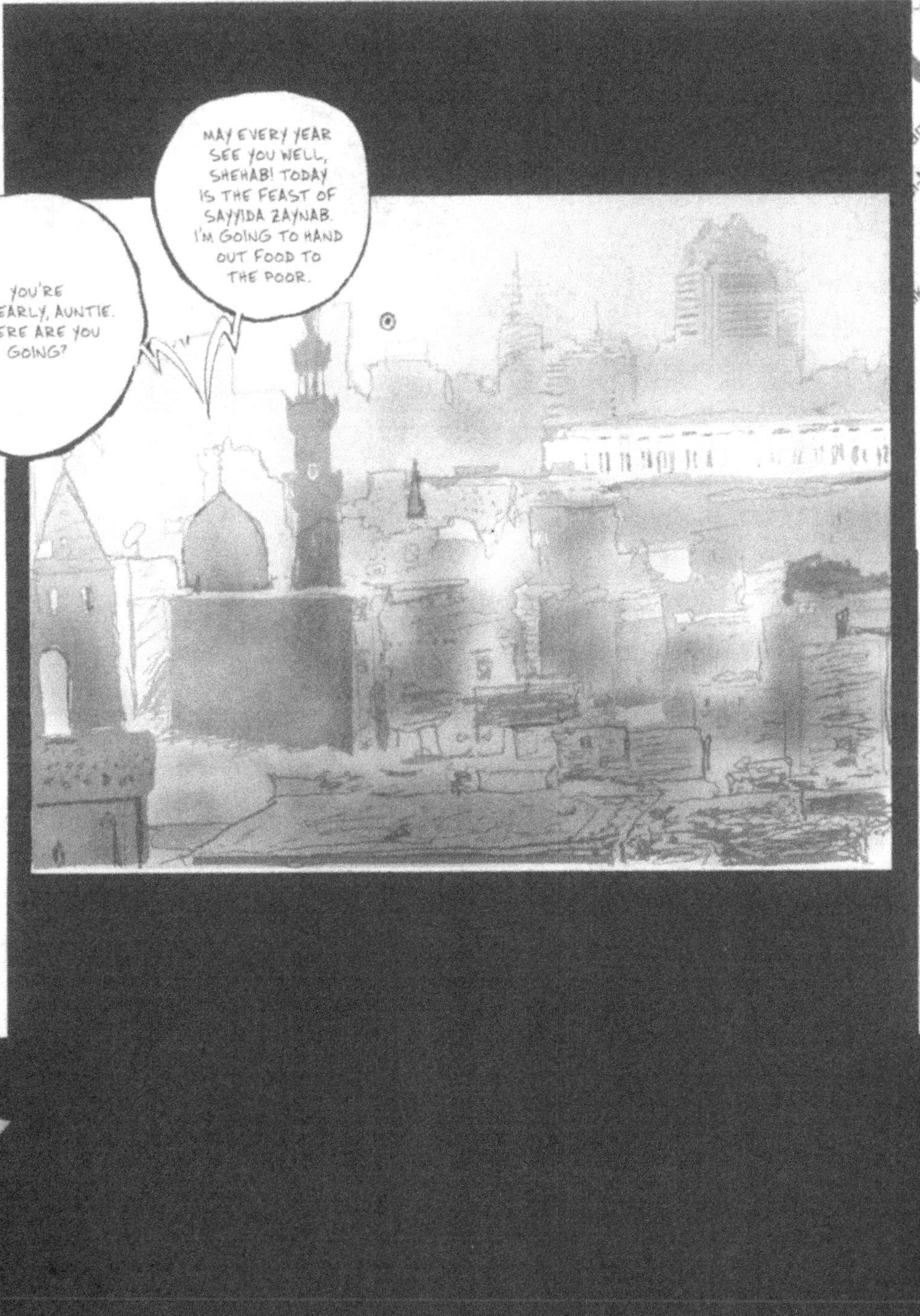

YOU'RE OFF EARLY, AUNTIE. WHERE ARE YOU GOING?
MAY EVERY YEAR SEE YOU WELL, SHEHAB! TODAY IS THE FEAST OF SAYYIDA ZAYNAB. I'M GOING TO HAND OUT FOOD TO THE POOR.

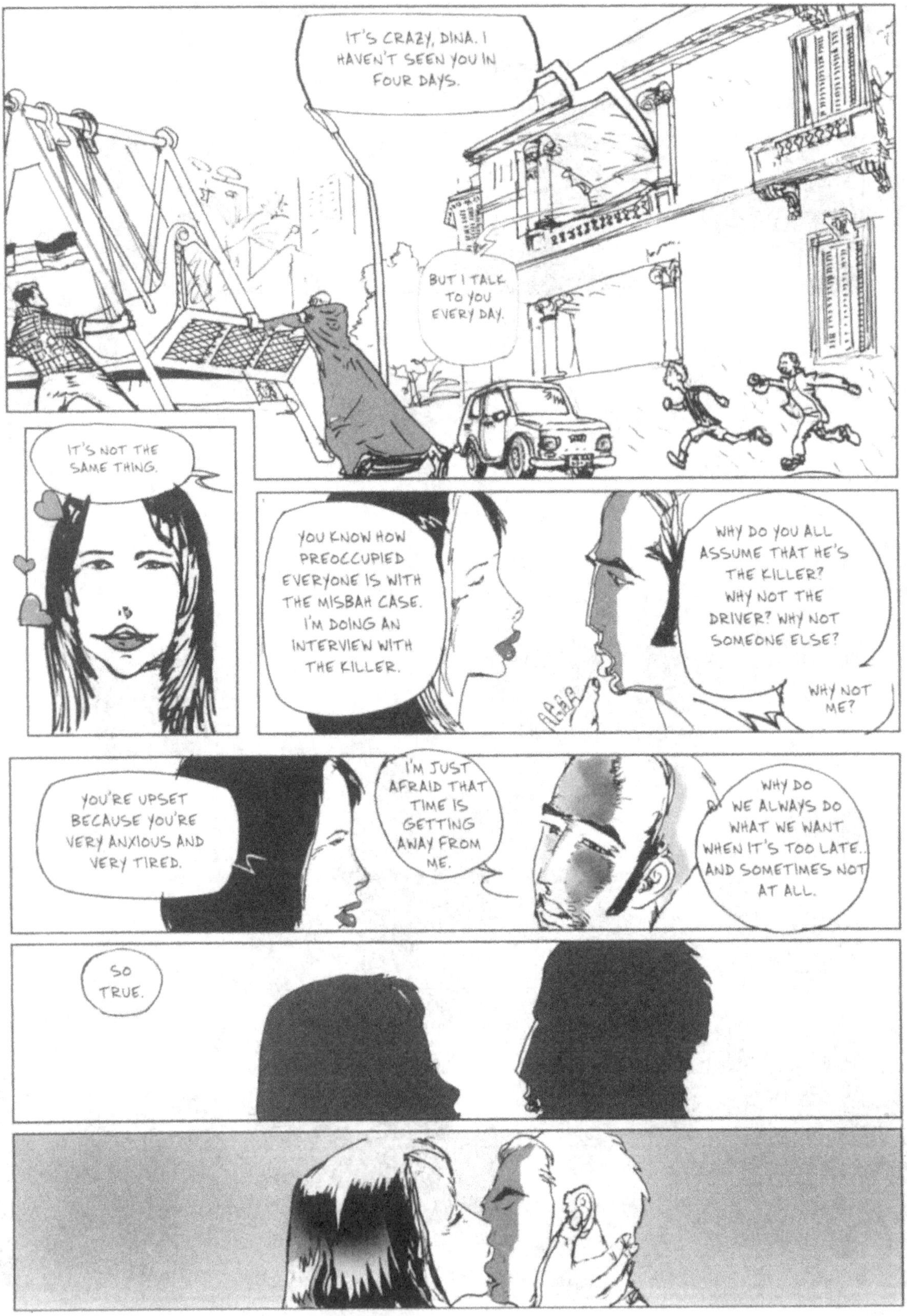
IT'S CRAZY, DINA. I HAVEN'T SEEN YOU IN FOUR DAYS.
BUT I TALK TO YOU EVERY DAY.
IT'S NOT THE SAME THING.
YOU KNOW HOW PREOCCUPIED EVERYONE IS WITH THE MISBAH CASE. I'M DOING AN INTERVIEW WITH THE KILLER.
WHY DO YOU ALL ASSUME THAT HE'S THE KILLER? WHY NOT THE DRIVER? WHY NOT SOMEONE ELSE?
WHY NOT ME?
YOU'RE UPSET BECAUSE YOU'RE VERY ANXIOUS AND VERY TIRED.
I'M JUST AFRAID THAT TIME IS GETTING AWAY FROM ME.
WHY DO WE ALWAYS DO WHAT WE WANT WHEN IT'S TOO LATE... AND SOMETIMES NOT AT ALL.
SO TRUE.

DINA,
I CAN'T MAKE YOU
ANY PROMISES.
JUST THAT YOU'RE
A VERY BIG DEAL TO ME.

SIGH· SIGH·SIGH·SIGH

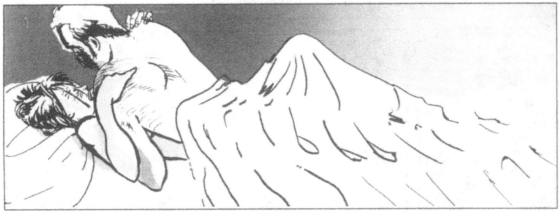

LOVE GIVEN IN EXCHANGE FOR SOMETHING IS CHEAP...

I CAN'T LOVE JUST
BECAUSE I'LL GET
SOMETHING IN
RETURN

NOT ALL MEN GET THAT, BUT YOU DO.

THAT'S WHY I LOVE YOU.

WHAT'S
THIS?

WHA—?

UH... DINA...

DON'T JUMP TO CONCLUSIONS... YOU HAVE TO UNDERSTAND.

A BLOODY KNIFE IN A BAG...

WHAT'S THERE TO UNDERSTAND?

YOU HAVE TO HEAR ME OUT!

I HAVE TO TELL SOMEONE THE TRUTH. I'LL TELL YOU, AND AFTER THAT, DO WHAT YOU LIKE.

I HAD NOTHING TO DO WITH IT. IT WAS PURE COINCIDENCE THAT I SAW WHO KILLED HAGG MISBAH.

AND MY CONSCIENCE IS KILLING ME. YOU KNOW WHY?

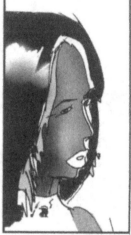

BECAUSE THE GUY YOU'VE ACCUSED IS INNOCENT... AND THE MAN WHO REALLY DID IT IS MISBAH'S DRIVER, ARAFA.

SO WHY HAVEN'T YOU GONE TO THE POLICE?

BECAUSE OF MY DEBTS, I CAN'T GO TO THE POLICE. BUT THE MOST IMPORTANT THING IN ALL THIS IS THAT THERE'S NO OBVIOUS MOTIVE.

BEFORE HE DIED, MISBAH ENTRUSTED ME WITH A SECRET, SOMETHING CALLED THE STABLE.

HELP ME FIND OUT WHO'S BEHIND THIS. YOU'LL GIVE ME BACK MY PEACE OF MIND. AND YOU'LL HELP MISBAH REST EASY IN HIS GRAVE. PLUS, IT'LL BE A SCOOP LIKE YOU'VE NEVER SEEN.

QUICK, CHIEF, THERE'S AN INTERVIEW WITH MISBAH'S KILLER ON TV.

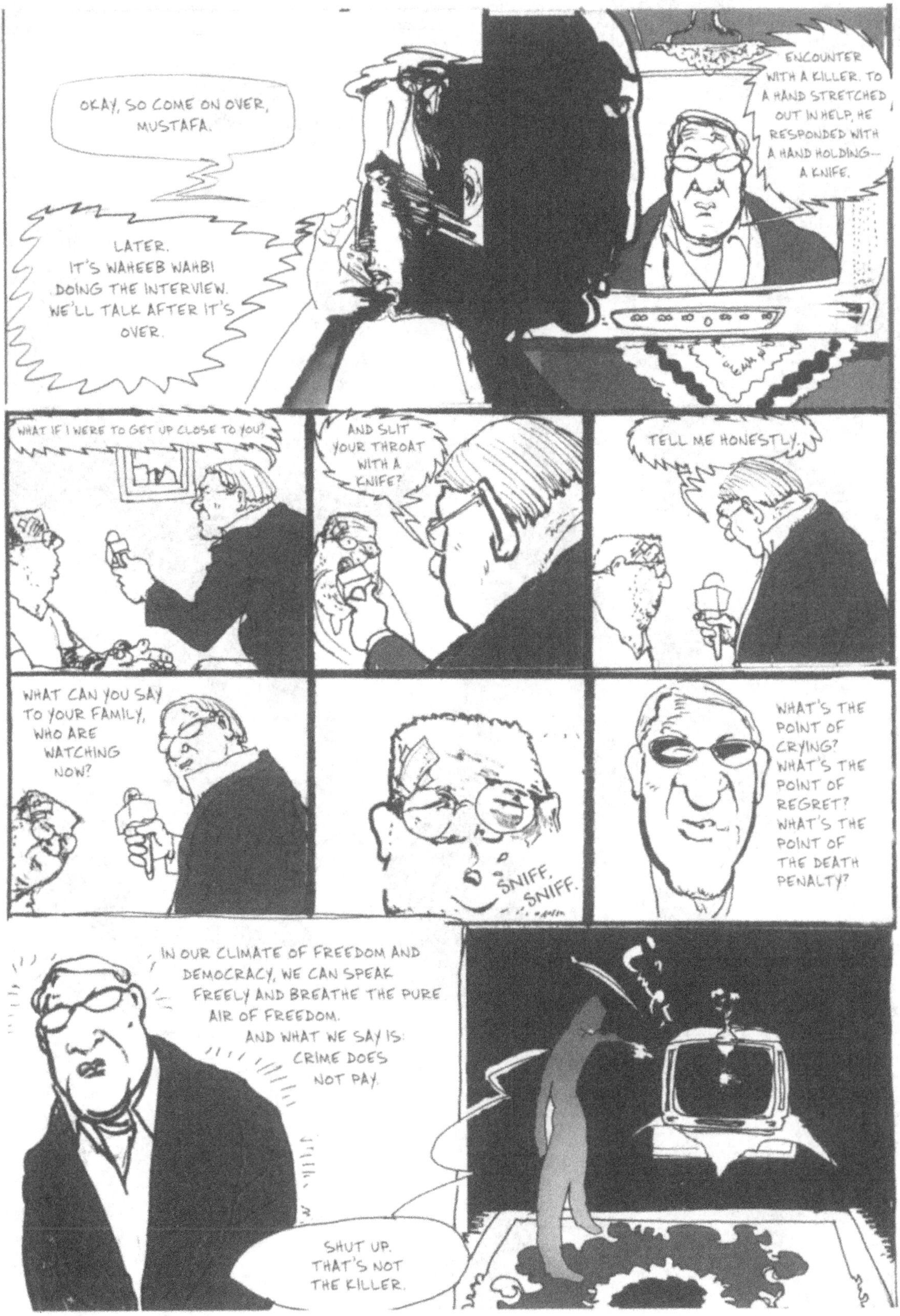
OKAY, SO COME ON OVER, MUSTAFA.
LATER. IT'S WAHEEB WAHBI DOING THE INTERVIEW. WE'LL TALK AFTER IT'S OVER.
ENCOUNTER WITH A KILLER. TO A HAND STRETCHED OUT IN HELP, HE RESPONDED WITH A HAND HOLDING... A KNIFE.
WHAT IF I WERE TO GET UP CLOSE TO YOU?
AND SLIT YOUR THROAT WITH A KNIFE?
TELL ME HONESTLY.
WHAT CAN YOU SAY TO YOUR FAMILY, WHO ARE WATCHING NOW?
...
SNIFF, SNIFF.
WHAT'S THE POINT OF CRYING? WHAT'S THE POINT OF REGRET? WHAT'S THE POINT OF THE DEATH PENALTY?
IN OUR CLIMATE OF FREEDOM AND DEMOCRACY, WE CAN SPEAK FREELY AND BREATHE THE PURE AIR OF FREEDOM.
AND WHAT WE SAY IS: CRIME DOES NOT PAY.
SHUT UP. THAT'S NOT THE KILLER.

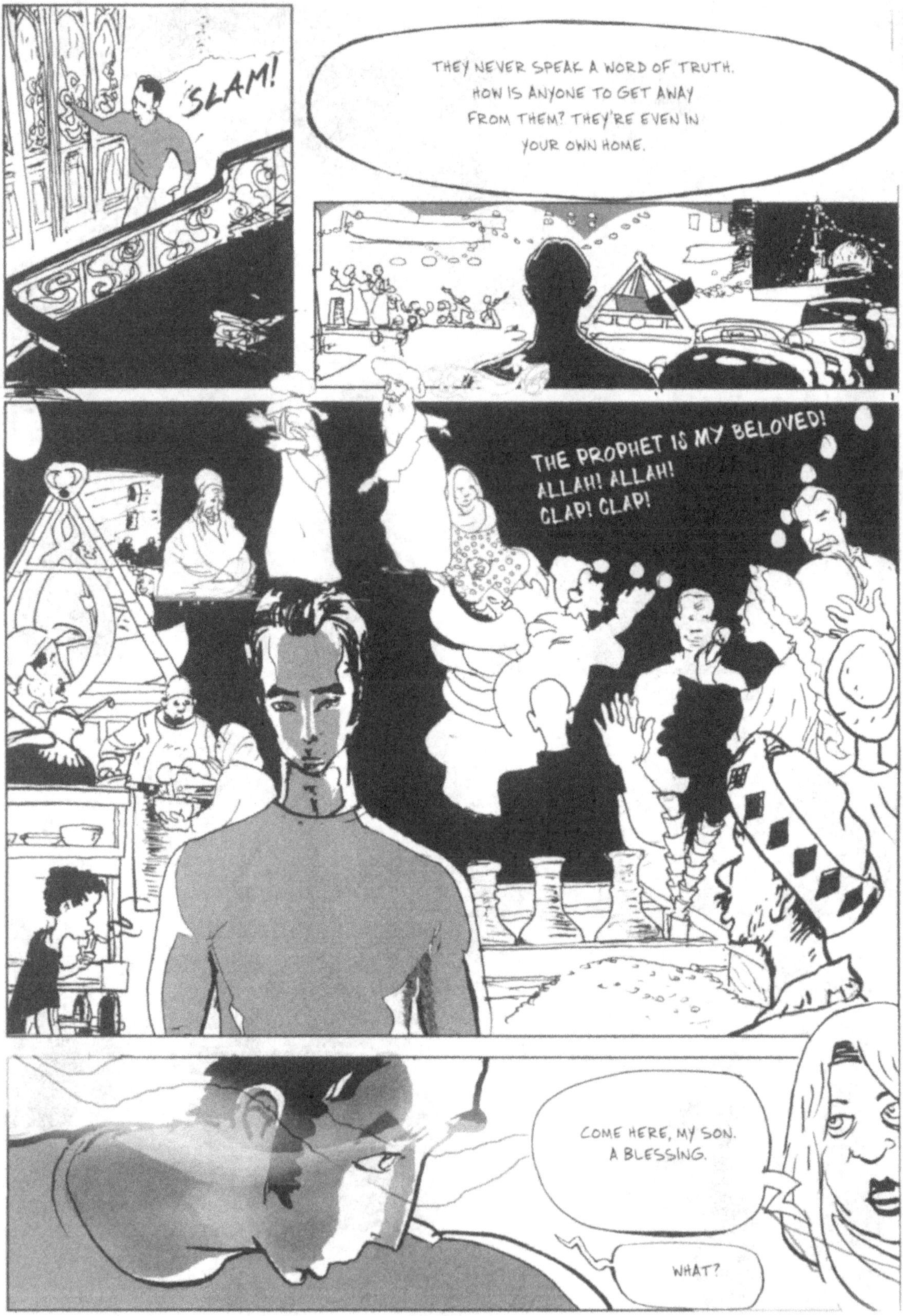
SLAM!
THEY NEVER SPEAK A WORD OF TRUTH. HOW IS ANYONE TO GET AWAY FROM THEM? THEY'RE EVEN IN YOUR OWN HOME.
THE PROPHET IS MY BELOVED! ALLAH! ALLAH! CLAP! CLAP!
COME HERE, MY SON. A BLESSING.
WHAT?

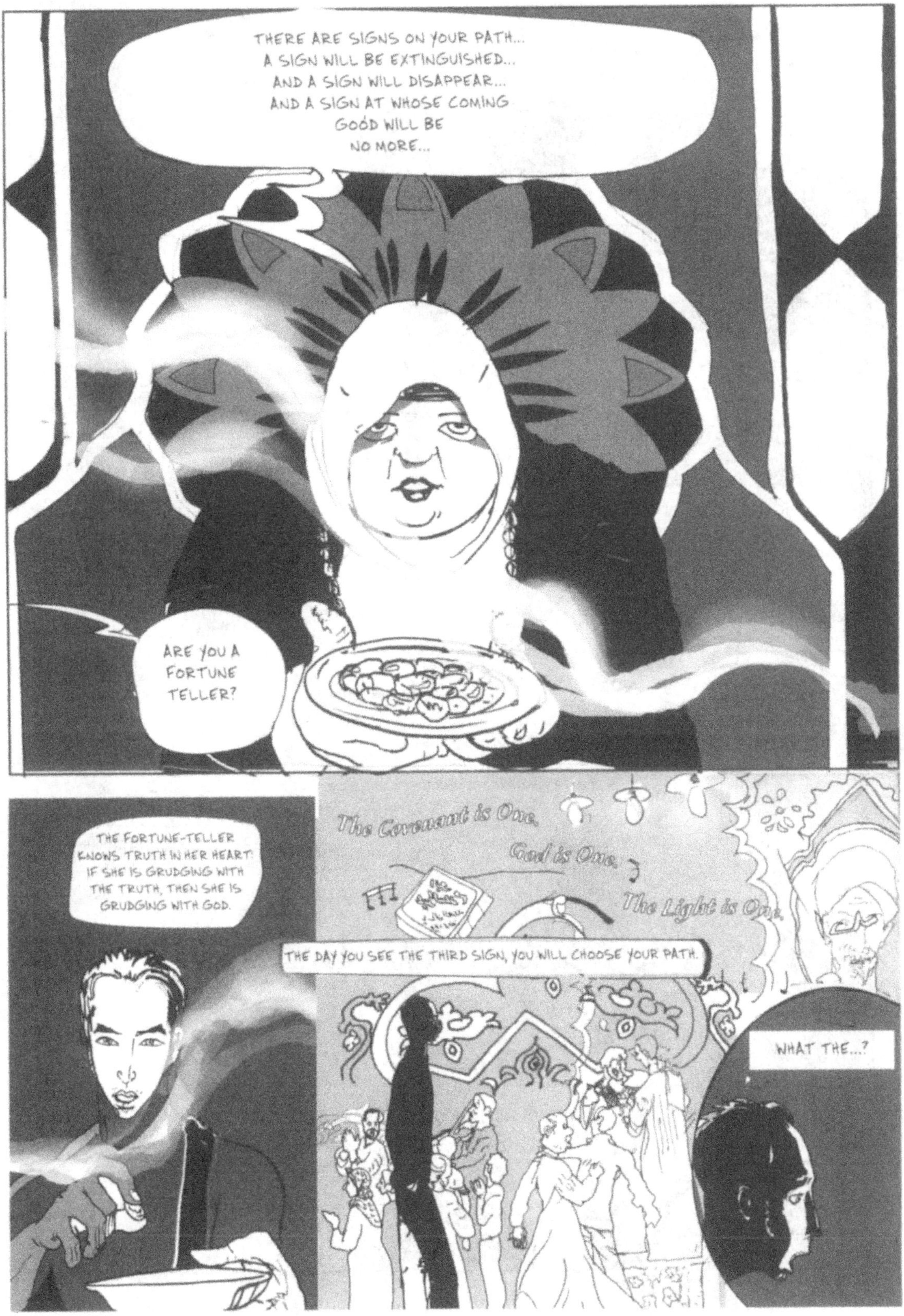
THERE ARE SIGNS ON YOUR PATH... A SIGN WILL BE EXTINGUISHED... AND A SIGN WILL DISAPPEAR... AND A SIGN AT WHOSE COMING GOOD WILL BE NO MORE...
ARE YOU A FORTUNE TELLER?
THE FORTUNE-TELLER KNOWS TRUTH IN HER HEART: IF SHE IS GRUDGING WITH THE TRUTH, THEN SHE IS GRUDGING WITH GOD.
The Covenant is One.
God is One.
The Light is One.
THE DAY YOU SEE THE THIRD SIGN, YOU WILL CHOOSE YOUR PATH.
WHAT THE...?

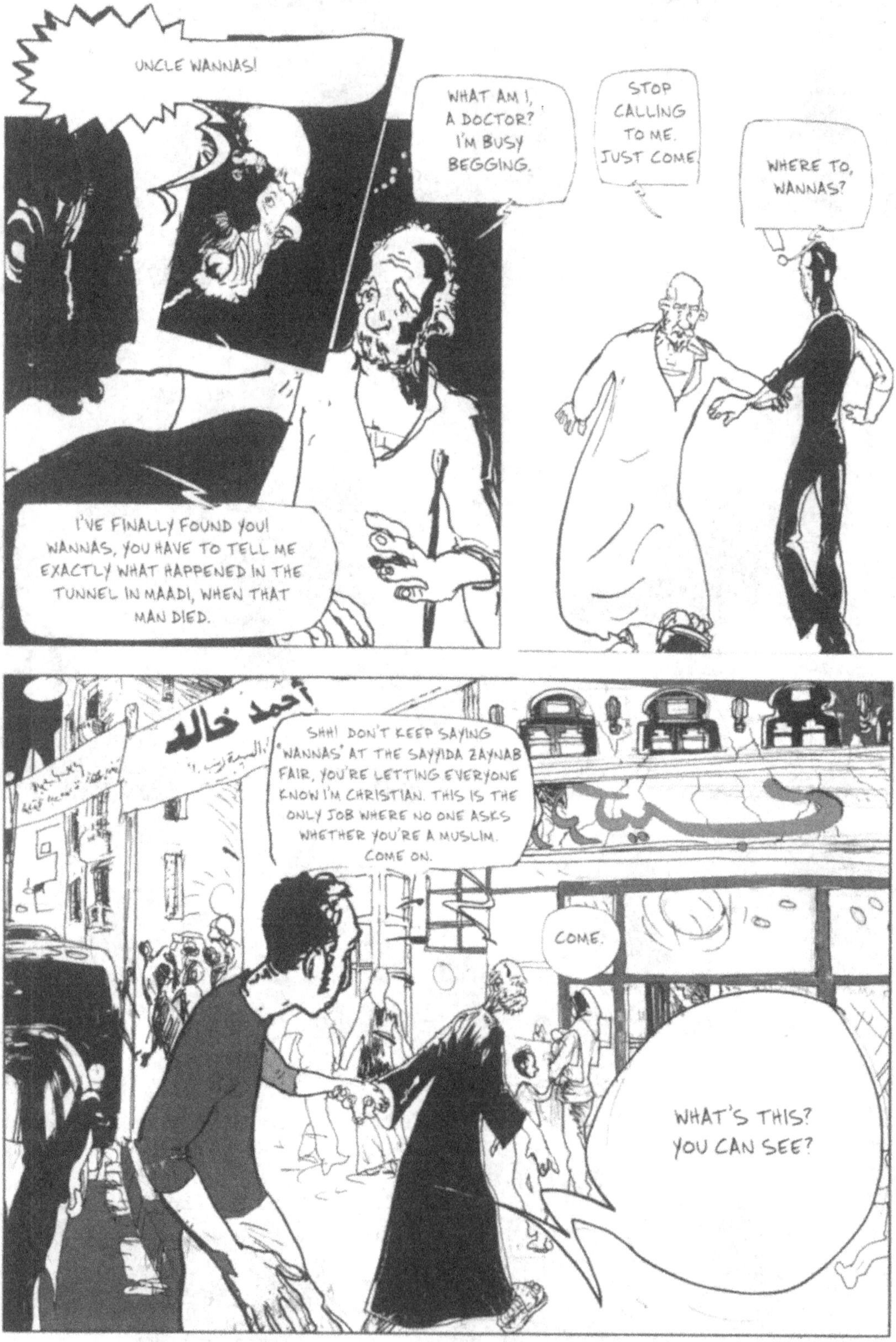
UNCLE WANNAS!
WHAT AM I, A DOCTOR? I'M BUSY BEGGING.
I'VE FINALLY FOUND YOU! WANNAS, YOU HAVE TO TELL ME EXACTLY WHAT HAPPENED IN THE TUNNEL IN MAADI, WHEN THAT MAN DIED.
STOP CALLING TO ME. JUST COME.
WHERE TO, WANNAS?
أحمد خالد
SHH! DON'T KEEP SAYING "WANNAS" AT THE SAYYIDA ZAYNAB FAIR, YOU'RE LETTING EVERYONE KNOW I'M CHRISTIAN. THIS IS THE ONLY JOB WHERE NO ONE ASKS WHETHER YOU'RE A MUSLIM. COME ON.
COME.
WHAT'S THIS? YOU CAN SEE?

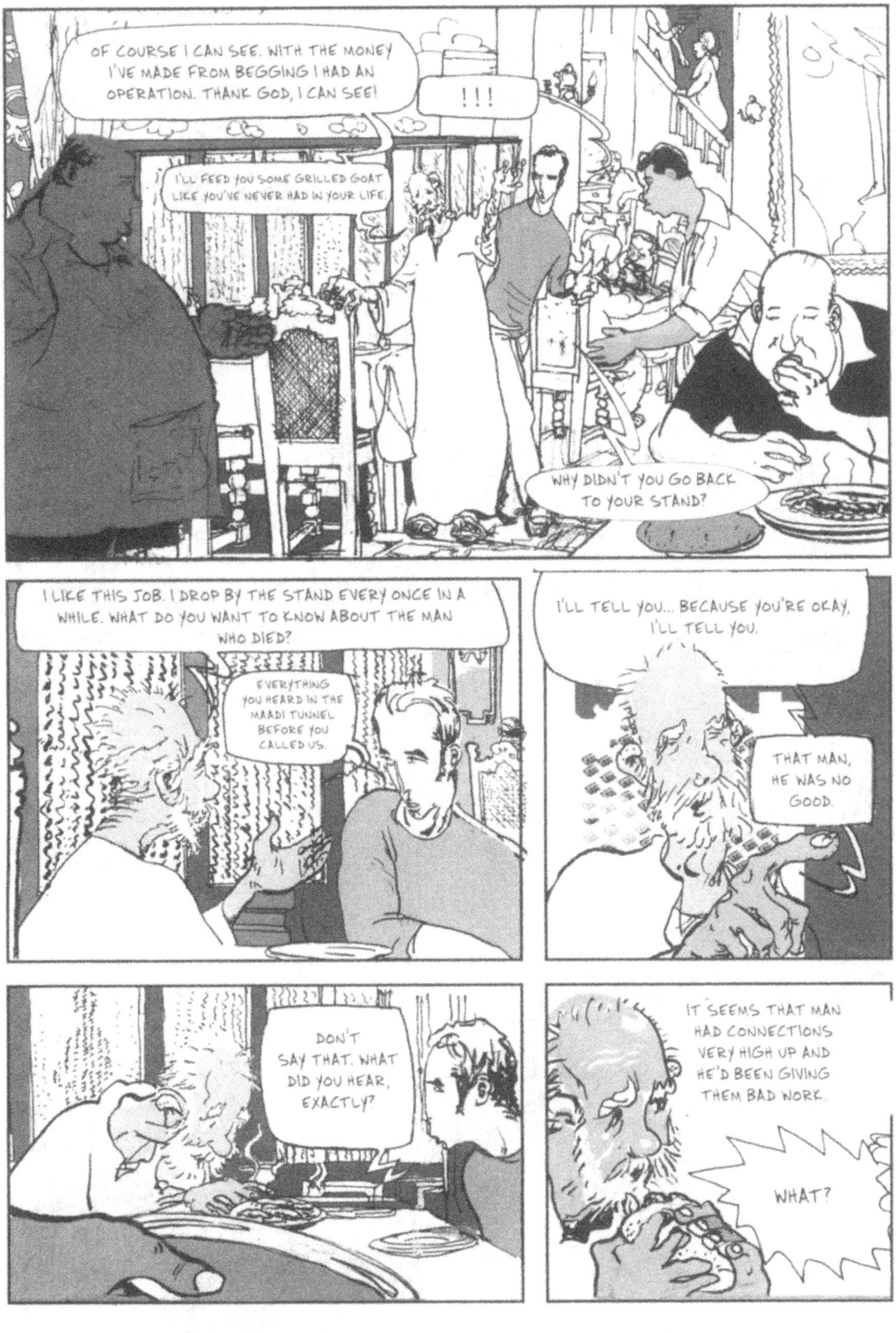
OF COURSE I CAN SEE. WITH THE MONEY I'VE MADE FROM BEGGING I HAD AN OPERATION. THANK GOD, I CAN SEE!
!!!
I'LL FEED YOU SOME GRILLED GOAT LIKE YOU'VE NEVER HAD IN YOUR LIFE.
WHY DIDN'T YOU GO BACK TO YOUR STAND?
I LIKE THIS JOB. I DROP BY THE STAND EVERY ONCE IN A WHILE. WHAT DO YOU WANT TO KNOW ABOUT THE MAN WHO DIED?
EVERYTHING YOU HEARD IN THE MAADI TUNNEL BEFORE YOU CALLED US.
I'LL TELL YOU... BECAUSE YOU'RE OKAY, I'LL TELL YOU.
THAT MAN, HE WAS NO GOOD.
DON'T SAY THAT. WHAT DID YOU HEAR, EXACTLY?
IT SEEMS THAT MAN HAD CONNECTIONS VERY HIGH UP AND HE'D BEEN GIVING THEM BAD WORK.
WHAT?

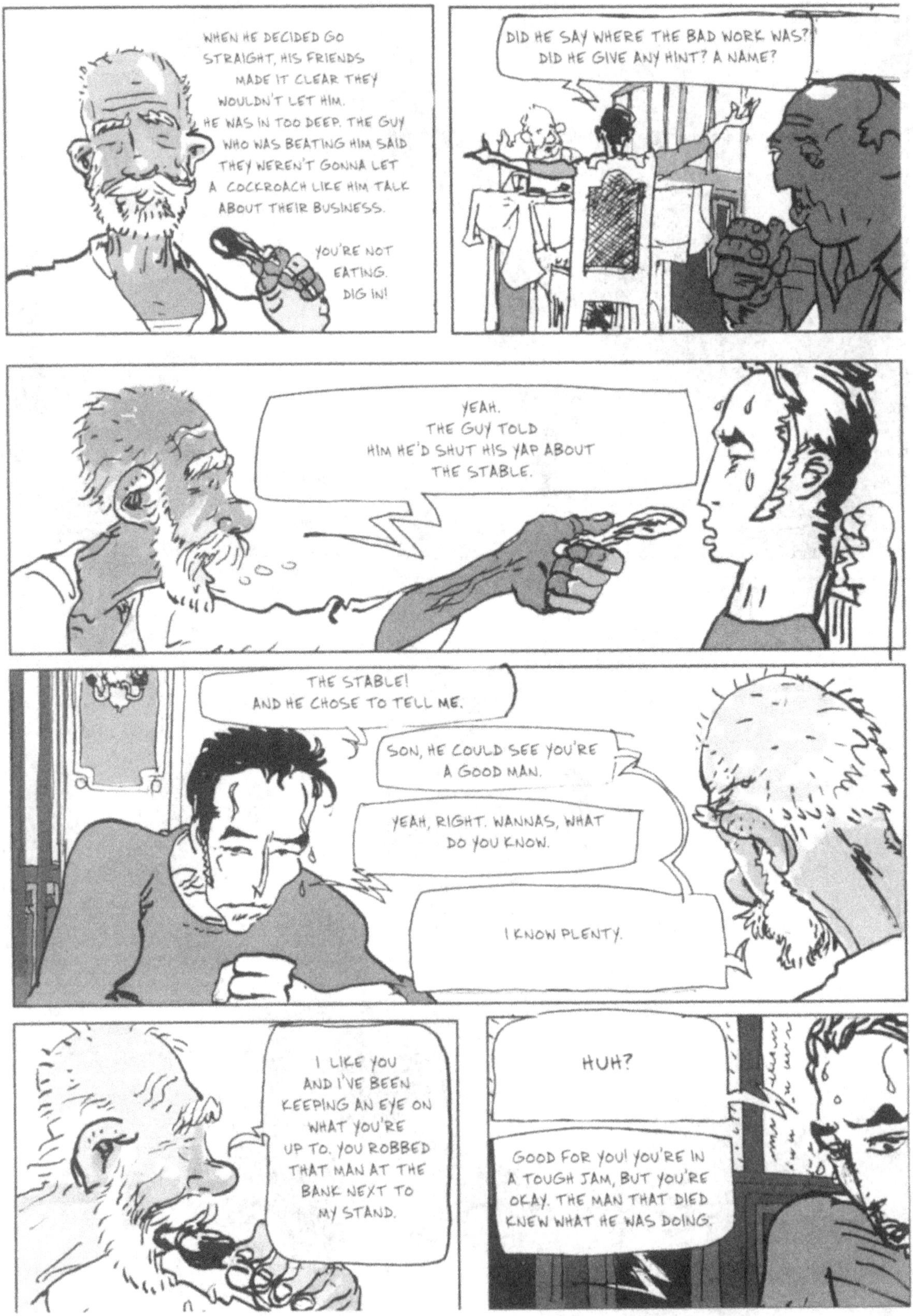

WHEN HE DECIDED GO STRAIGHT, HIS FRIENDS MADE IT CLEAR THEY WOULDN'T LET HIM. HE WAS IN TOO DEEP. THE GUY WHO WAS BEATING HIM SAID THEY WEREN'T GONNA LET A COCKROACH LIKE HIM TALK ABOUT THEIR BUSINESS.
YOU'RE NOT EATING. DIG IN!
DID HE SAY WHERE THE BAD WORK WAS? DID HE GIVE ANY HINT? A NAME?
YEAH. THE GUY TOLD HIM HE'D SHUT HIS YAP ABOUT THE STABLE.
THE STABLE! AND HE CHOSE TO TELL ME.
SON, HE COULD SEE YOU'RE A GOOD MAN.
YEAH, RIGHT. WANNAS, WHAT DO YOU KNOW.
I KNOW PLENTY.
I LIKE YOU AND I'VE BEEN KEEPING AN EYE ON WHAT YOU'RE UP TO. YOU ROBBED THAT MAN AT THE BANK NEXT TO MY STAND.
HUH?
GOOD FOR YOU! YOU'RE IN A TOUGH JAM, BUT YOU'RE OKAY. THE MAN THAT DIED KNEW WHAT HE WAS DOING.

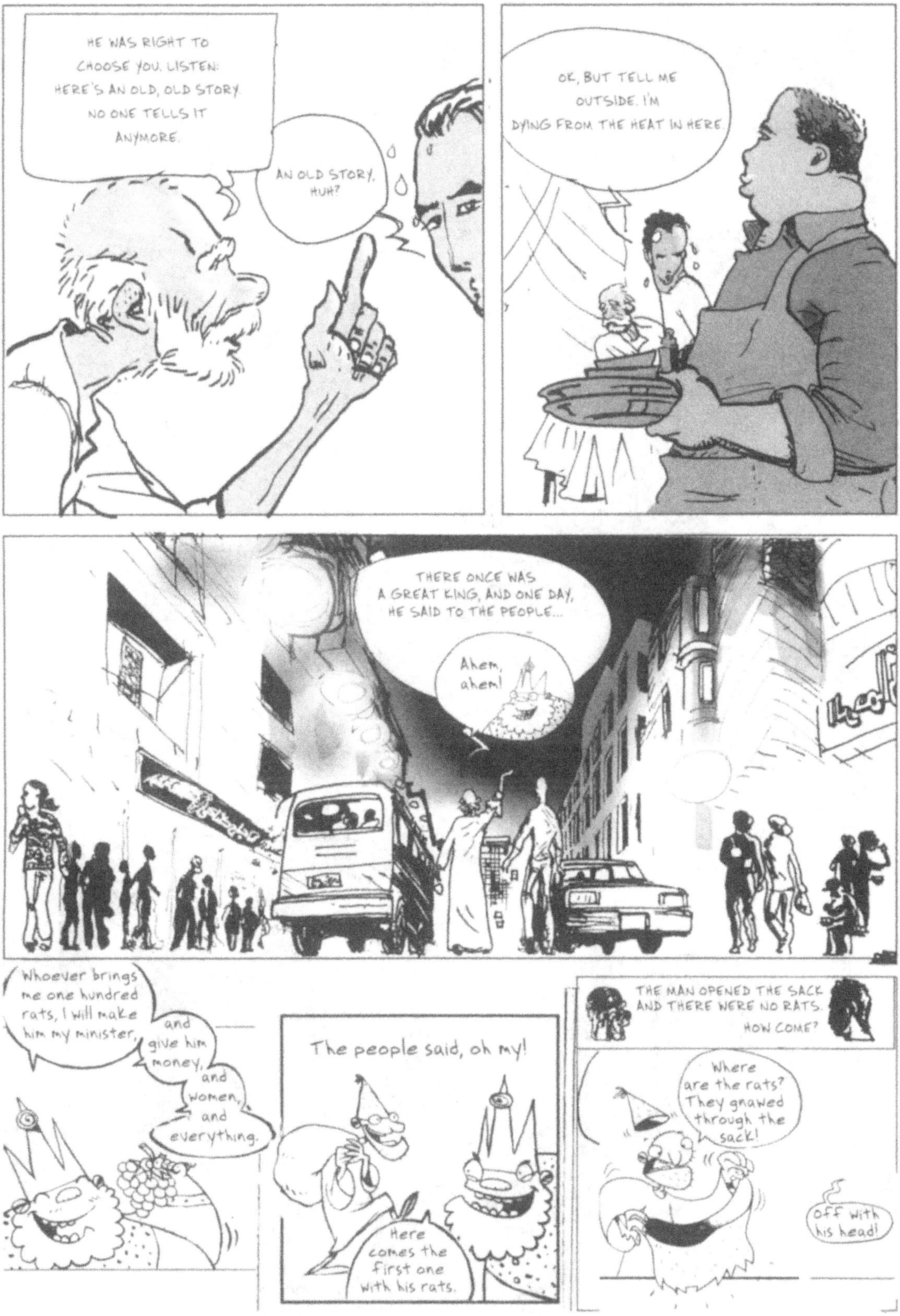
HE WAS RIGHT TO CHOOSE YOU. LISTEN: HERE'S AN OLD, OLD STORY. NO ONE TELLS IT ANYMORE.
AN OLD STORY, HUH?
OK, BUT TELL ME OUTSIDE. I'M DYING FROM THE HEAT IN HERE.
THERE ONCE WAS A GREAT KING, AND ONE DAY, HE SAID TO THE PEOPLE...
Ahem, ahem!
Whoever brings me one hundred rats, I will make him my minister,
and give him money,
and women,
and everything.
The people said, oh my!
Here comes the first one with his rats.
THE MAN OPENED THE SACK AND THERE WERE NO RATS.
HOW COME?
Where are the rats? They gnawed through the sack!
Off with his head!

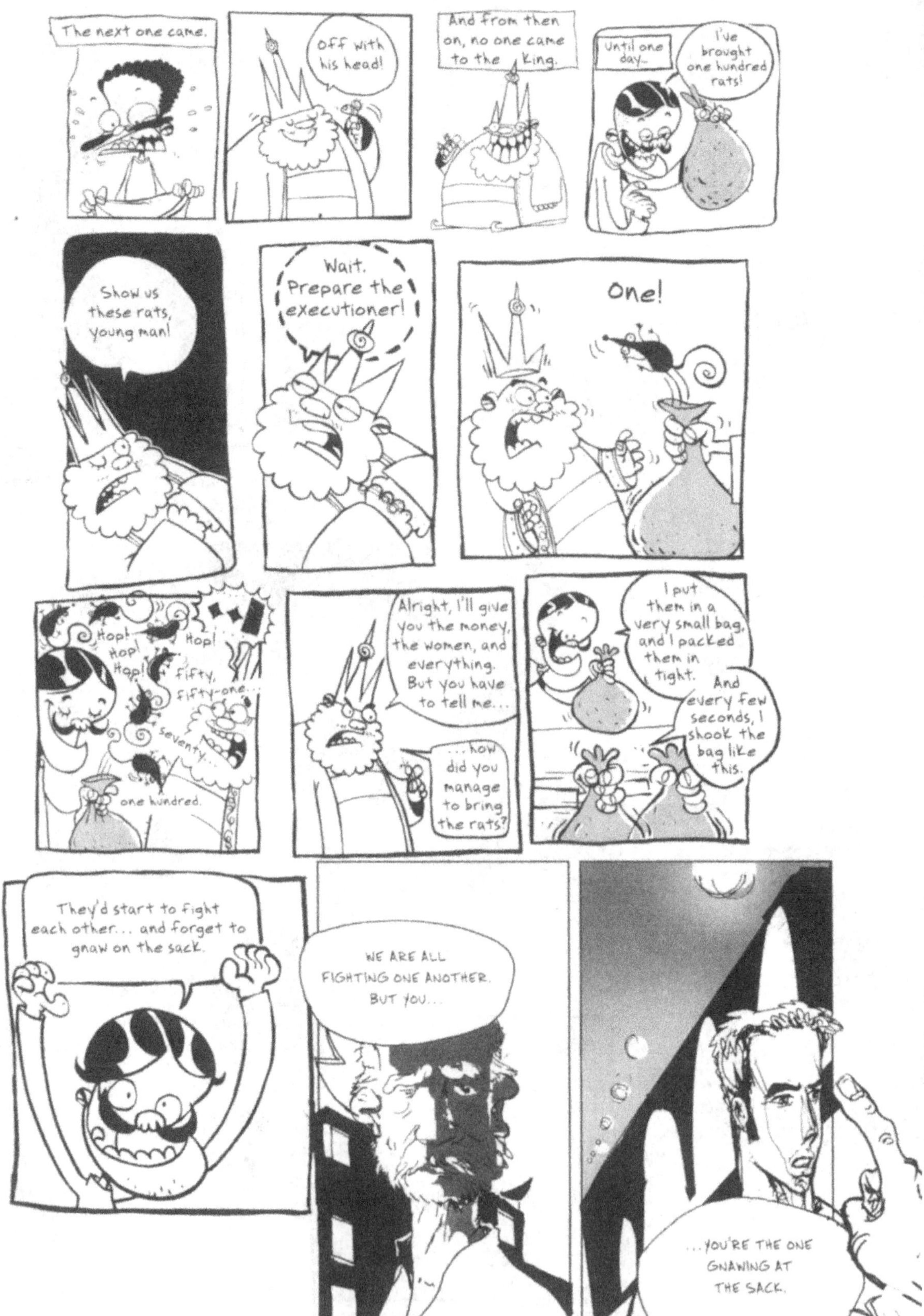
The next one came.
Off with his head!
And from then on, no one came to the King.
Until one day...
I've brought one hundred rats!
Show us these rats, young man!
Wait. Prepare the executioner!
One!
Hop! Hop! Hop!
Hop!
fifty, fifty-one...
seventy...
one hundred.
Alright, I'll give you the money, the women, and everything. But you have to tell me...
...how did you manage to bring the rats?
I put them in a very small bag, and I packed them in tight.
And every few seconds, I shook the bag like this.
They'd start to fight each other... and forget to gnaw on the sack.
WE ARE ALL FIGHTING ONE ANOTHER. BUT YOU...
...YOU'RE THE ONE GNAWING AT THE SACK.

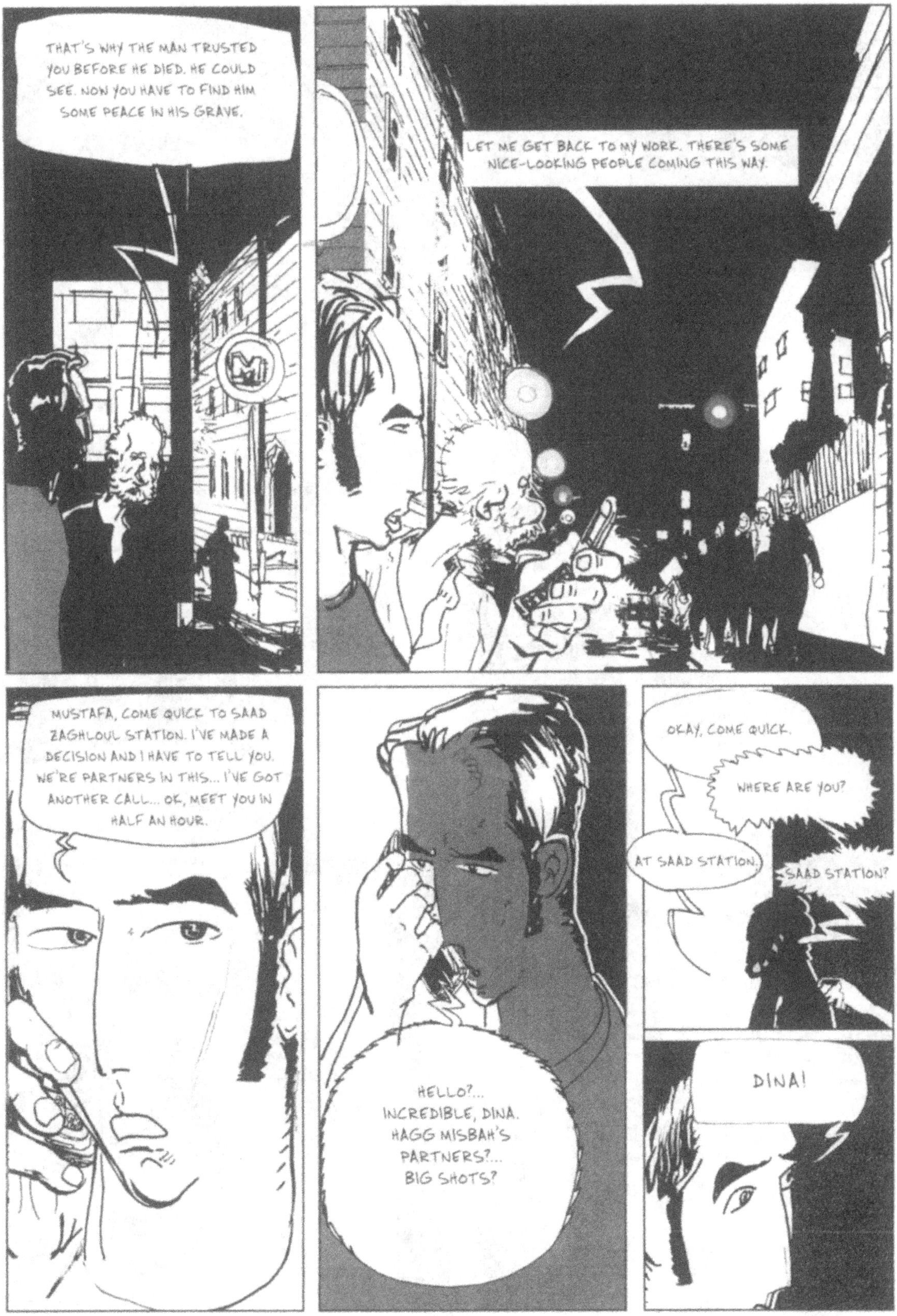
THAT'S WHY THE MAN TRUSTED YOU BEFORE HE DIED. HE COULD SEE. NOW YOU HAVE TO FIND HIM SOME PEACE IN HIS GRAVE.
LET ME GET BACK TO MY WORK. THERE'S SOME NICE-LOOKING PEOPLE COMING THIS WAY.
MUSTAFA, COME QUICK TO SAAD ZAGHLOUL STATION. I'VE MADE A DECISION AND I HAVE TO TELL YOU. WE'RE PARTNERS IN THIS... I'VE GOT ANOTHER CALL... OK, MEET YOU IN HALF AN HOUR.
HELLO?... INCREDIBLE, DINA. HAGG MISBAH'S PARTNERS?... BIG SHOTS?
OKAY, COME QUICK.
WHERE ARE YOU?
AT SAAD STATION.
SAAD STATION?
DINA!

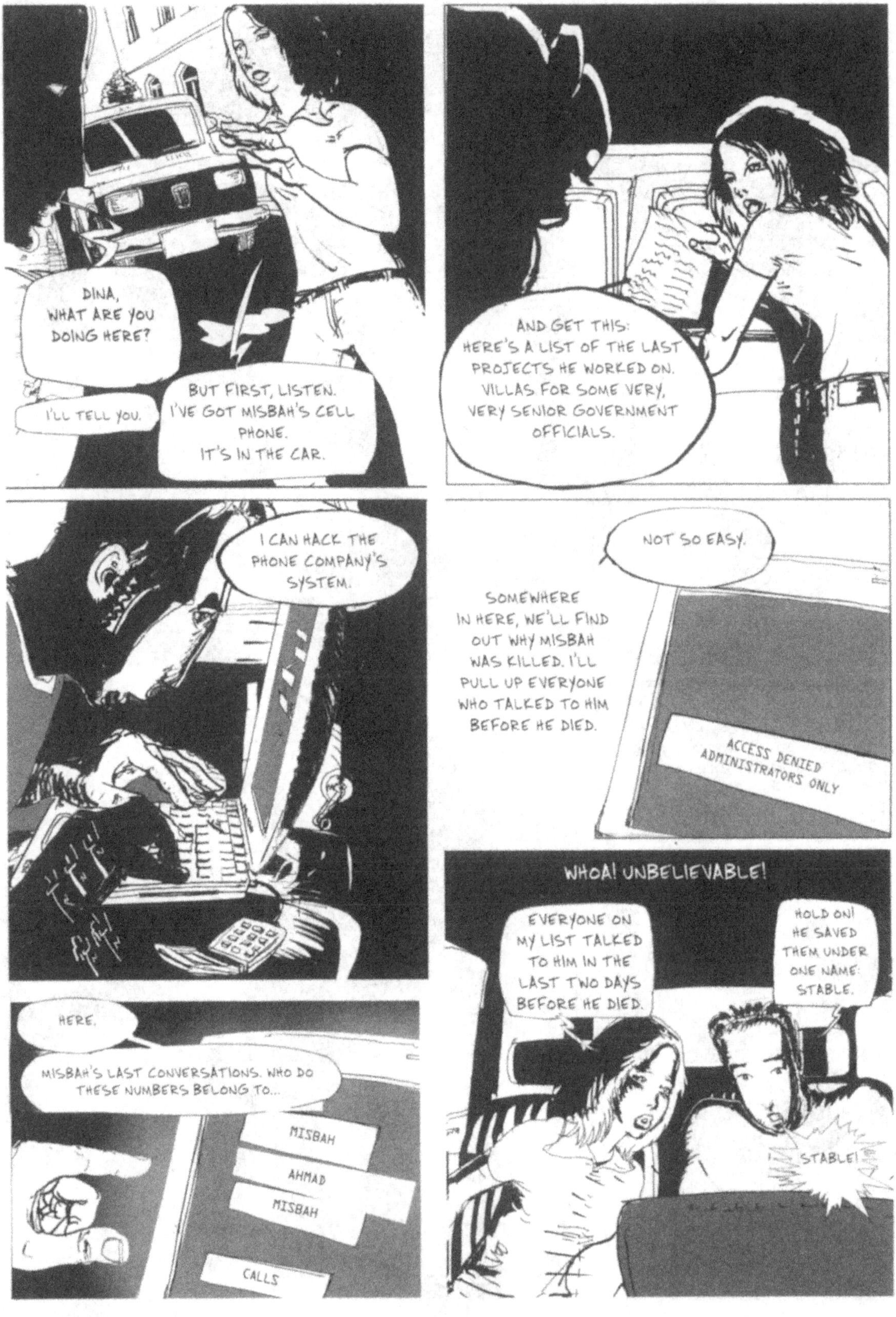
DINA, WHAT ARE YOU DOING HERE?
I'LL TELL YOU.
BUT FIRST, LISTEN. I'VE GOT MISBAH'S CELL PHONE. IT'S IN THE CAR.
AND GET THIS: HERE'S A LIST OF THE LAST PROJECTS HE WORKED ON. VILLAS FOR SOME VERY, VERY SENIOR GOVERNMENT OFFICIALS.
I CAN HACK THE PHONE COMPANY'S SYSTEM.
NOT SO EASY.
SOMEWHERE IN HERE, WE'LL FIND OUT WHY MISBAH WAS KILLED. I'LL PULL UP EVERYONE WHO TALKED TO HIM BEFORE HE DIED.
ACCESS DENIED ADMINISTRATORS ONLY
HERE.
MISBAH'S LAST CONVERSATIONS. WHO DO THESE NUMBERS BELONG TO...
MISBAH
AHMAD
MISBAH
CALLS
WHOA! UNBELIEVABLE!
EVERYONE ON MY LIST TALKED TO HIM IN THE LAST TWO DAYS BEFORE HE DIED.
HOLD ON! HE SAVED THEM UNDER ONE NAME: STABLE.
STABLE!

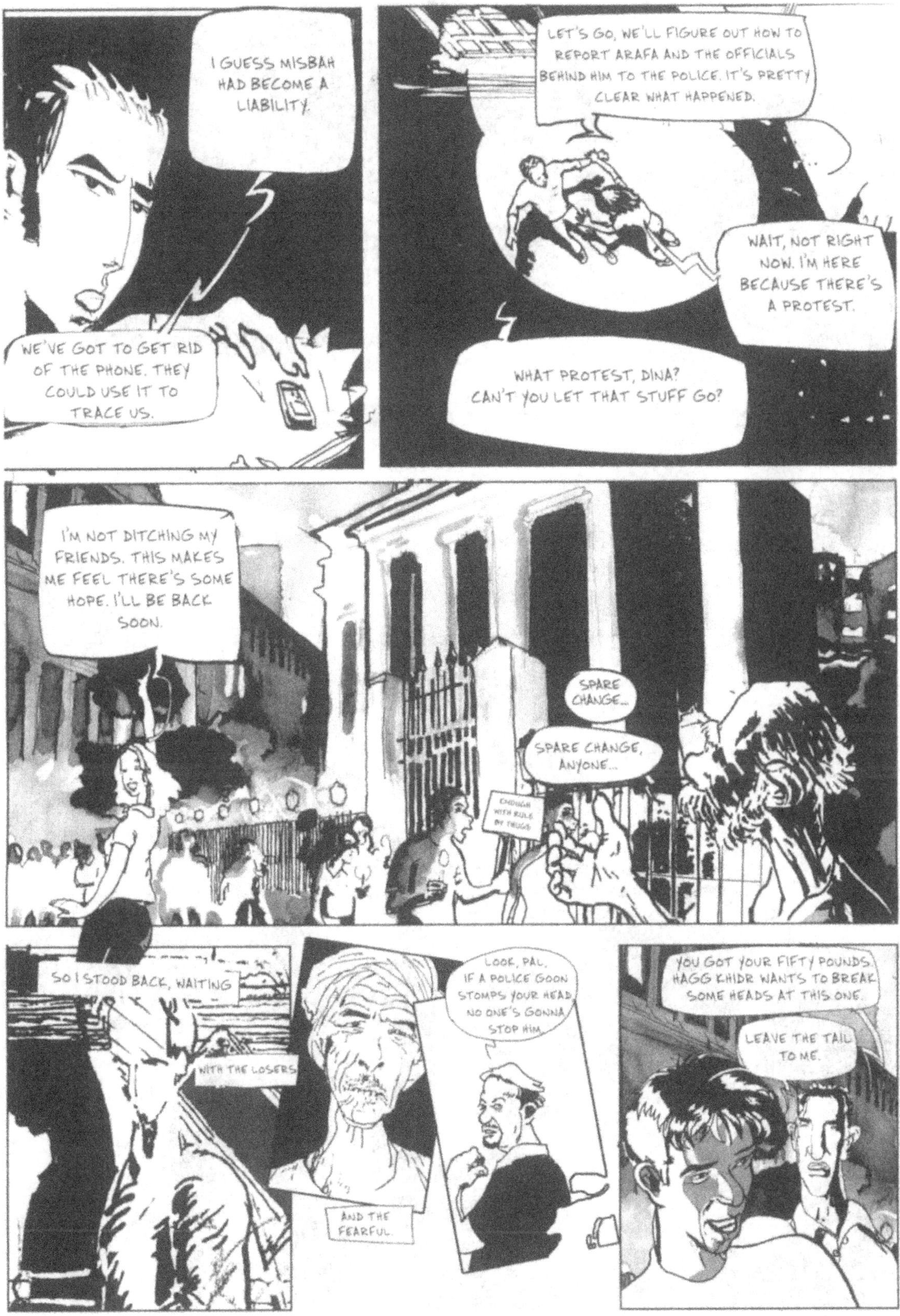
I GUESS MISBAH HAD BECOME A LIABILITY.
WE'VE GOT TO GET RID OF THE PHONE. THEY COULD USE IT TO TRACE US.
LET'S GO, WE'LL FIGURE OUT HOW TO REPORT ARAFA AND THE OFFICIALS BEHIND HIM TO THE POLICE. IT'S PRETTY CLEAR WHAT HAPPENED.
WAIT, NOT RIGHT NOW. I'M HERE BECAUSE THERE'S A PROTEST.
WHAT PROTEST, DINA? CAN'T YOU LET THAT STUFF GO?
I'M NOT DITCHING MY FRIENDS. THIS MAKES ME FEEL THERE'S SOME HOPE. I'LL BE BACK SOON.
SPARE CHANGE...
SPARE CHANGE, ANYONE...
ENOUGH WITH RULE BY THUGS
SO I STOOD BACK, WAITING
WITH THE LOSERS
AND THE FEARFUL.
LOOK, PAL, IF A POLICE GOON STOMPS YOUR HEAD NO ONE'S GONNA STOP HIM.
YOU GOT YOUR FIFTY POUNDS. HAGG KHIDR WANTS TO BREAK SOME HEADS AT THIS ONE.
LEAVE THE TAIL TO ME.

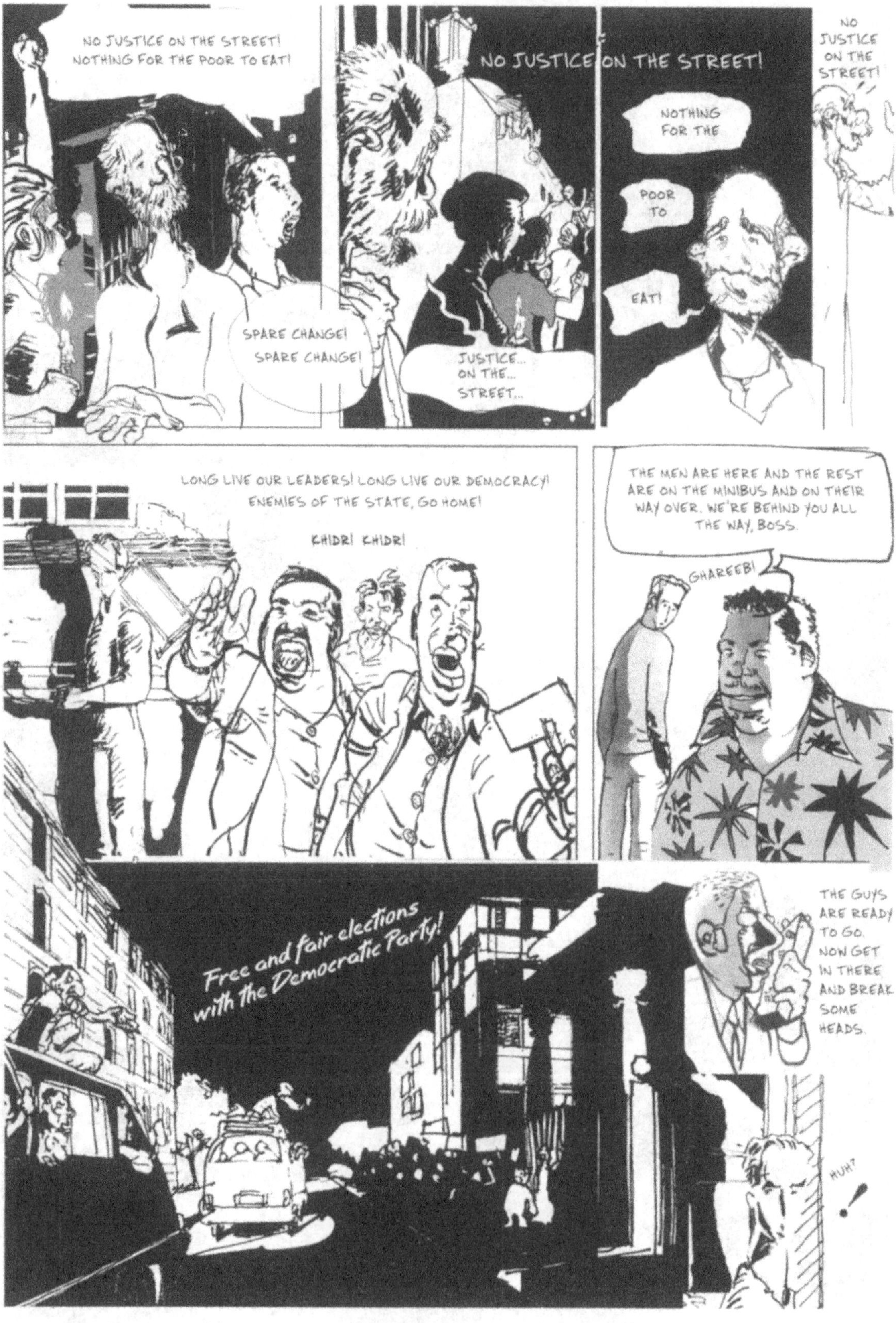
NO JUSTICE ON THE STREET! NOTHING FOR THE POOR TO EAT!
SPARE CHANGE! SPARE CHANGE!
NO JUSTICE ON THE STREET!
JUSTICE... ON THE... STREET...
NOTHING FOR THE
POOR TO
EAT!
NO JUSTICE ON THE STREET!
LONG LIVE OUR LEADERS! LONG LIVE OUR DEMOCRACY! ENEMIES OF THE STATE, GO HOME!
KHIDR! KHIDR!
THE MEN ARE HERE AND THE REST ARE ON THE MINIBUS AND ON THEIR WAY OVER. WE'RE BEHIND YOU ALL THE WAY, BOSS.
GHAREEB!
Free and fair elections with the Democratic Party!
THE GUYS ARE READY TO GO. NOW GET IN THERE AND BREAK SOME HEADS.
HUH?

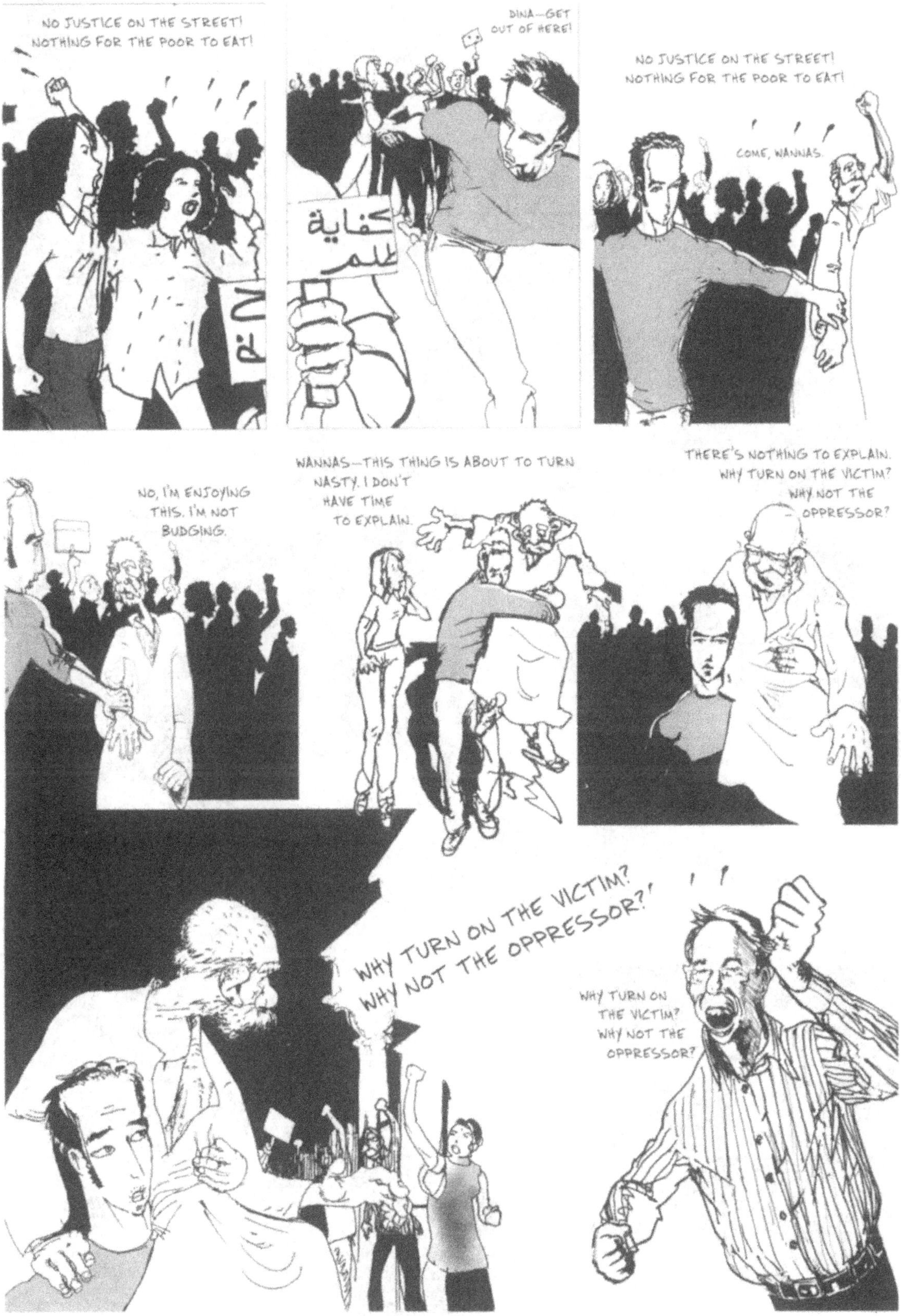
NO JUSTICE ON THE STREET!
NOTHING FOR THE POOR TO EAT!
DINA—GET OUT OF HERE!
كفاية
ظلم
NO JUSTICE ON THE STREET!
NOTHING FOR THE POOR TO EAT!
COME, WANNAS.
NO, I'M ENJOYING THIS. I'M NOT BUDGING.
WANNAS—THIS THING IS ABOUT TO TURN NASTY. I DON'T HAVE TIME TO EXPLAIN.
THERE'S NOTHING TO EXPLAIN. WHY TURN ON THE VICTIM? WHY NOT THE OPPRESSOR?
WHY TURN ON THE VICTIM? WHY NOT THE OPPRESSOR?
WHY TURN ON THE VICTIM? WHY NOT THE OPPRESSOR?

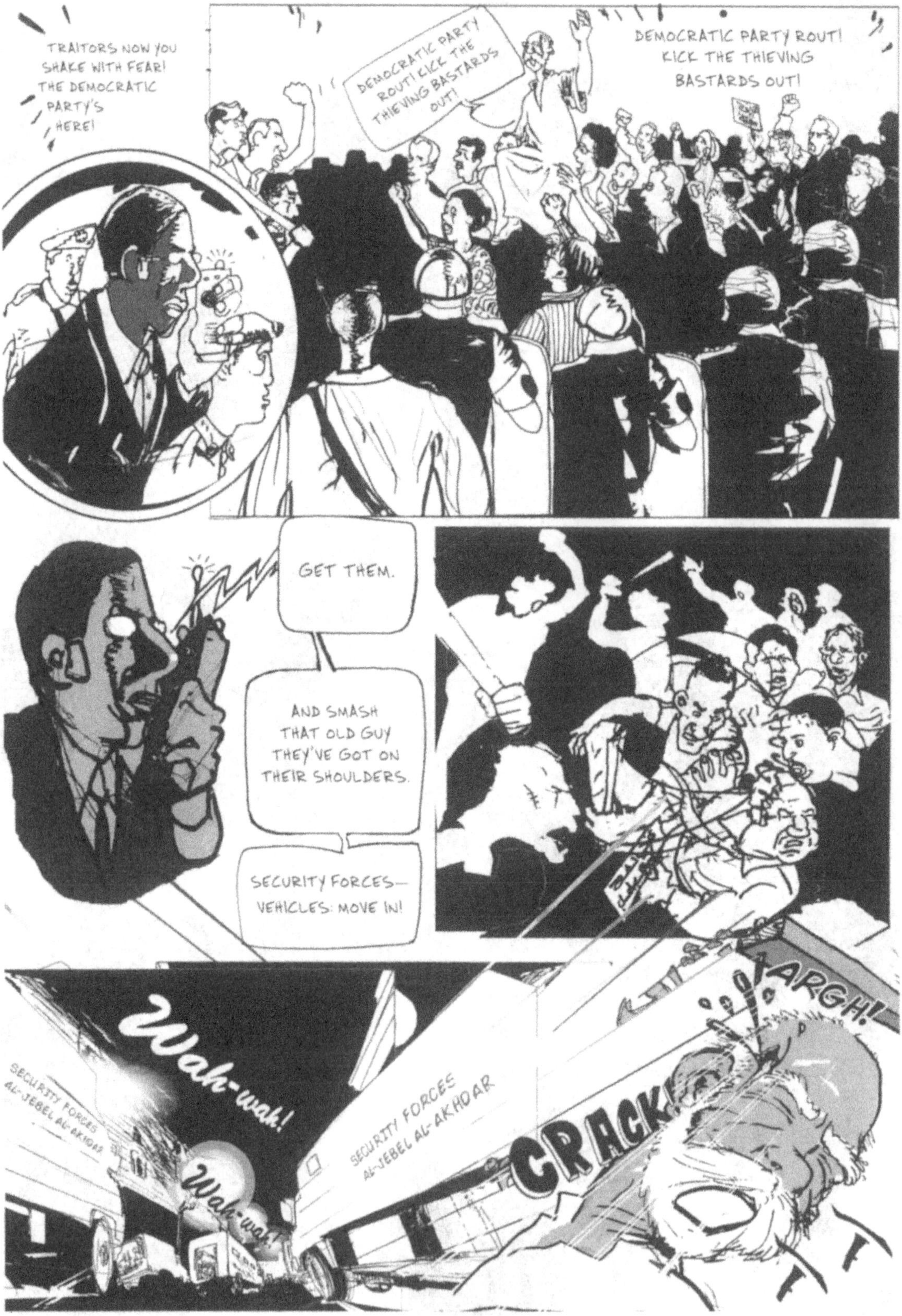
TRAITORS NOW YOU SHAKE WITH FEAR! THE DEMOCRATIC PARTY'S HERE!
DEMOCRATIC PARTY ROUT! KICK THE THIEVING BASTARDS OUT!
DEMOCRATIC PARTY ROUT! KICK THE THIEVING BASTARDS OUT!
GET THEM.
AND SMASH THAT OLD GUY THEY'VE GOT ON THEIR SHOULDERS.
SECURITY FORCES— VEHICLES: MOVE IN!
Wah-wah!
Wah-wah!
SECURITY FORCES AL-JEBEL AL-AKHDAR
SECURITY FORCES AL-JEBEL AL-AKHDAR
CRACK!
ARGH!

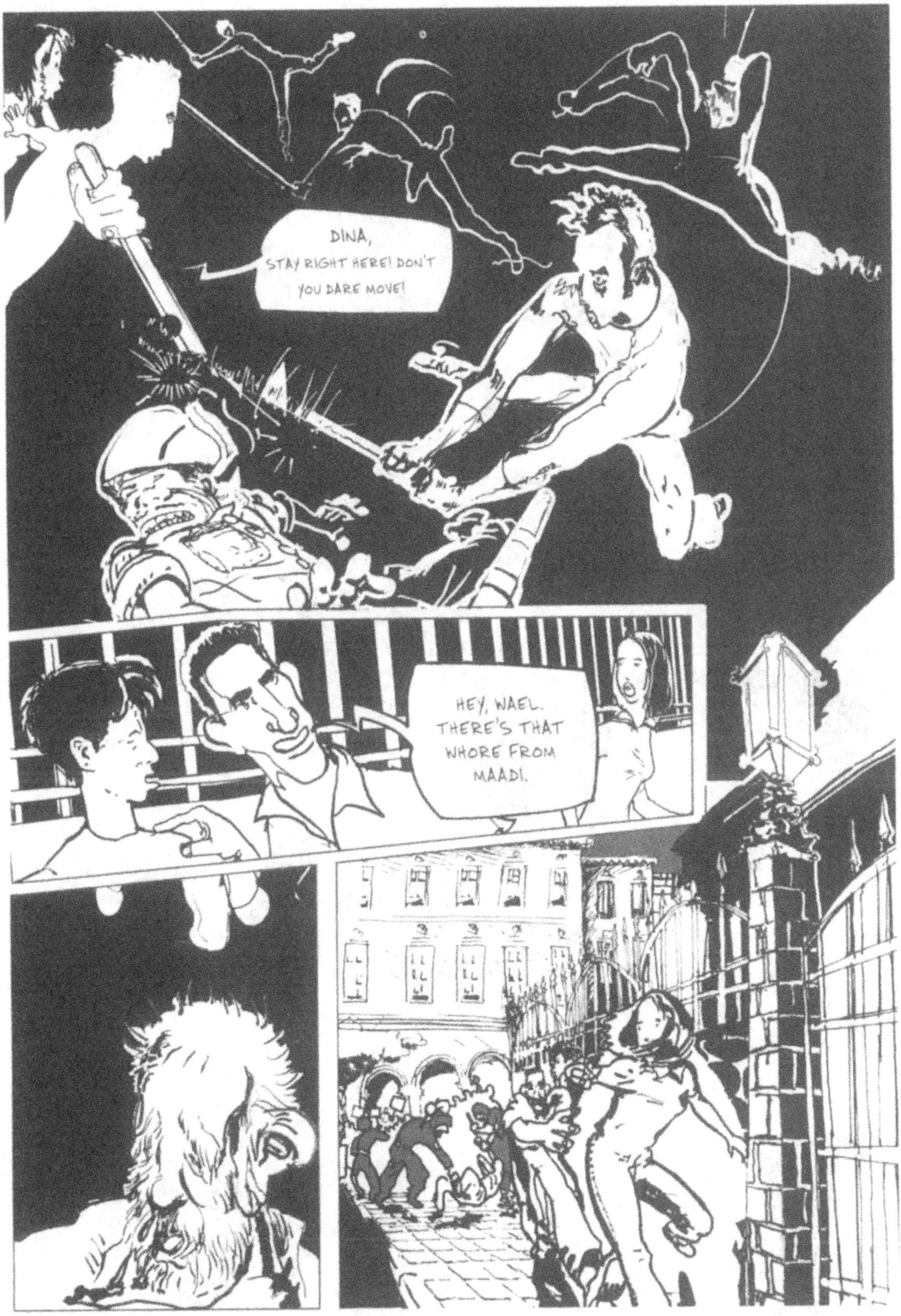
DINA,
STAY RIGHT HERE! DON'T
YOU DARE MOVE!
HEY, WAEL.
THERE'S THAT
WHORE FROM
MAADI.

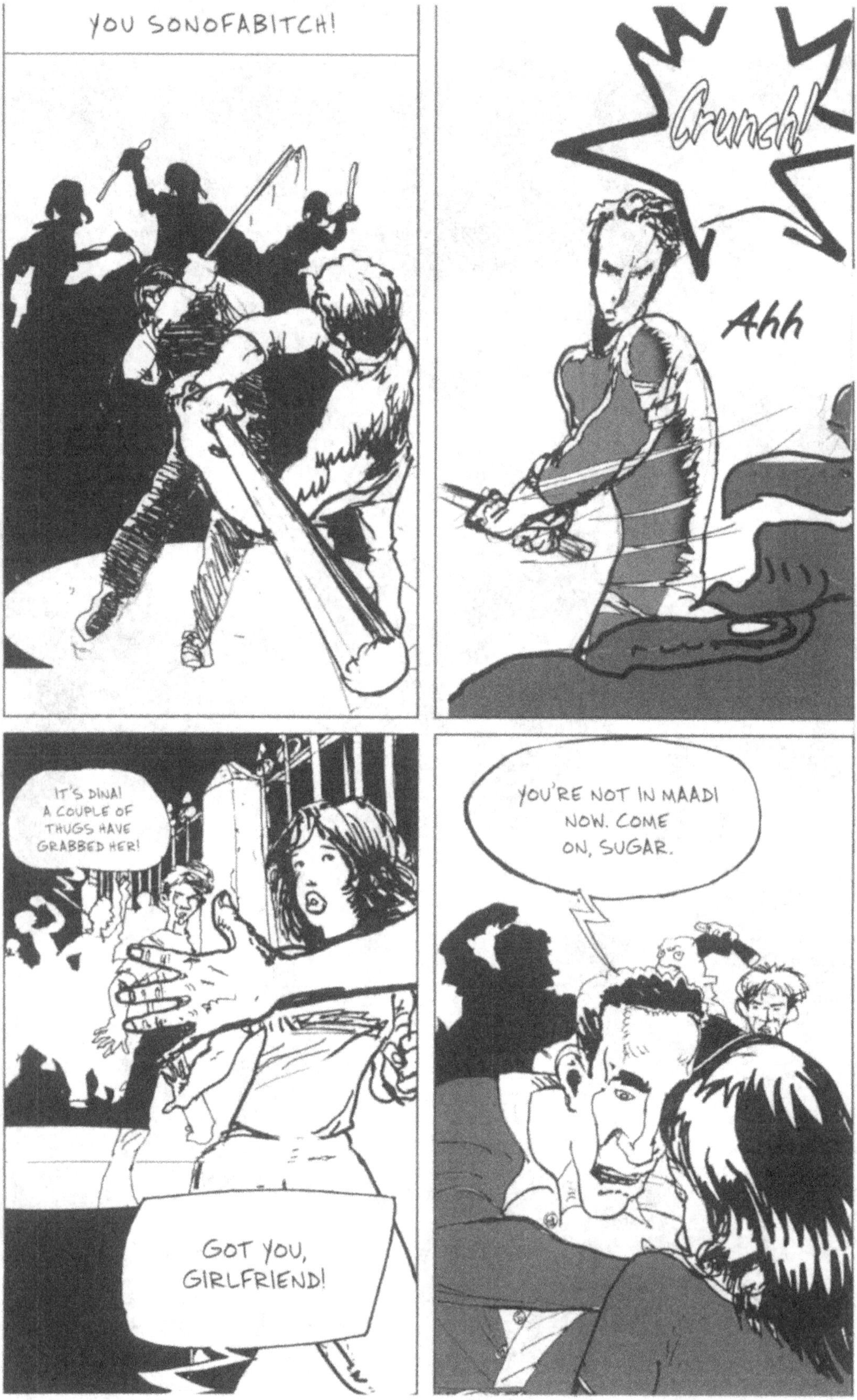
YOU SONOFABITCH!
Crunch!
Ahh
IT'S DINA! A COUPLE OF THUGS HAVE GRABBED HER!
GOT YOU, GIRLFRIEND!
YOU'RE NOT IN MAADI NOW. COME ON, SUGAR.

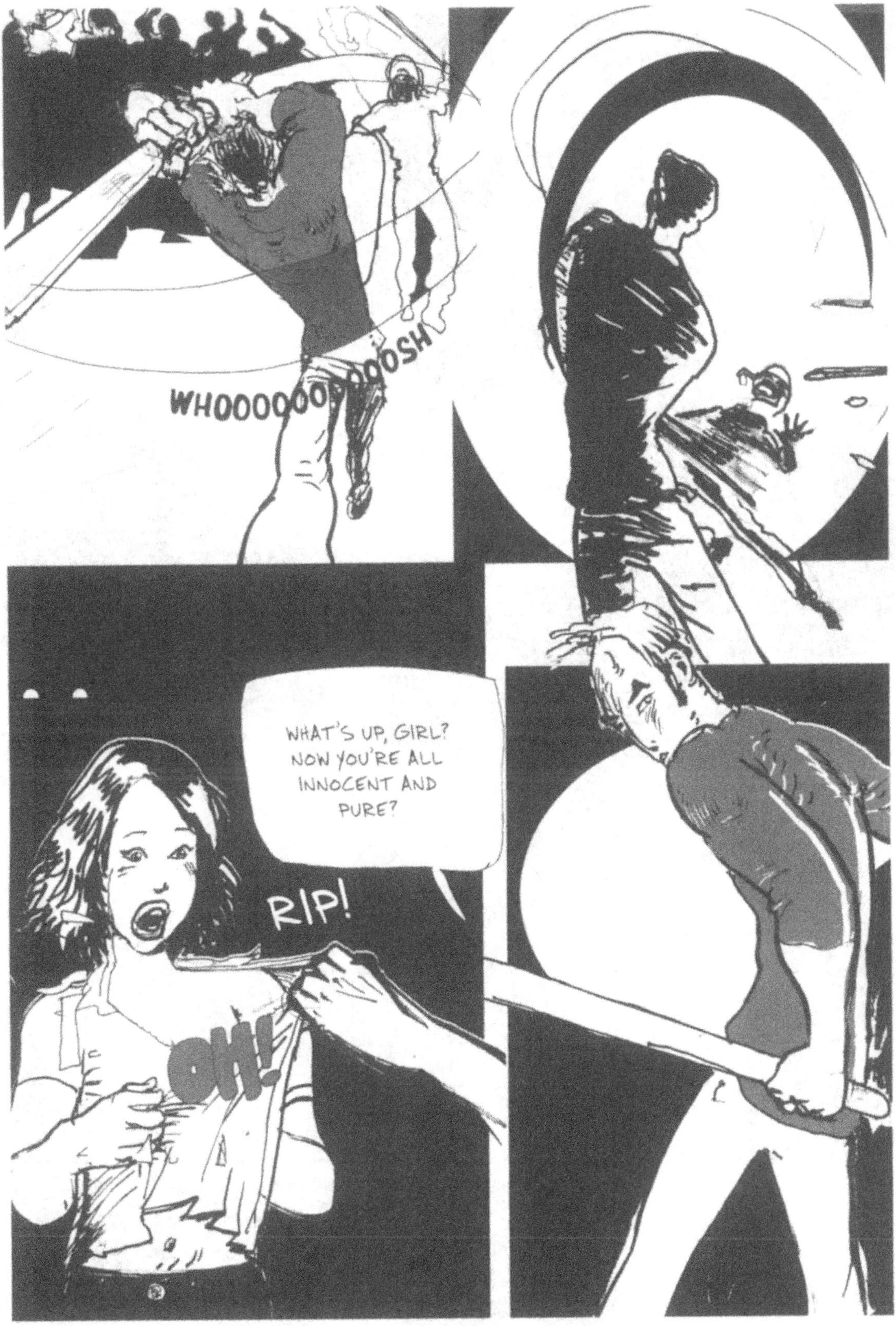
WHOOOOOOOOOOSH
WHAT'S UP, GIRL? NOW YOU'RE ALL INNOCENT AND PURE?
RIP!
OH!

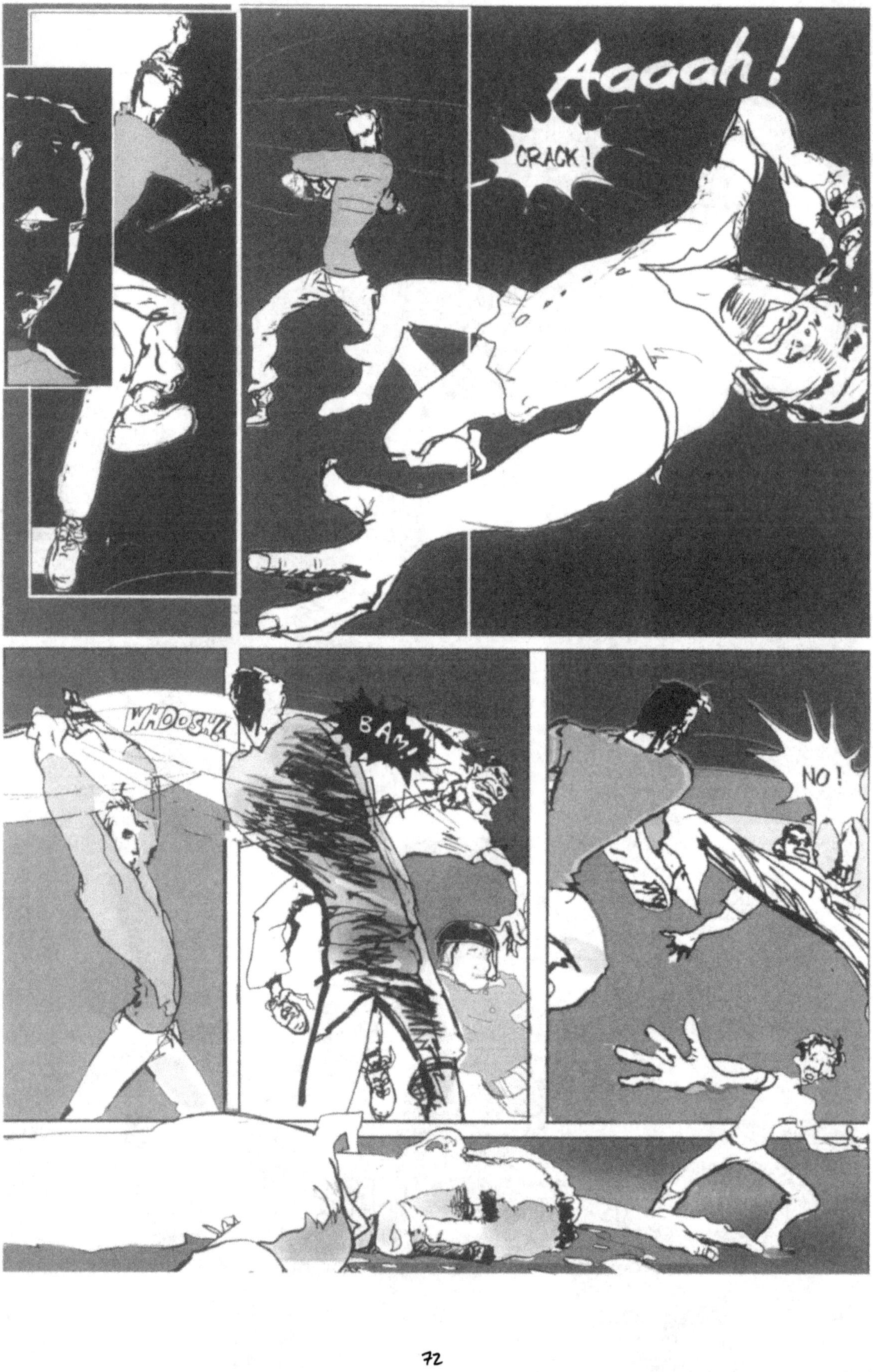
Aaaah!
CRACK!
WHOOSH!
BAM!
NO!

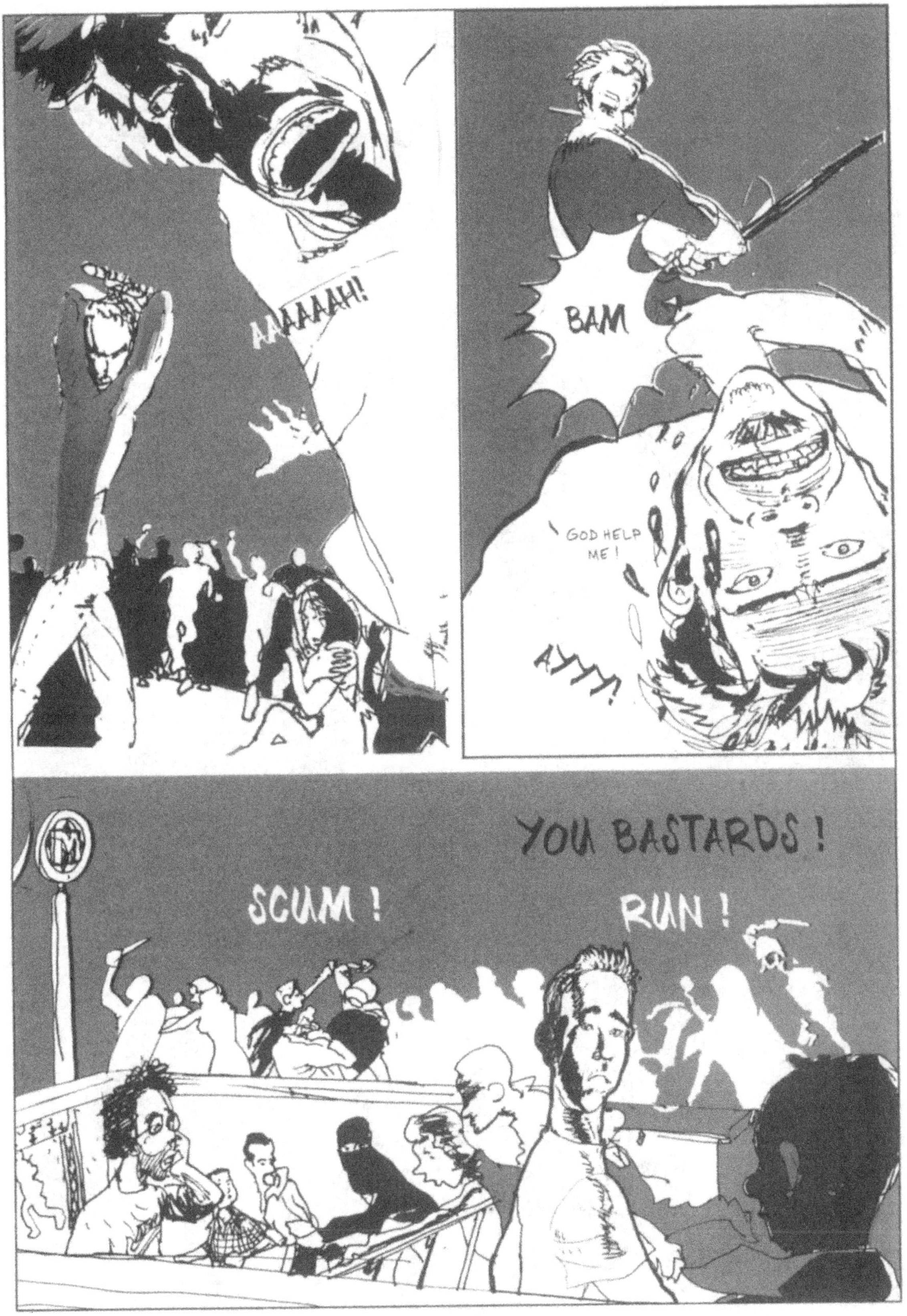
AAAAAAH!
BAM
GOD HELP ME!
AYYY!
YOU BASTARDS!
SCUM!
RUN!

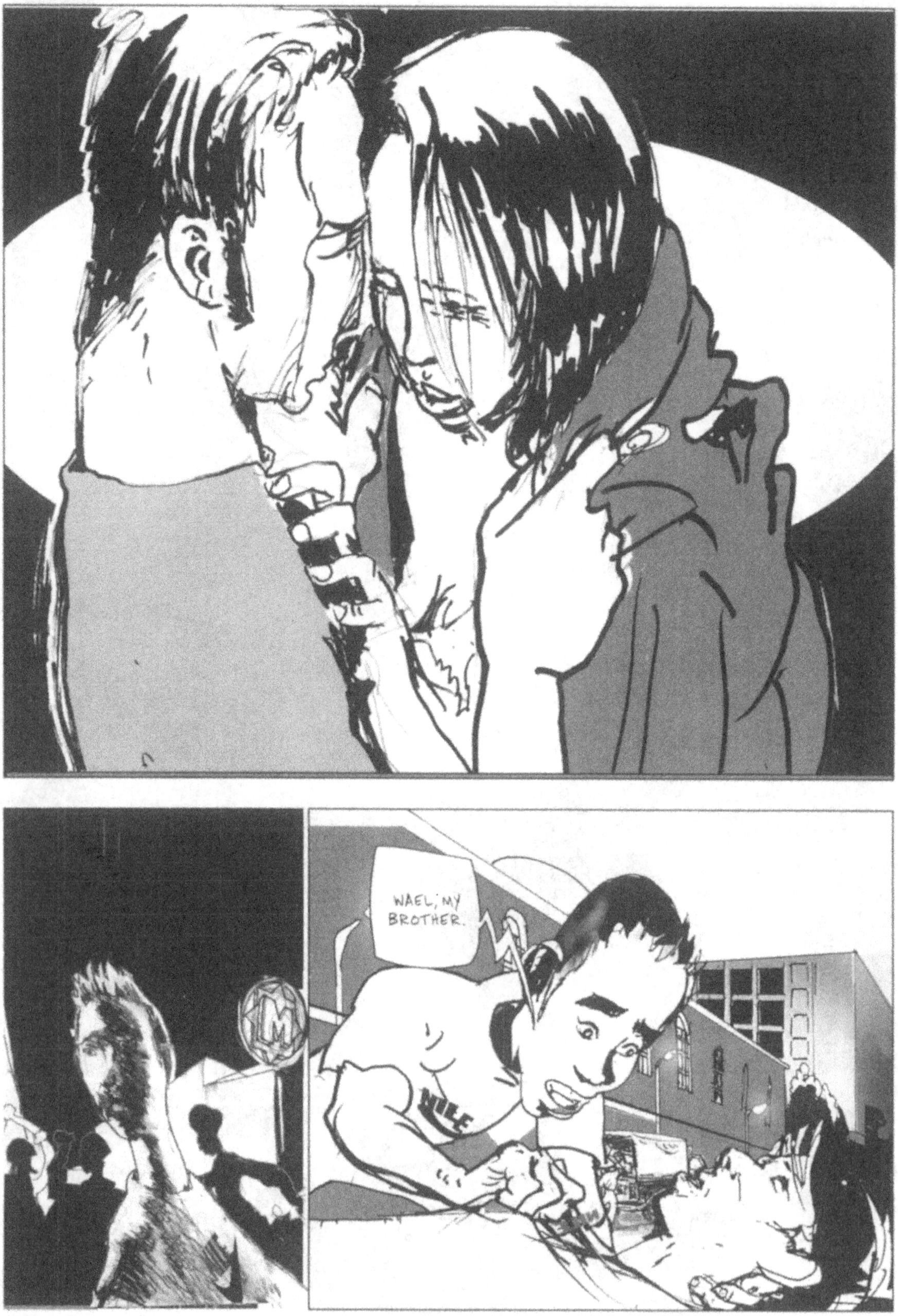
WAEL, MY BROTHER.

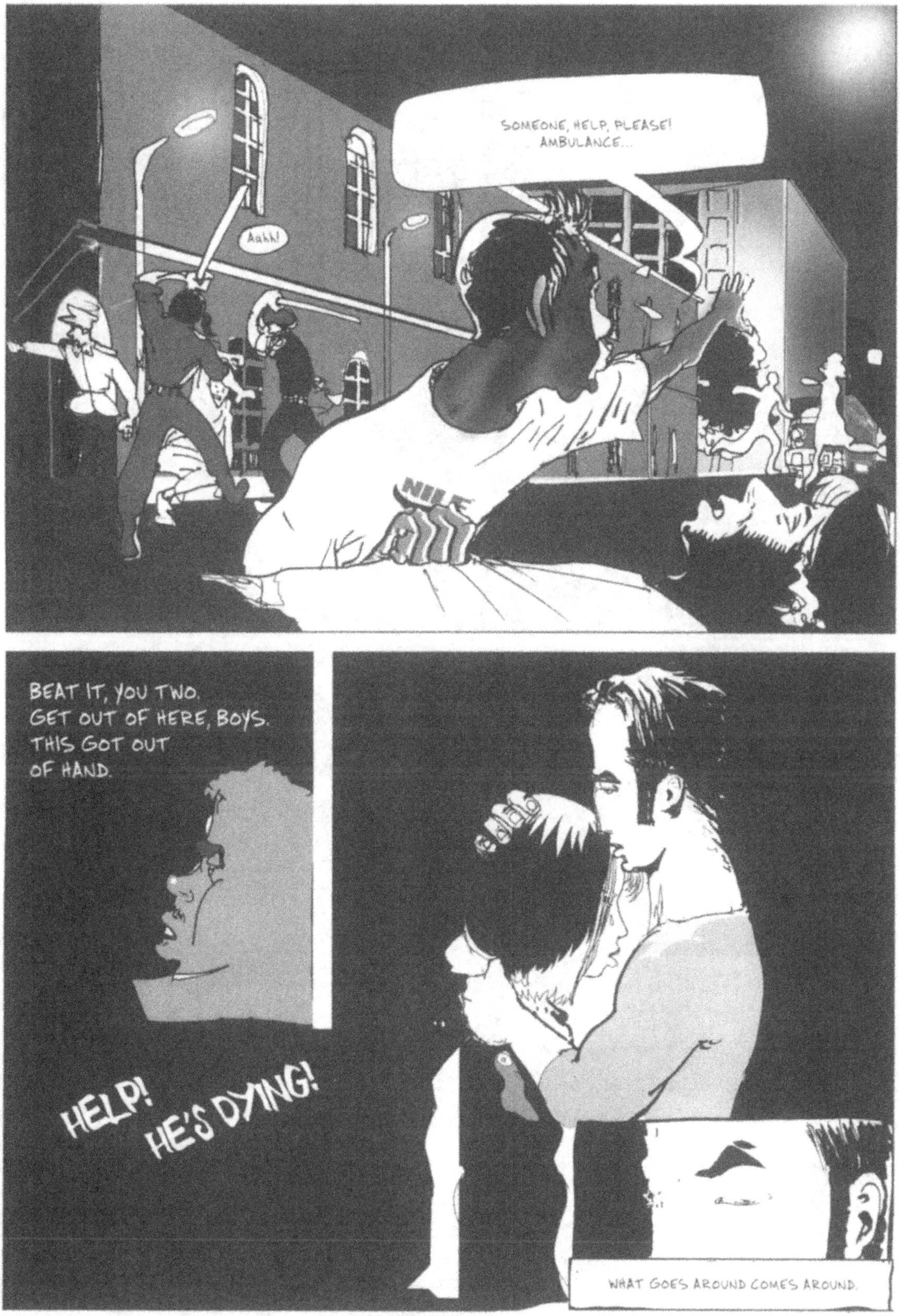
SOMEONE, HELP, PLEASE!
AMBULANCE...
Aahh!
NILE
BEAT IT, YOU TWO.
GET OUT OF HERE, BOYS.
THIS GOT OUT
OF HAND.
HELP!
HE'S DYING!
WHAT GOES AROUND COMES AROUND.

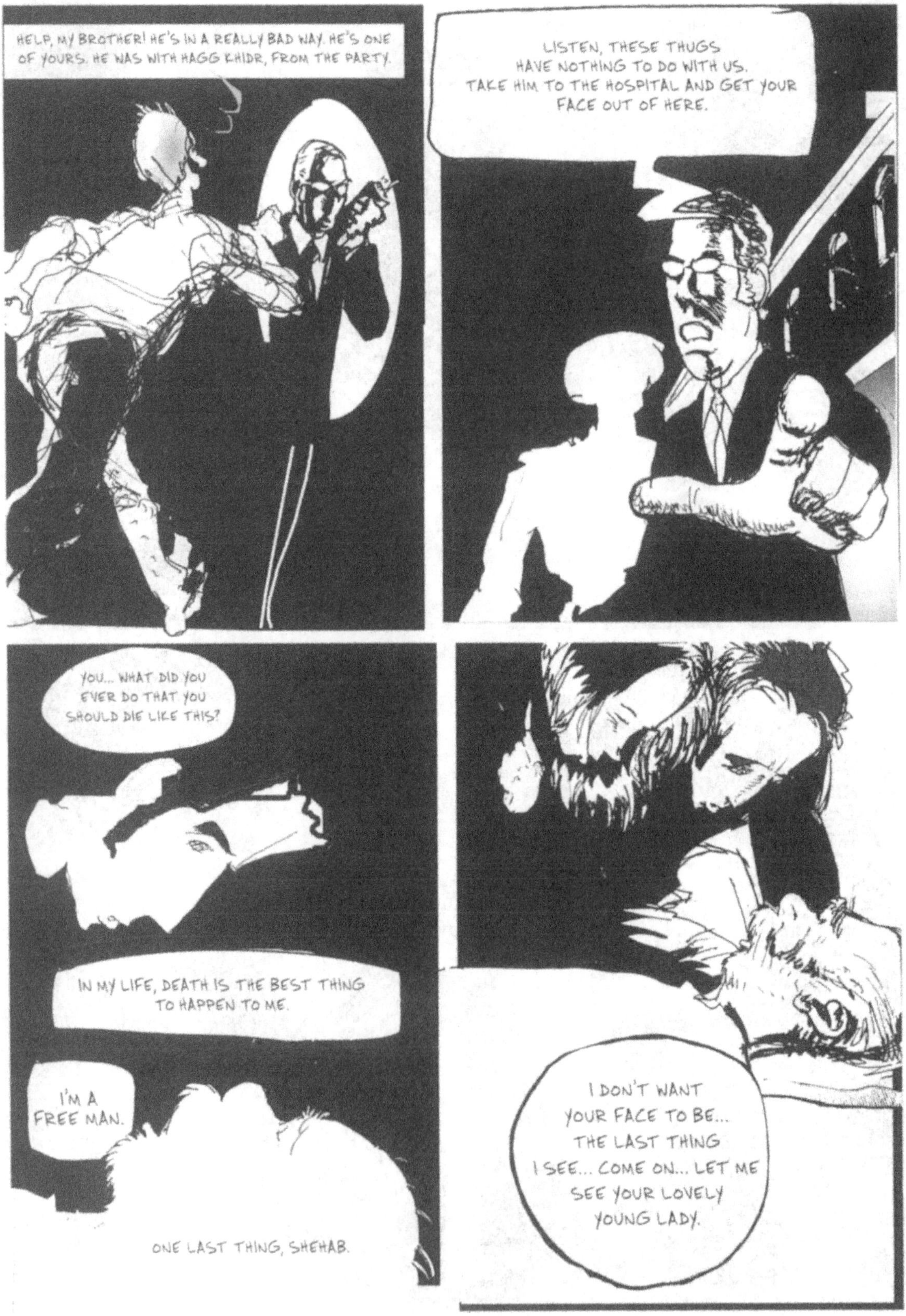
HELP, MY BROTHER! HE'S IN A REALLY BAD WAY. HE'S ONE OF YOURS. HE WAS WITH HAGG KHIDR, FROM THE PARTY.
LISTEN, THESE THUGS HAVE NOTHING TO DO WITH US. TAKE HIM TO THE HOSPITAL AND GET YOUR FACE OUT OF HERE.
YOU... WHAT DID YOU EVER DO THAT YOU SHOULD DIE LIKE THIS?
IN MY LIFE, DEATH IS THE BEST THING TO HAPPEN TO ME.
I'M A FREE MAN.
ONE LAST THING, SHEHAB.
I DON'T WANT YOUR FACE TO BE... THE LAST THING I SEE... COME ON... LET ME SEE YOUR LOVELY YOUNG LADY.

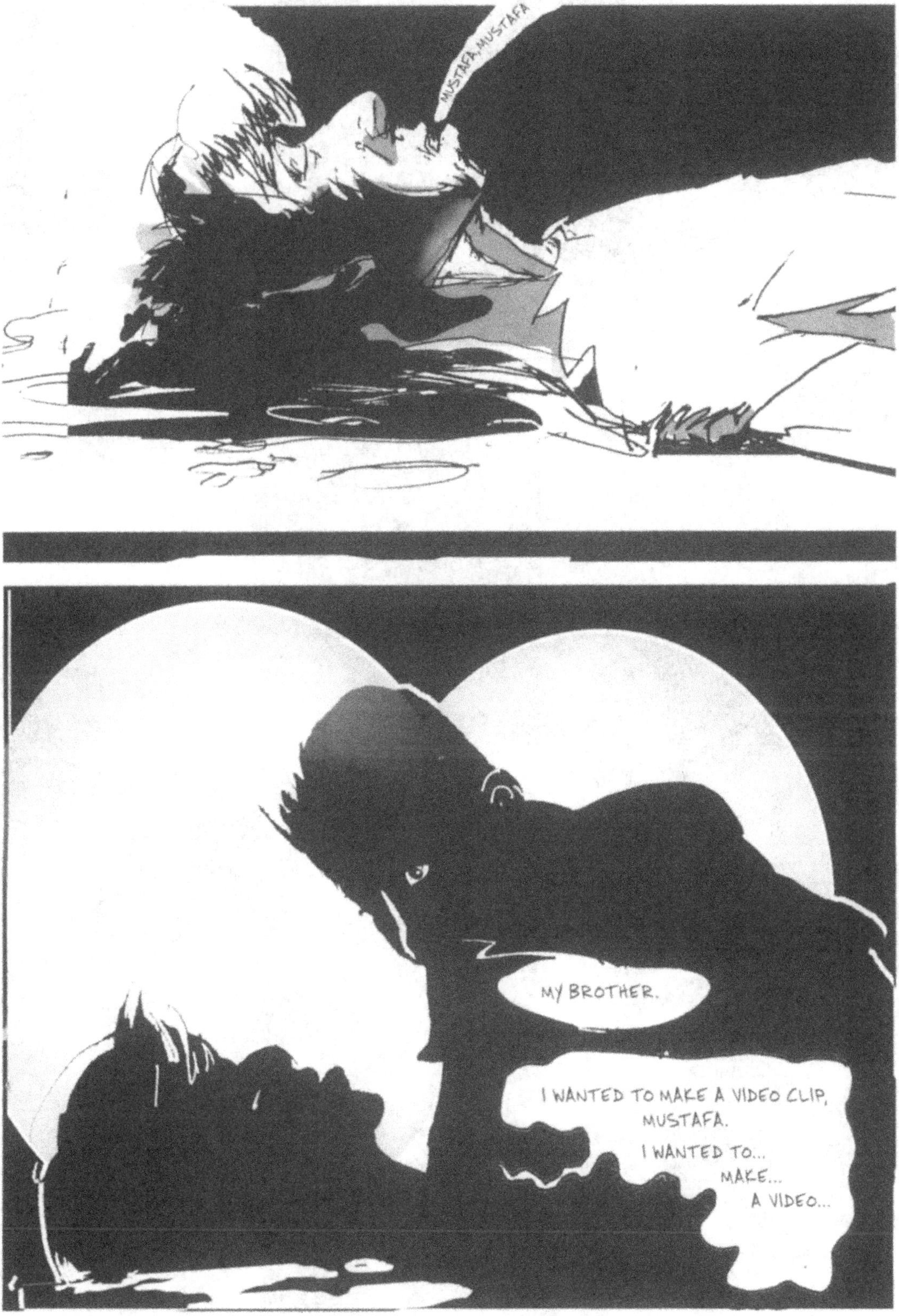
MUSTAFA, MUSTAFA
MY BROTHER.
I WANTED TO MAKE A VIDEO CLIP, MUSTAFA.
I WANTED TO... MAKE... A VIDEO...

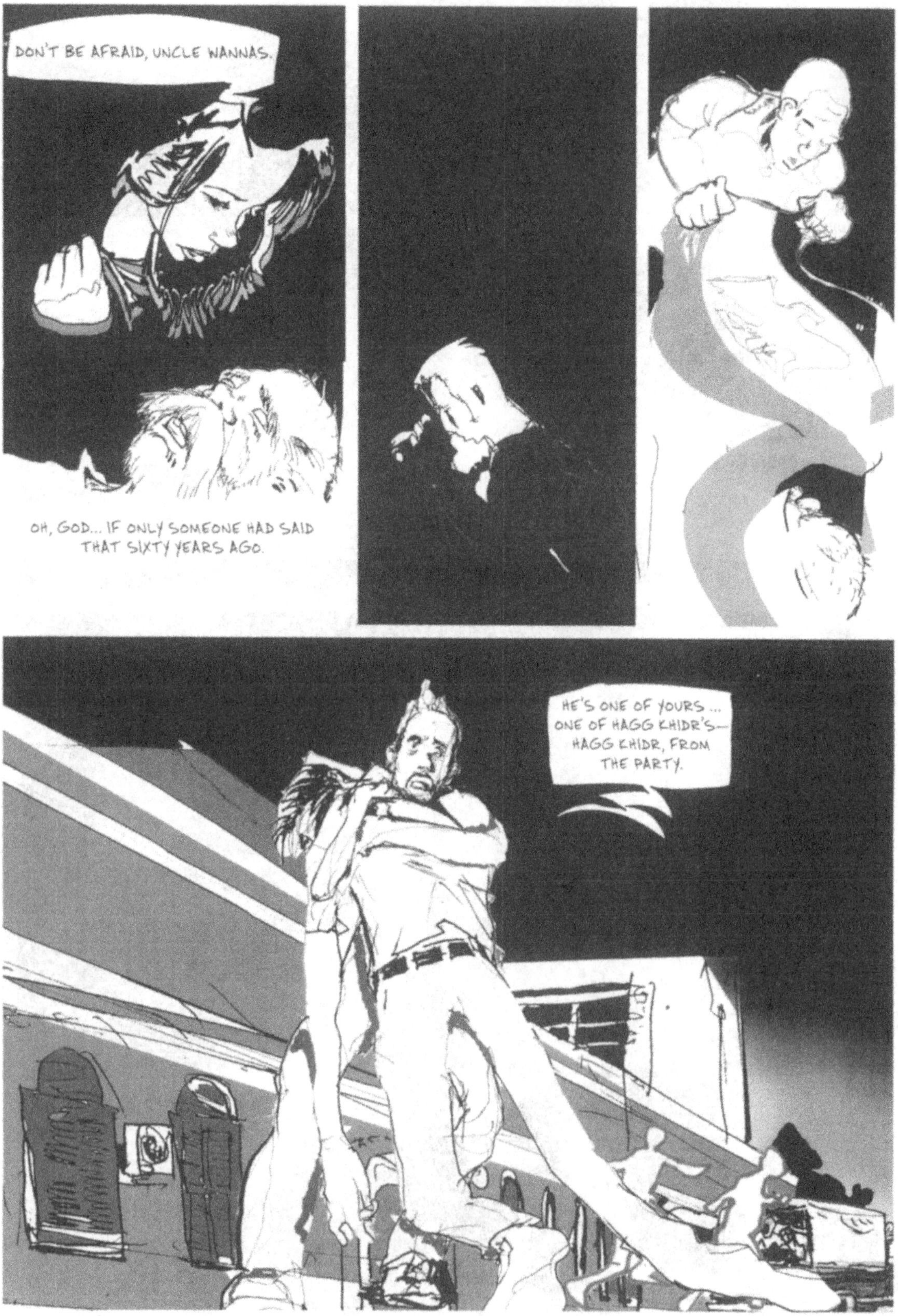
DON'T BE AFRAID, UNCLE WANNAS.
OH, GOD... IF ONLY SOMEONE HAD SAID THAT SIXTY YEARS AGO.
HE'S ONE OF YOURS ... ONE OF HAGG KHIDR'S— HAGG KHIDR, FROM THE PARTY.

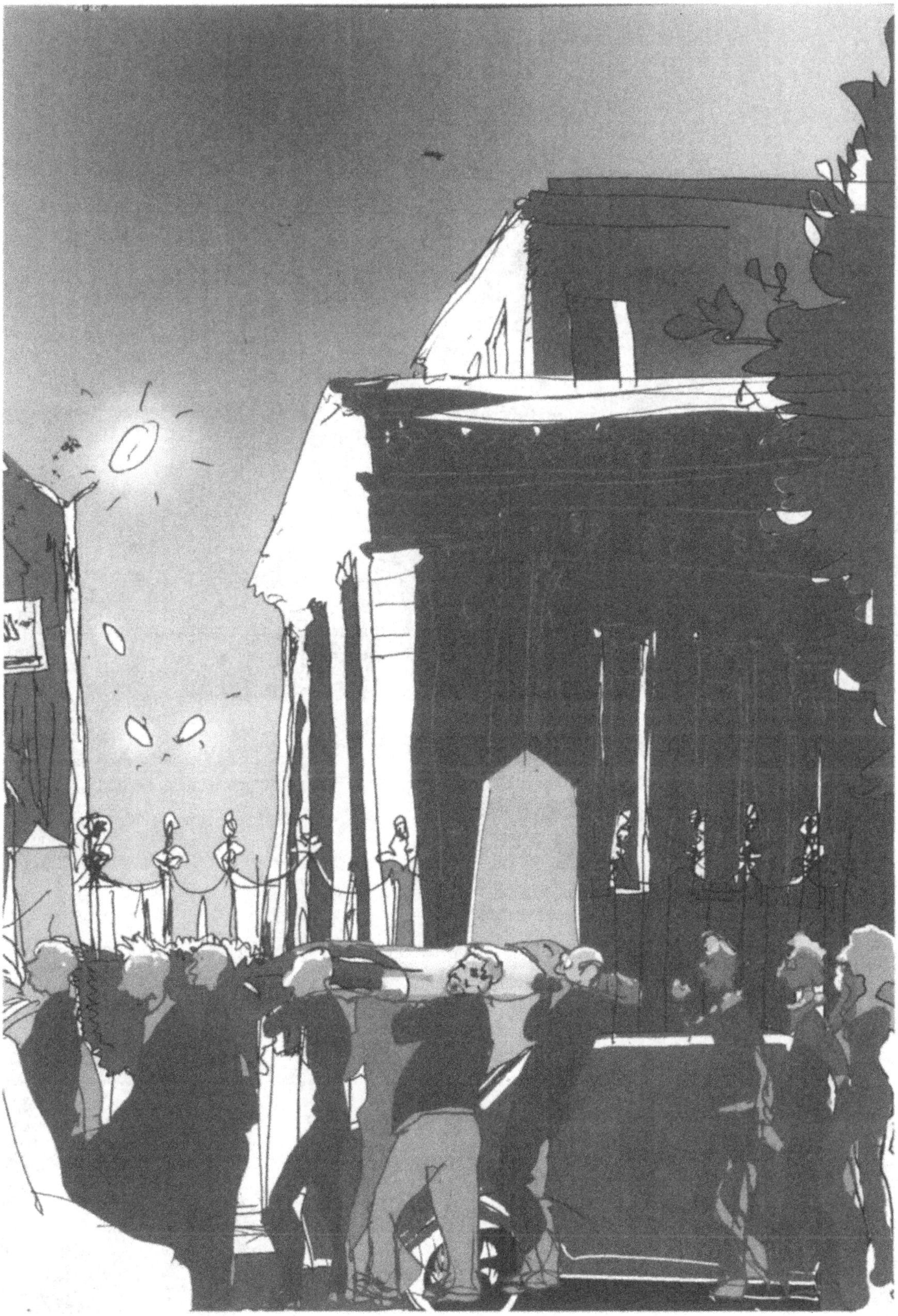

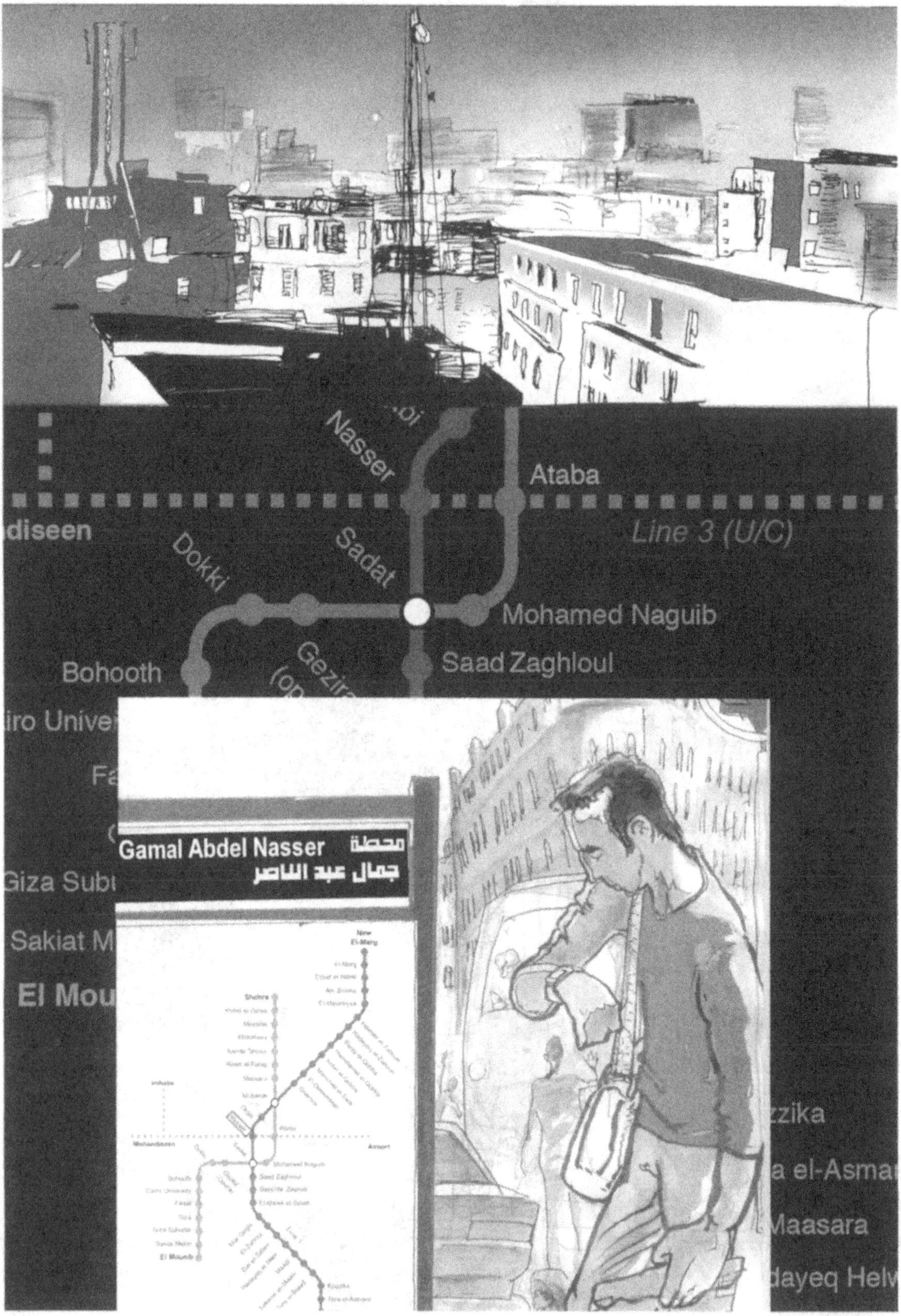
Nasser
Ataba
diseen
Line 3 (U/C)
Dokki
Sadat
Mohamed Naguib
Bohooth
Saad Zaghloul
iro Unive
Giza Sub
Sakiat M
El Mou
Gamal Abdel Nasser
محطة
جمال عبد الناصر
zzika
a el-Asma
Maasara
dayeq Helw

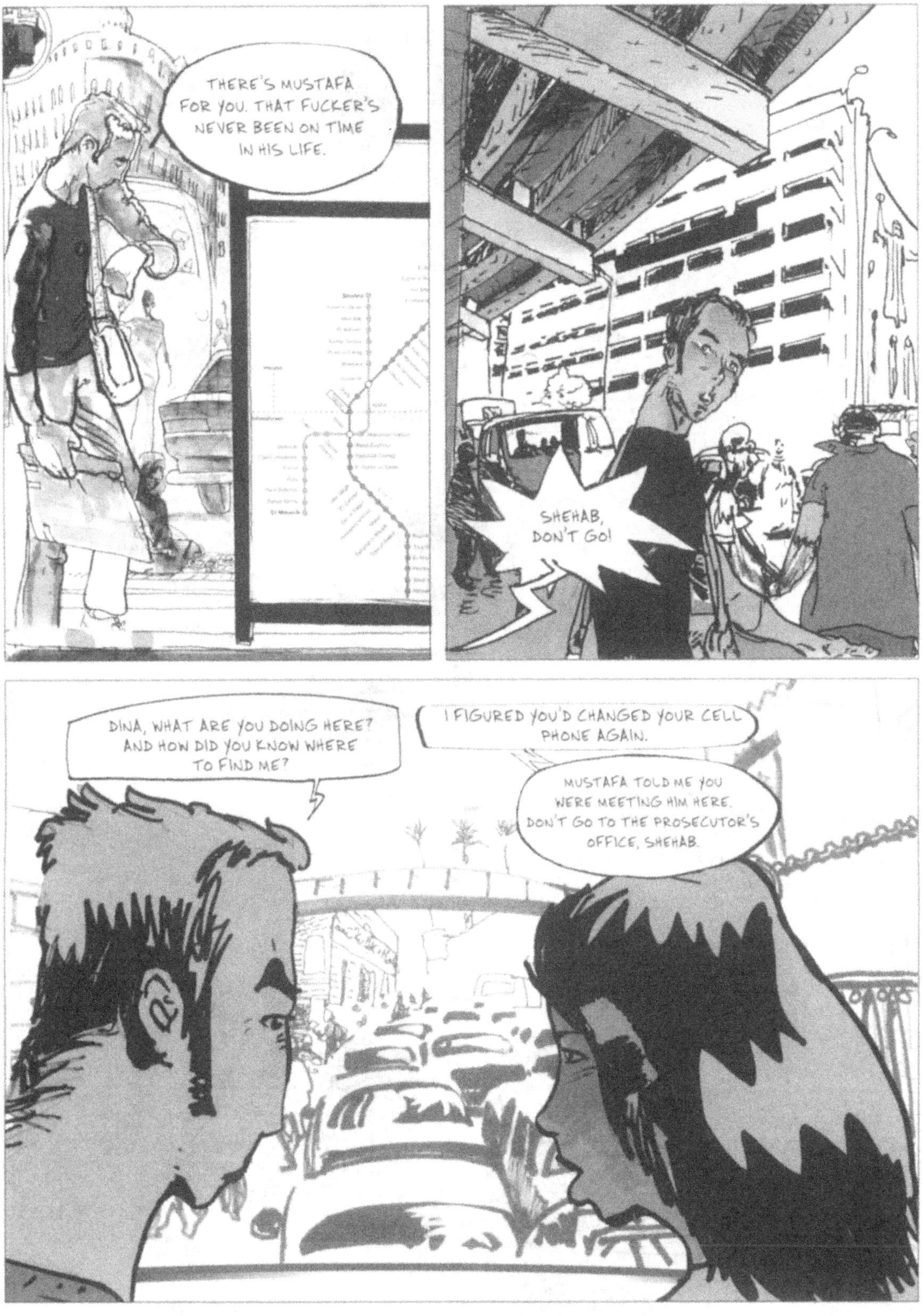
THERE'S MUSTAFA FOR YOU. THAT FUCKER'S NEVER BEEN ON TIME IN HIS LIFE.
SHEHAB, DON'T GO!
DINA, WHAT ARE YOU DOING HERE? AND HOW DID YOU KNOW WHERE TO FIND ME?
I FIGURED YOU'D CHANGED YOUR CELL PHONE AGAIN.
MUSTAFA TOLD ME YOU WERE MEETING HIM HERE. DON'T GO TO THE PROSECUTOR'S OFFICE, SHEHAB.

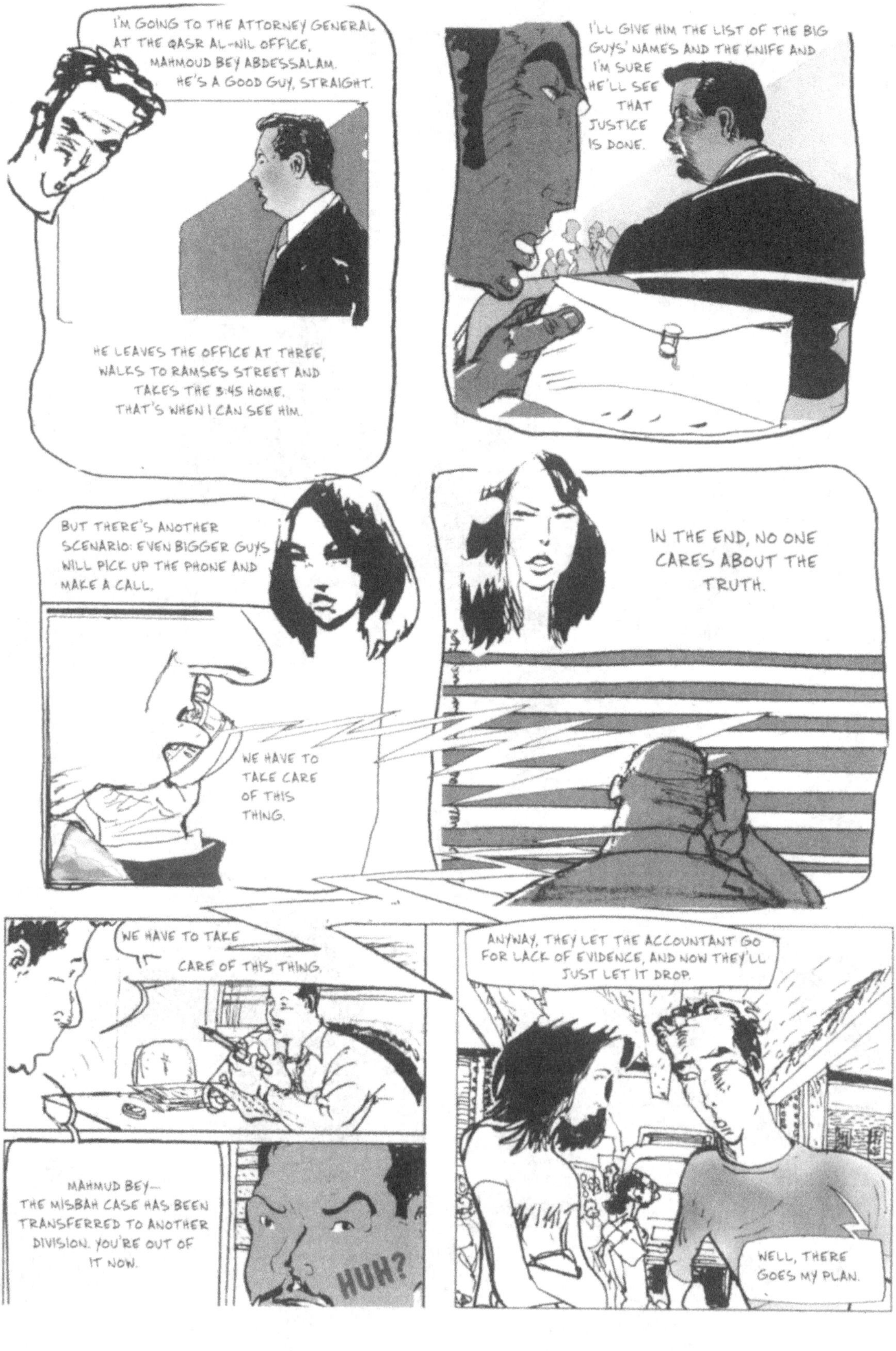
I'M GOING TO THE ATTORNEY GENERAL AT THE QASR AL-NIL OFFICE, MAHMOUD BEY ABDESSALAM. HE'S A GOOD GUY, STRAIGHT.
HE LEAVES THE OFFICE AT THREE, WALKS TO RAMSES STREET AND TAKES THE 3:45 HOME. THAT'S WHEN I CAN SEE HIM.
I'LL GIVE HIM THE LIST OF THE BIG GUYS' NAMES AND THE KNIFE AND I'M SURE HE'LL SEE THAT JUSTICE IS DONE.
BUT THERE'S ANOTHER SCENARIO: EVEN BIGGER GUYS WILL PICK UP THE PHONE AND MAKE A CALL.
IN THE END, NO ONE CARES ABOUT THE TRUTH.
WE HAVE TO TAKE CARE OF THIS THING.
WE HAVE TO TAKE CARE OF THIS THING.
MAHMUD BEY— THE MISBAH CASE HAS BEEN TRANSFERRED TO ANOTHER DIVISION. YOU'RE OUT OF IT NOW.
HUH?
ANYWAY, THEY LET THE ACCOUNTANT GO FOR LACK OF EVIDENCE, AND NOW THEY'LL JUST LET IT DROP.
WELL, THERE GOES MY PLAN.

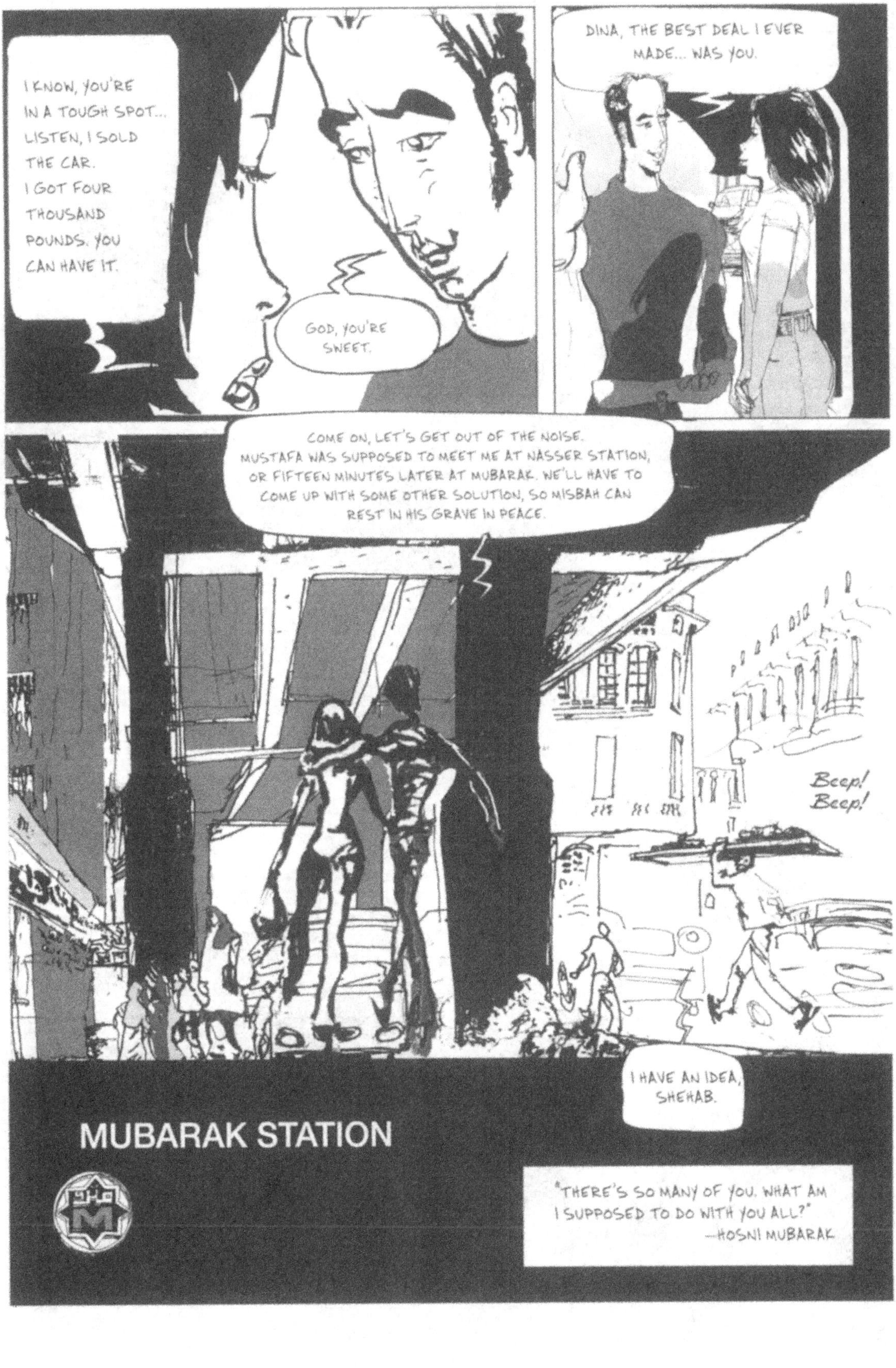
I KNOW, YOU'RE IN A TOUGH SPOT... LISTEN, I SOLD THE CAR. I GOT FOUR THOUSAND POUNDS. YOU CAN HAVE IT.
GOD, YOU'RE SWEET.
DINA, THE BEST DEAL I EVER MADE... WAS YOU.
COME ON, LET'S GET OUT OF THE NOISE. MUSTAFA WAS SUPPOSED TO MEET ME AT NASSER STATION, OR FIFTEEN MINUTES LATER AT MUBARAK. WE'LL HAVE TO COME UP WITH SOME OTHER SOLUTION, SO MISBAH CAN REST IN HIS GRAVE IN PEACE.
Beep! Beep!
I HAVE AN IDEA, SHEHAB.
MUBARAK STATION
"THERE'S SO MANY OF YOU. WHAT AM I SUPPOSED TO DO WITH YOU ALL?"
—HOSNI MUBARAK

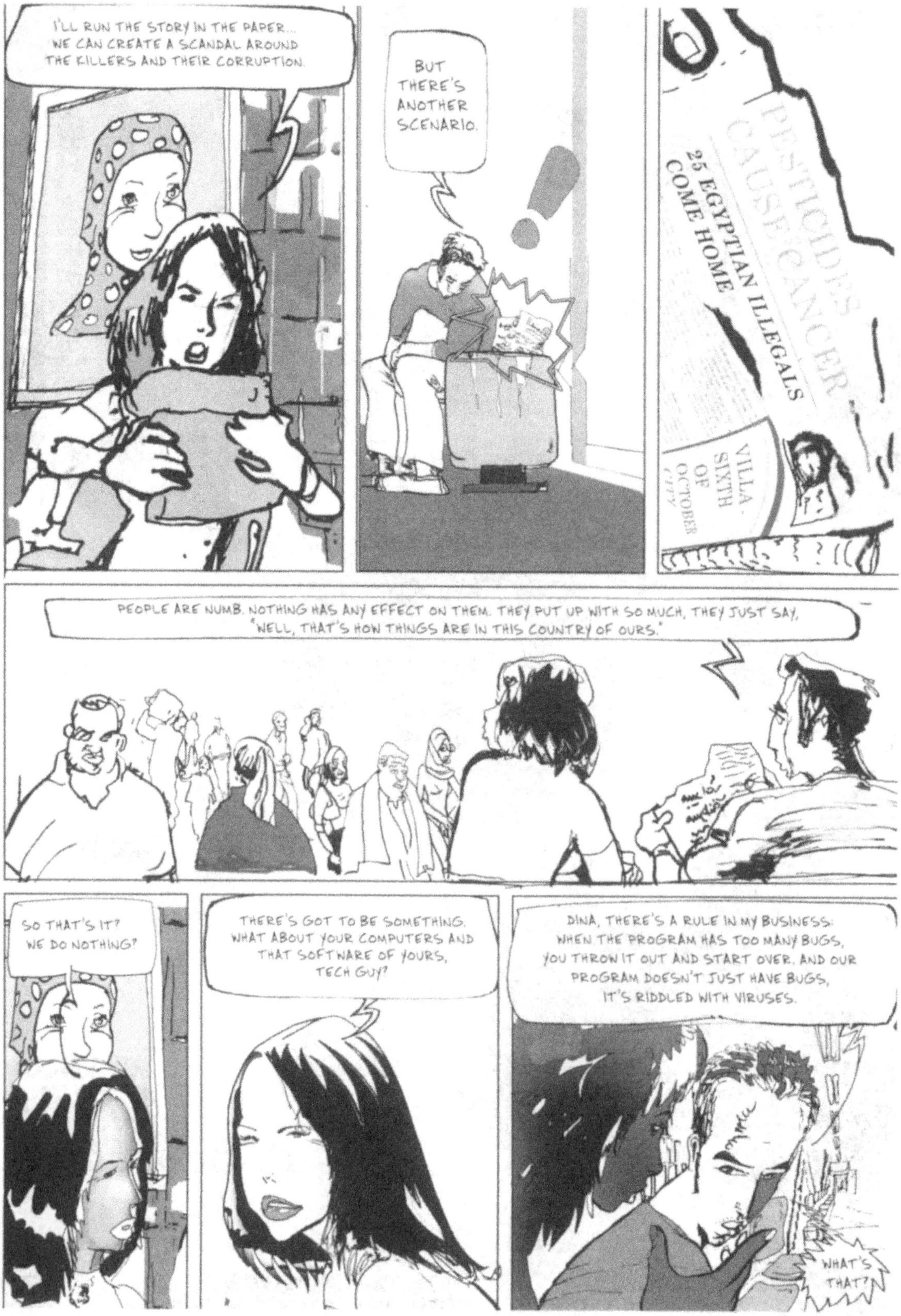
I'LL RUN THE STORY IN THE PAPER... WE CAN CREATE A SCANDAL AROUND THE KILLERS AND THEIR CORRUPTION.
BUT THERE'S ANOTHER SCENARIO.
PESTICIDES CAUSE CANCER
25 EGYPTIAN ILLEGALS COME HOME
VILLA SIXTH OF OCTOBER CITY
PEOPLE ARE NUMB. NOTHING HAS ANY EFFECT ON THEM. THEY PUT UP WITH SO MUCH, THEY JUST SAY, "WELL, THAT'S HOW THINGS ARE IN THIS COUNTRY OF OURS."
SO THAT'S IT? WE DO NOTHING?
THERE'S GOT TO BE SOMETHING. WHAT ABOUT YOUR COMPUTERS AND THAT SOFTWARE OF YOURS, TECH GUY?
DINA, THERE'S A RULE IN MY BUSINESS: WHEN THE PROGRAM HAS TOO MANY BUGS, YOU THROW IT OUT AND START OVER. AND OUR PROGRAM DOESN'T JUST HAVE BUGS, IT'S RIDDLED WITH VIRUSES.
WHAT'S THAT?

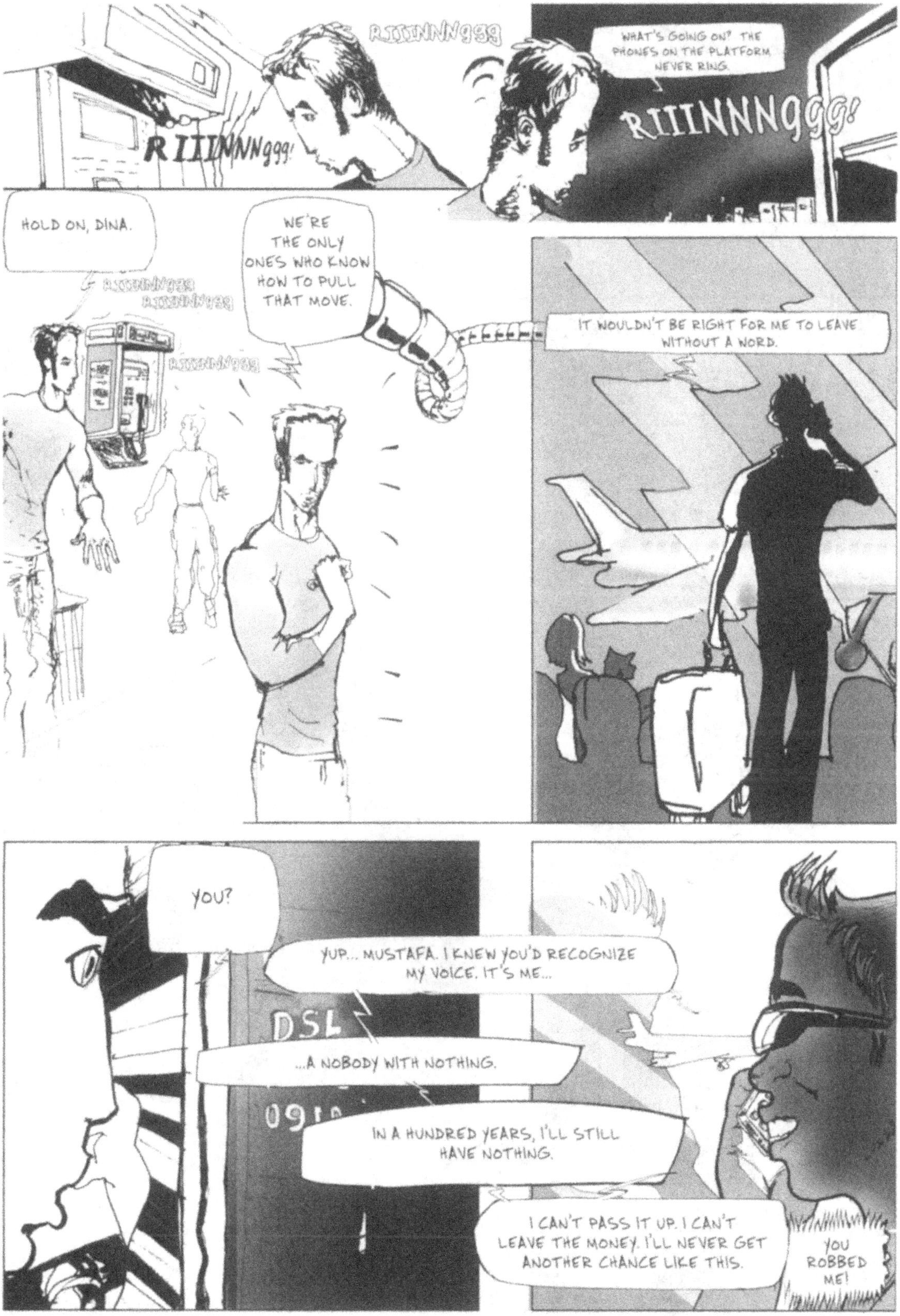
RIIINNNggg
RIIINNNggg!
WHAT'S GOING ON? THE PHONES ON THE PLATFORM NEVER RING.
RIIINNNggg!
HOLD ON, DINA.
WE'RE THE ONLY ONES WHO KNOW HOW TO PULL THAT MOVE.
IT WOULDN'T BE RIGHT FOR ME TO LEAVE WITHOUT A WORD.
YOU?
YUP... MUSTAFA. I KNEW YOU'D RECOGNIZE MY VOICE. IT'S ME...
DSL
...A NOBODY WITH NOTHING.
IN A HUNDRED YEARS, I'LL STILL HAVE NOTHING.
I CAN'T PASS IT UP. I CAN'T LEAVE THE MONEY. I'LL NEVER GET ANOTHER CHANCE LIKE THIS.
YOU ROBBED ME!

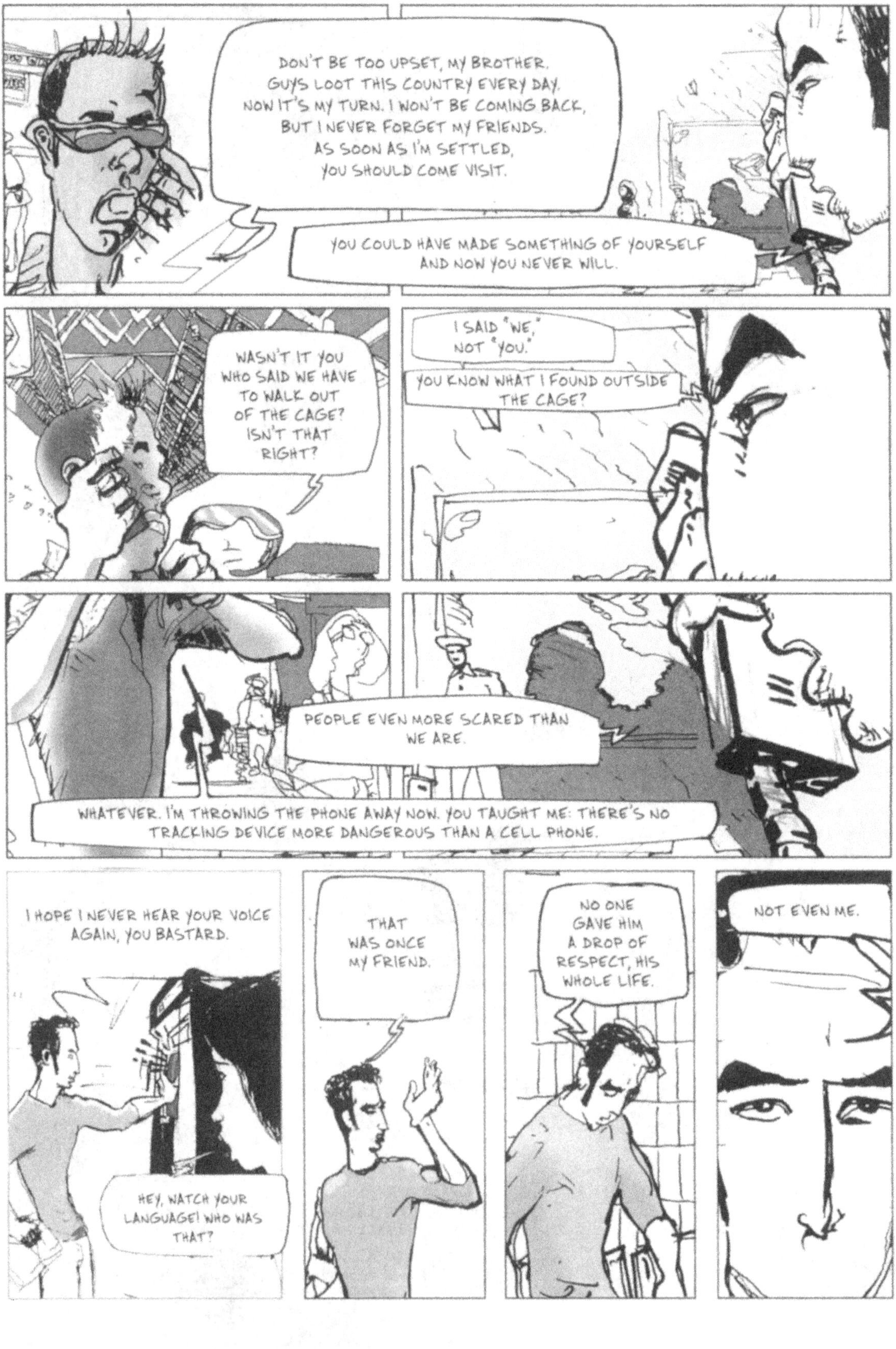
DON'T BE TOO UPSET, MY BROTHER. GUYS LOOT THIS COUNTRY EVERY DAY. NOW IT'S MY TURN. I WON'T BE COMING BACK, BUT I NEVER FORGET MY FRIENDS. AS SOON AS I'M SETTLED, YOU SHOULD COME VISIT.
YOU COULD HAVE MADE SOMETHING OF YOURSELF AND NOW YOU NEVER WILL.
WASN'T IT YOU WHO SAID WE HAVE TO WALK OUT OF THE CAGE? ISN'T THAT RIGHT?
I SAID "WE," NOT "YOU."
YOU KNOW WHAT I FOUND OUTSIDE THE CAGE?
PEOPLE EVEN MORE SCARED THAN WE ARE.
WHATEVER. I'M THROWING THE PHONE AWAY NOW. YOU TAUGHT ME: THERE'S NO TRACKING DEVICE MORE DANGEROUS THAN A CELL PHONE.
I HOPE I NEVER HEAR YOUR VOICE AGAIN, YOU BASTARD.
HEY, WATCH YOUR LANGUAGE! WHO WAS THAT?
THAT WAS ONCE MY FRIEND.
NO ONE GAVE HIM A DROP OF RESPECT, HIS WHOLE LIFE.
NOT EVEN ME.

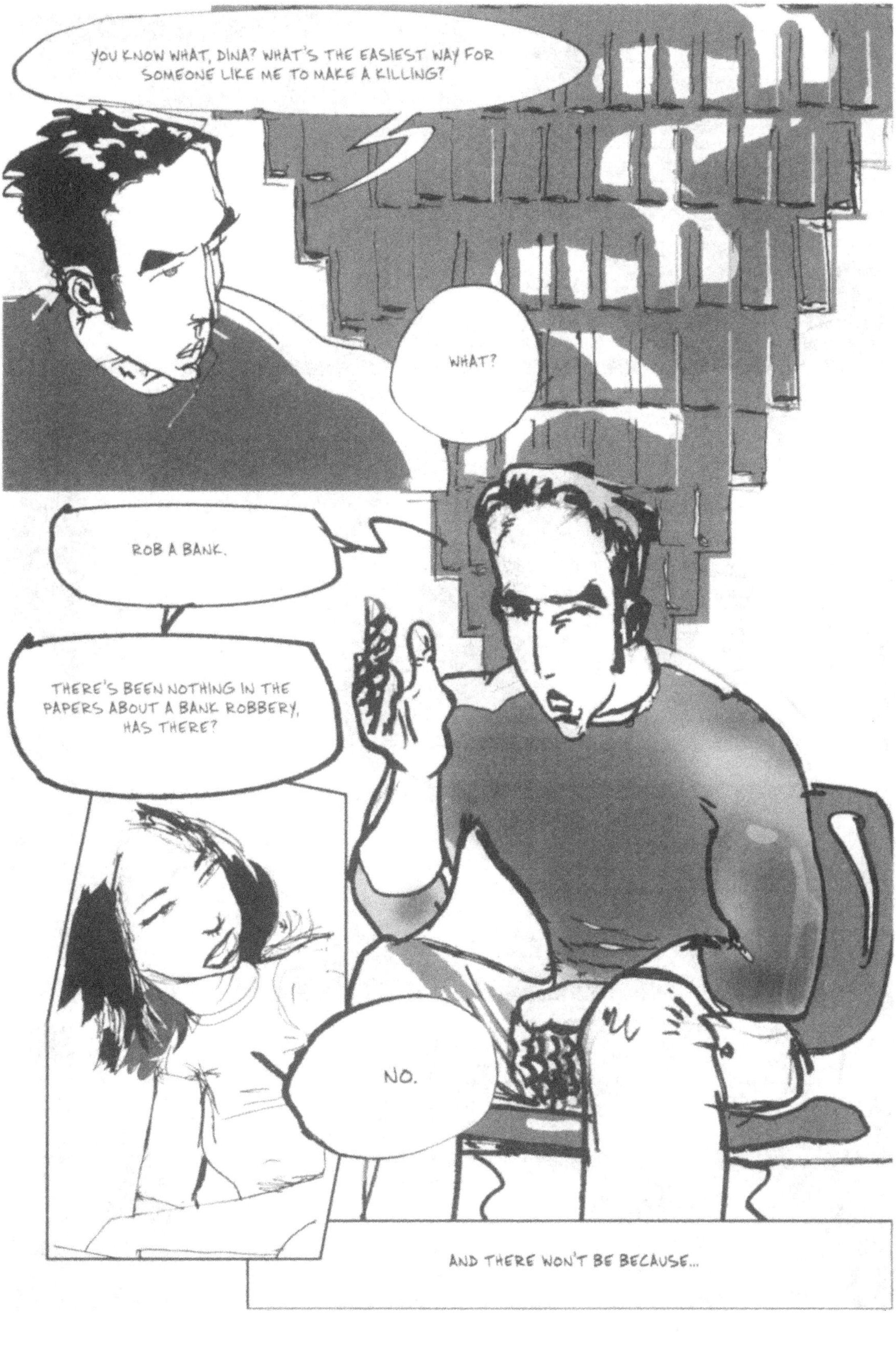
YOU KNOW WHAT, DINA? WHAT'S THE EASIEST WAY FOR SOMEONE LIKE ME TO MAKE A KILLING?
WHAT?
ROB A BANK.
THERE'S BEEN NOTHING IN THE PAPERS ABOUT A BANK ROBBERY, HAS THERE?
NO.
AND THERE WON'T BE BECAUSE...

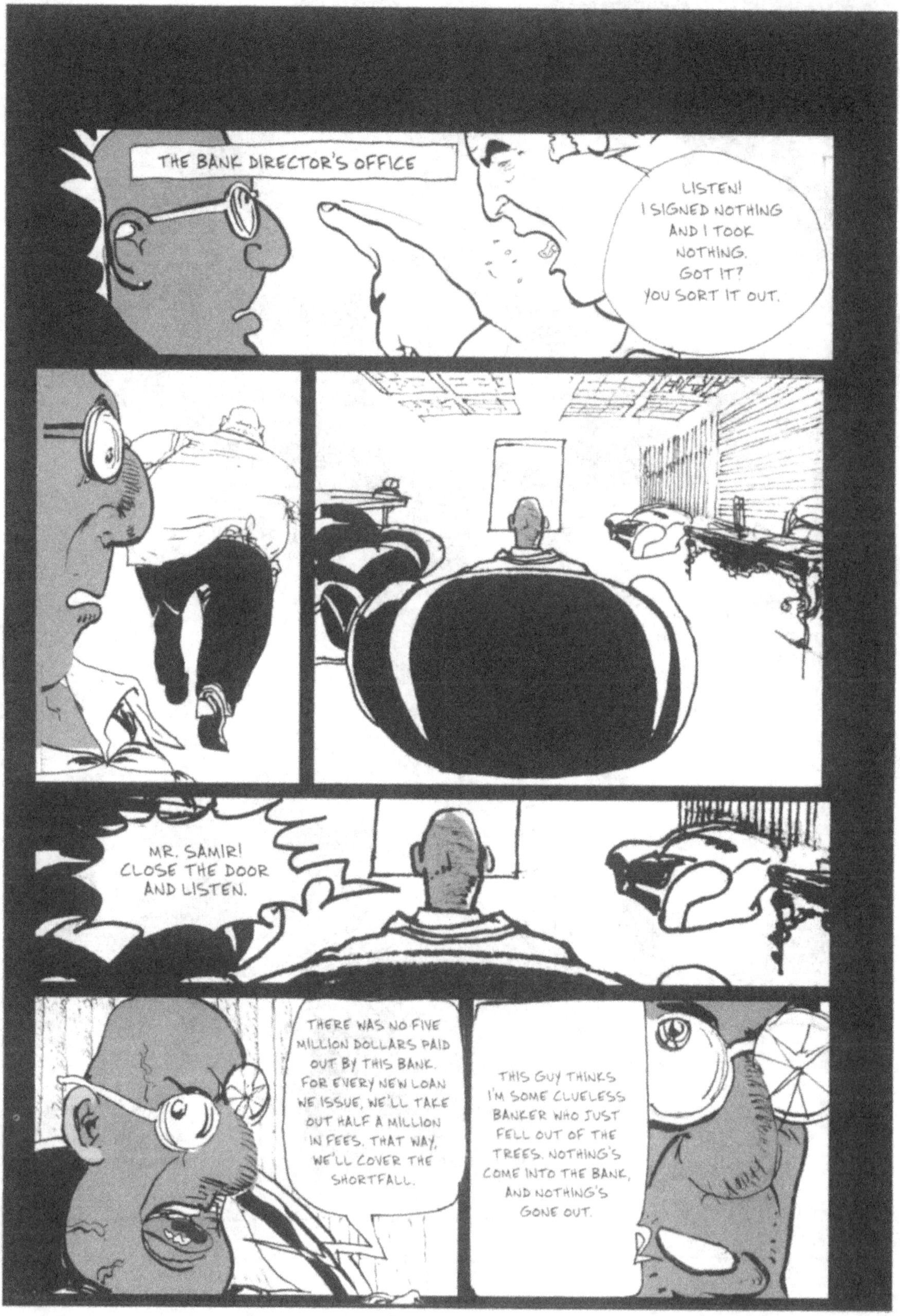
THE BANK DIRECTOR'S OFFICE
LISTEN! I SIGNED NOTHING AND I TOOK NOTHING. GOT IT? YOU SORT IT OUT.
MR. SAMIR! CLOSE THE DOOR AND LISTEN.
THERE WAS NO FIVE MILLION DOLLARS PAID OUT BY THIS BANK. FOR EVERY NEW LOAN WE ISSUE, WE'LL TAKE OUT HALF A MILLION IN FEES. THAT WAY, WE'LL COVER THE SHORTFALL.
THIS GUY THINKS I'M SOME CLUELESS BANKER WHO JUST FELL OUT OF THE TREES. NOTHING'S COME INTO THE BANK, AND NOTHING'S GONE OUT.

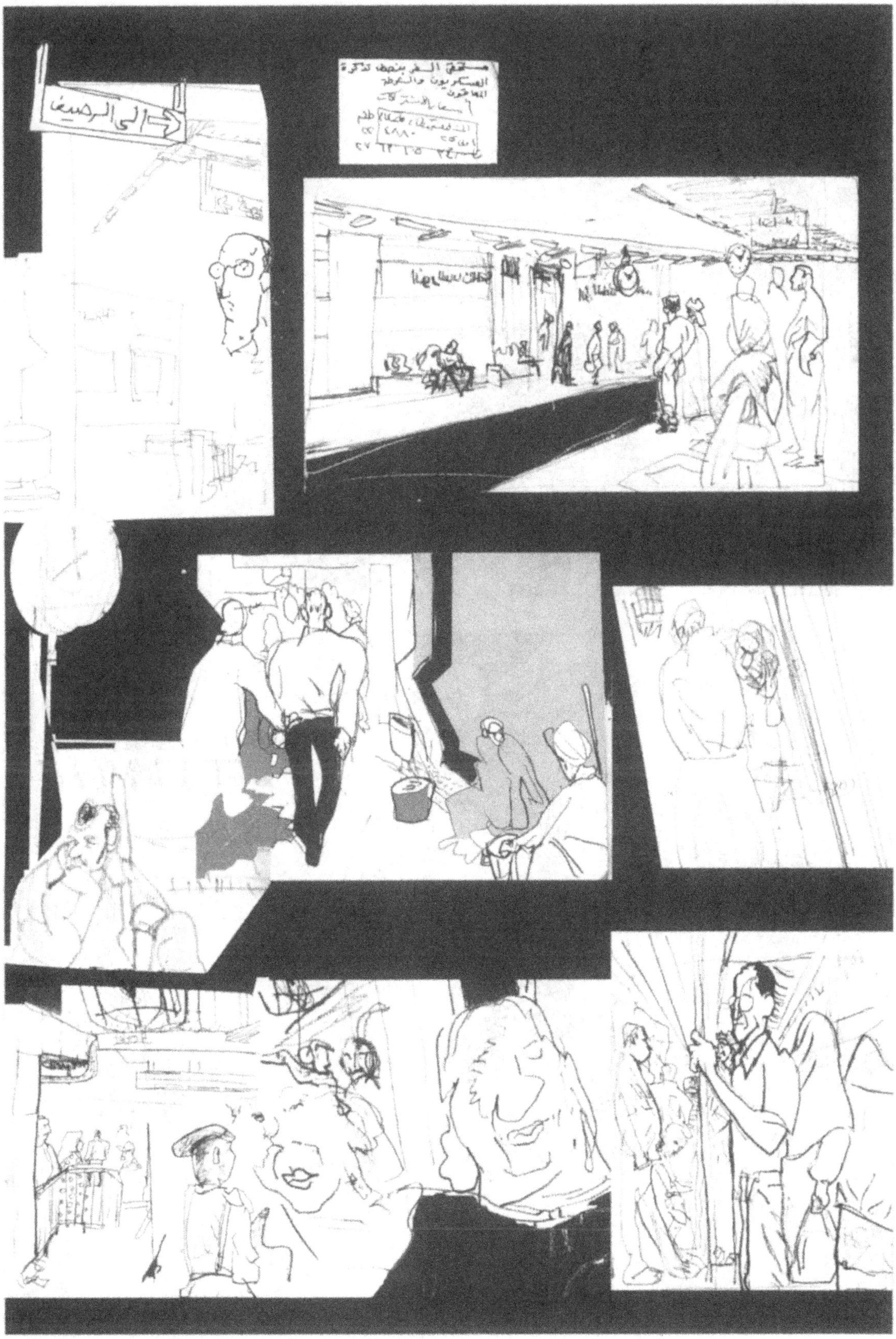
الى الرصيف
مستحق السفر بنصف تذكرة
العسكريون والشرطة
المعاقون

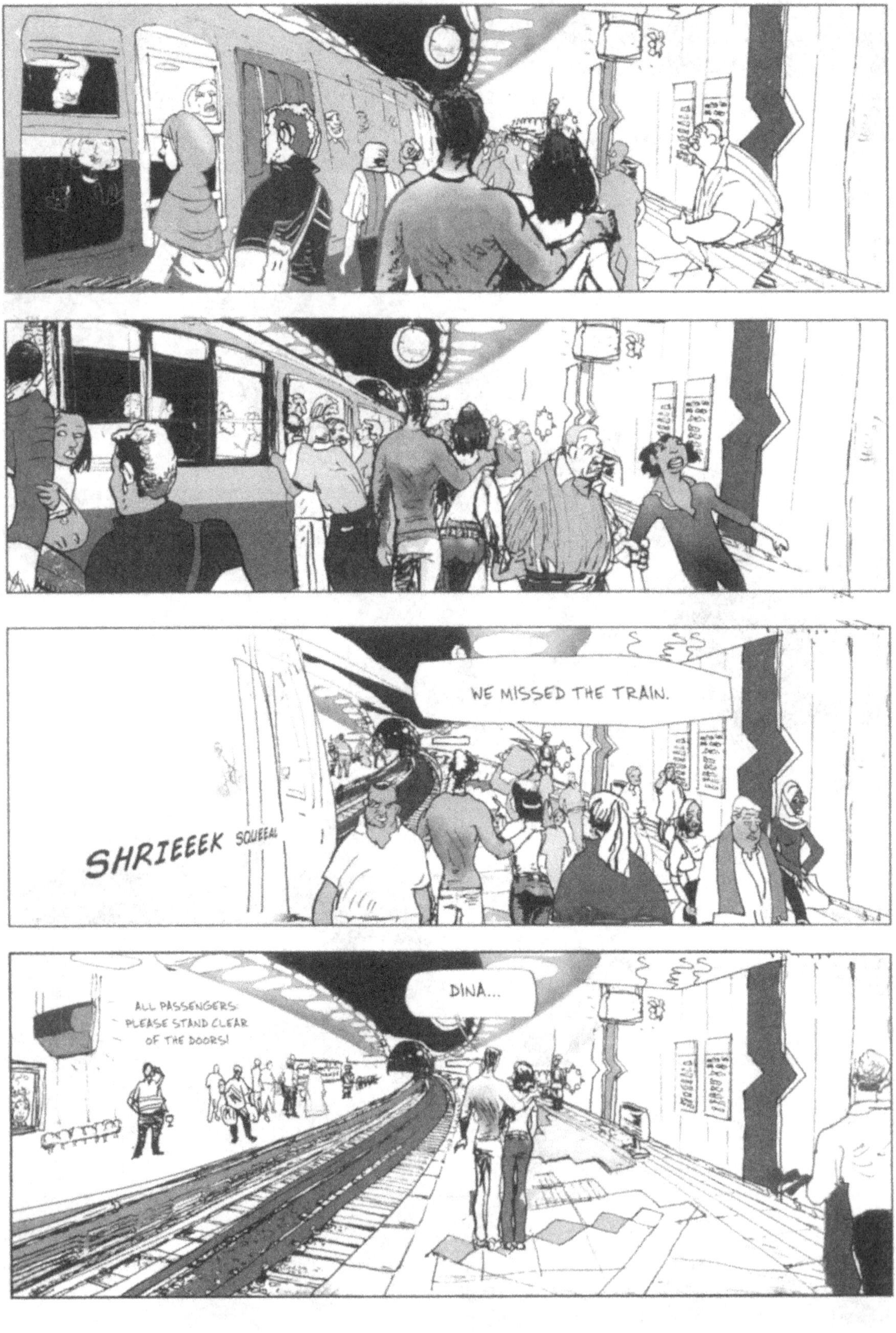
WE MISSED THE TRAIN.
SHRIEEEK
SQUEEAL
ALL PASSENGERS: PLEASE STAND CLEAR OF THE DOORS!
DINA...

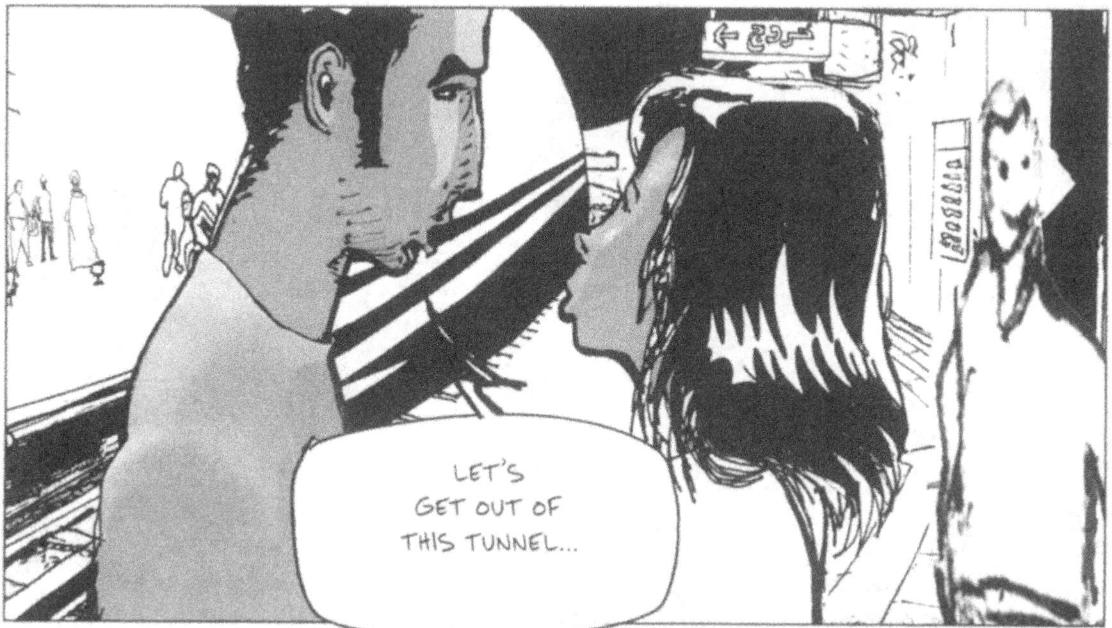
LET'S GET OUT OF THIS TUNNEL...

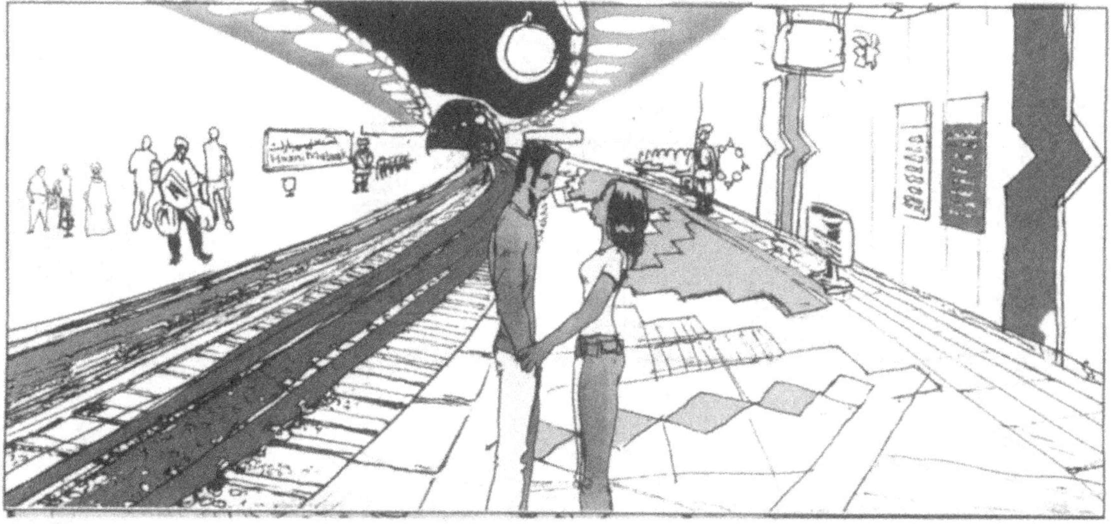

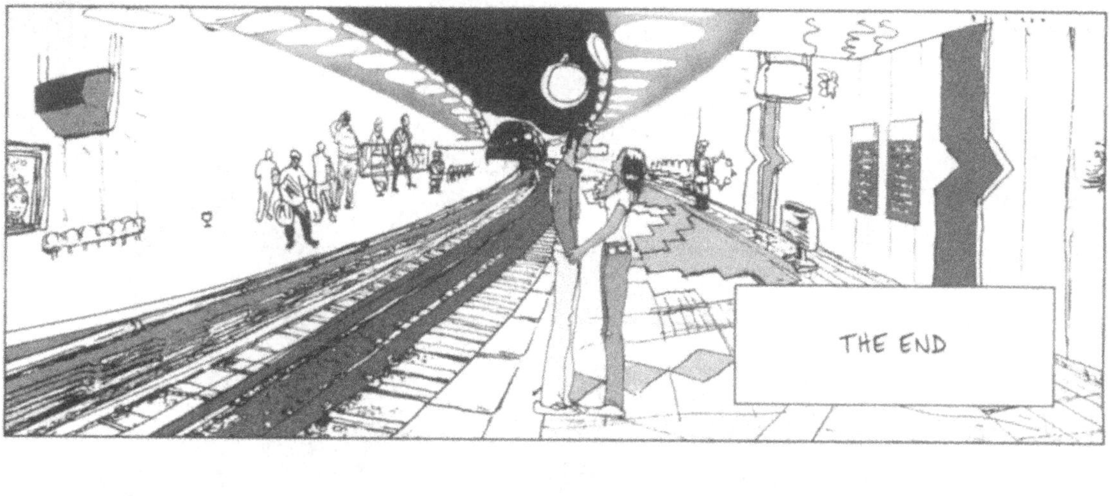
THE END

A SPECIAL THANK YOU

The idea for this book came to me in 2003, and my close friends pushed me to write it, so I thank them from the bottom of my heart for having had confidence in me. Special thanks to the talented Ahmad Alaidy, who helped refine the plot. I cannot leave out the sensitivity and encouragement of my brother, friend, and graphic novel comrade, Hatim Fathy, or the valuable advice I received from artists Golo and Philippe Bayun.

I started work in 2005 with the help of talented writers Basim Sharaf, Muhammad Hamad, and Tamer Abdelhamid, as well as Wa'el Saad, a loyal companion on this journey. I am grateful for the vote of confidence they gave when I showed them the story. If not for their approval, comments, revisions, and continual support, I would never have finished this book.

The artist Ahmad Khalid kept up my spirits and supplied some amazing photos of *moulid* festivals, which he had collected for his work with the writer Muhammad Alaa al-Din. I was as impressed by his skill as a photographer as his talent as a writer.

I benefited from the time and contributions of artist Sharif Mustafa and the actor and director Sharif Shaaban: they joined me at some of the locations in the story and Sharif Mustafa took some inspired photos of Shaaban, on whom I modeled Shehab's appearance. I offer these words of thanks in response to their great friendship.

Thanks to the man who taught us to see: Professor Mohy al-Din al-Labad, who is also father of my friend Ahmad al-Labad. The advice that he gave me in late 2006 to concentrate on finishing the book was invaluable. Without his intervention, I wouldn't have completed it. All my love and respect to you; I am indebted to you both.

To the man we call "our generation's professor," Ibrahim Eissa: my apologies for leaving your newspaper, *Dustour*. I love the people who work there. When I went to show Ibrahim Eissa some of what I'd written, he put it down and said one word: "Sold." I left his office soaring like a bird. I flew because of you, Professor Ibrahim.

All my thanks as well to my dear loyal friends Muhammad Fathy, Walid Abu al Saoud, and Muhammad Abd al-Aziz.

My special thanks to the great renowned illustrator Muhammad Sayyid Tawfiq, who generously allowed the use of his art on pages 61–62.

As for my beloved wife, I don't know how to repay all the tolerance and kindness you have lavished on me, except to dedicate my work to you.

Magdy El Shafee

TRANSLATOR'S ACKNOWLEDGMENTS

As translator, I would like to thank Magdy El Shafee for his assistance answering questions about his text, and also Mariam Bazeed for the invaluable help she gave to this *khawaga* as I made my way through the manuscript: her advice and guidance on cultural points and knotty passages were invaluable. Last, my gratitude to Riva Hocherman at Metropolitan Books for her work in improving and polishing the translation, and to Grigory Tovbis for his smooth management of operations. I am grateful for their assistance, but as always, any errors in translation are solely my own.

Chip Rossetti

ABOUT THE AUTHOR

Born in Libya in 1961, MAGDY EL SHAFEE is an Egyptian cartoonist, writer, and illustrator who has also worked in the pharmaceutical industry. In 2006, UNESCO honored El Shafee's comics series "Yasmin and Amina," written with writer Wa'el Saad and published in the weekly *Alaa Eddin*, for its depiction of migration and racism. *Metro*, which addresses Egyptian corruption, poverty, and injustice, was banned on publication in 2008 for "offending public morals" and is unavailable in Arabic. It is El Shafee's first full-length book. He lives in Cairo, where he edits *El Doshma*, a comics journal for young adults, and is working on his next graphic novel.

CPSIA information can be obtained
at www.ICGtesting.com
Printed in the USA
LVHW060532080722
722780LV00006BA/330